To all our friends, old and new,
who really make every festival, every feast
– a celebration.

VIVEK SINGH'S
INDIAN FESTIVAL FEASTS

Absolute Press
An imprint of Bloomsbury Publishing Plc

50 Bedford Square	1385 Broadway
London	New York
WC1B 3DP	NY 10018
UK	USA

www.bloomsbury.com

ABSOLUTE PRESS and the A. logo are trademarks of Bloomsbury Publishing Plc

First published 2017

British Library Cataloguing-in-Publication Data
A catalogue record for this book is available from the British Library.

Library of Congress Cataloguing-in-Publication data has been applied for.

ISBN:
HB: 9781472938466
ePDF: 9781472938480
ePub: 9781472938473

2 4 6 8 10 9 7 5 3 1

Printed and bound in China by C&C Offset

Bloomsbury Publishing Plc makes every effort to ensure that the papers used in the manufacture of our books are natural, recyclable products made from wood grown in well-managed forests. Our manufacturing processes conform to the environmental regulations of the country of origin.

To find out more about our authors and books visit www.bloomsbury.com. Here you will find extracts, author interviews, details of forthcoming events and the option to sign up for our newsletters.

Introduction

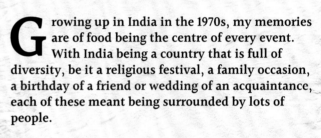

Growing up in India in the 1970s, my memories are of food being the centre of every event. With India being a country that is full of diversity, be it a religious festival, a family occasion, a birthday of a friend or wedding of an acquaintance, each of these meant being surrounded by lots of people.

India's festivals are as diverse as the country's landscapes and as lively as its people, bringing together a blend of cultures, religions and understanding for people to celebrate. Celebrations often have long, drawn-out preparation, with weeks and months of planning; I recall women, especially of my mother's and grandmother's generations, getting together in each other's kitchens to prepare the ever-important Diwali snacks. And with many days of preparation would come several days of recovery, post-festival.

Looking back at those events, and in writing this book, I can't help but notice that food was an expression of the sentiment, the emotion that people would feel for the particular event. Indian food is as diverse as India, so the kind of food that would be served would vary from festival to festival, family to family, region to region. Nevertheless, food is at the heart of these celebrations, regardless of numerous cultures and religious nuances. Often, food was traditionally incorporated into the festival as an offering to a deity, and then communities or families would gather to share in a feast, so indeed one may say that these festivals are incomplete without food. It is often said 'we eat to live', but here, more than anywhere, it seems like 'we live to eat'! Somehow, almost miraculously, the food element

Indian villagers celebrate Holi at the Nandji Temple. (Manan Vatsyayana/AFP/Getty)

of festivals and celebrations would evoke similar emotions of happiness and joy, and bring friends and family together in a way that would be unique to that occasion.

This collection is an effort to pick out some of the most favoured celebrations from my childhood memories. Weaving through the calendar, I dip in and out of festivals (trust me, India has more festivals and celebrations than there are days in the year!): from al fresco picnics on Makar Sankranti in my father's colliery town to Saraswati Puja (the veneration for the Goddess of Knowledge) in the middle of January, or from vibrant Holi, Easter, community weddings or Dussehra all the way through to Diwali or Christmas. The festivals included here are just a beginning; it's probably true to suggest that if an Indian were to engage in all celebrations, they would have no time left for anything else in life.

Each of the occasions included here is marked by the unique kind of food that is prepared and served at the event. With some of these dishes only being eaten once a year during the festival, the preparation and presentation tell a story of celebration in India; a combination of colours, energy, music, communities and, of course, flavours and styles of cooking.

Fast forwarding from the celebrations of my childhood, today's modern society has become even more of a cultural melting pot; there is now so much interest, understanding and interaction between various communities. As a result, in India, the festivals and the feasts are more and more being shared beyond the initial boundaries of the festival, with neighbours of different religions being invited to share the celebrations. And even beyond India, festivals such as Holi and Diwali have become increasingly familiar in London and across the world; celebrated with immense fervour amongst people of all backgrounds, extending much further than just the people of the festival's ethnic origins. Indeed, at The Cinnamon Kitchen in central London we host 'Play Holi in the City' and invite Londoners to join our celebrations with paints and Holi-themed cocktails and canapés – it's a joy to be part of it.

This book shares a collection of recipes for the kind of food that is enjoyed at festivals and celebrations in India, combined with regional nuances and religious differences in the subcontinent. These carefully chosen recipes, in their own unique way, paint a festive picture, and a sense of sharing and being together, through their vibrant colours, special ingredients, big feasting platters and unique flavours. For example, in the Holi section you can expect to find samosas and chaats of various combinations, alongside cool lentil dumplings in yoghurt dressing. Other recipes like malpuas and *thandhai* will just finish off the meal... If you're looking for ideas for a wedding meal, skip to my collection of Bengali wedding dishes for ideas, including a rich and creamy prawn curry redolent with cardamom, sweet spiced slow-cooked mutton curry and a punchy fish curry with mustard. The community pot of biryani and *seviyaan* – a rich dessert of fine vermicelli cooked in milk – are simply not to be missed at Eid.

As a result of travel, migration and globalisation, various festivals are being celebrated in places far away from their place of birth. It's good that people are able to stay connected to their culture and tradition through continuing these celebrations in faraway lands; however what is not so good is that as these festivals move away from the place of their origin, the ingredients, the menus and, with them, the expression of the festival change beyond its traditions.

As I see it, there are both positives and negatives of India, and indeed the world, turning into a melting pot. I am sure this has been happening all the time, but when I speak to my friends in Delhi and ask how they celebrate Vaisakhi, when the response is 'we have vodka and chicken sandwiches in the club', something suddenly dies inside me – it is not the celebration that I remember.

But then I think about how relatively recent some of our favourite ingredients and dishes are, and I'm amazed at the pace of change. I think of tomatoes, which are no more than 150 years old in India; potatoes and chillies, both brought to India by the British and the Portuguese respectively; and *rossogolla*, Bengal's favourite sweet, which was only invented less than 500 years ago. I think of a tandoor and its myriad offering of kebabs coming in from Persia and Central Asia with the Mughals – yes, domesticated chicken was an Indian invention but tandoori chicken was an innovation – and India's favourite curry, the butter chicken or Murgh Makhani, was only invented in the 1940s to use up leftover tandoori chicken. Chaat – the epitome of Indian street food that has recently gained so much popularity all over the world, owing much of its success to its wide array of components that allow for incredible flexibility of choice and potential for customisation – was only invented in the early seventeenth century when Shahjahan moved the capital to Delhi and established Shahjahanabad (now old Delhi) on the banks of the River Yamuna. It was believed that the water in Yamuna was not drinkable and would lead to all kinds of illnesses for its population. The royal doctors prescribed using heavily spiced food cooked in large amounts of fat (ghee) as an antidote. Now, this was fine for those that were meat eaters, but for the vegetarian population, they invented chaats, which could be deep-fried potato cakes, samosas, crisp wheat biscuits, etc, all served with an array of sharp, tangy and spicy sweet chutneys, spice mixes and dressings.

As is becoming abundantly clear, the cuisine of India has been greatly shaped by the influences that various rulers brought with them at different points of time in history, and so have the festivals and feasts. And both will no doubt continue to evolve.

One note of caution though: not all of the recipes listed in this book are ones that you will immediately fall in love with. In actual fact, some sweets and Indian desserts can require quite a specialised skill and takes years of practice to get right. Others, though, can be recreated with just a couple of practice runs! You will notice some festivals use very limited ingredients but use them again and again in different proportions to create an illusion of a banquet! Feel free to substitute ingredients you can't find with similar alternatives, or even to mix different dishes from various chapters to create your own personal Indian feast.

Our society has always been receiving, sending and sharing new influences and new ideas in all walks of life, and our cooking, cuisine and celebrations are the same. Even today, the influences and exchanges continue with migration, through movies and, more recently, through social media. The role that Instagram, Twitter, Snapchat and Facebook have played in spreading awareness of celebrations that were once limited to specific parts of the world is mind-boggling. The world was always fluid, as it is now, but now we have truly turned into a melting pot with ideas being exchanged almost instantaneously. We're connected with the world all the time, which in essence was the point of these festivals and celebrations.

I, for one, am all for evolving and adapting with the times, and staying connected to the roots but not chained by tradition. I also realise that our role is not to fight change but to merely be a connection between the past and the future. I feel extremely fortunate to realise that there are so many festivals, so many celebrations, so many religions and yet food is the common expression of them all. So what if the offering changes with time – that is inevitable. I would love for food to remain at the centre of these expressions in the years to come.

Vivek Singh
London, January 2017

Pongal

This is one of the few Hindu festivals that falls on the same date every year – 14th January – and is traditionally meant to symbolise the day after the winter solstice. Celebrated all over India, Nepal and Bangladesh in various cultural forms, it is essentially a Hindu harvest festival, celebrating the (imminent) arrival of spring.

It is known by different names in different regions, including Pongal, Makar Sankranti, Uttarayan, Maghi, Bhogali Bihu, Shishur Saenkraat, Khichdi and Makara Sankramana. Pongal takes its name from the Tamil Nadu version of the festival, in which rice is boiled with milk and jaggery, topped with brown sugar, cashew nuts and raisins, and when the pot boils over the tradition is to shout 'Pongal, Pongal', announcing the blessing of a new year.

As a child I remember the period from just after Diwali to Pongal or Sankranti as being a period quite devoid of any festivities or celebrations. Thank goodness for more cosmopolitan and modern-day festivities such New Year's Eve; otherwise, in strict Hindu faith, that period is quite possibly the longest time without any celebration worth noting.

From Pongal onwards things start looking up and the winter doesn't seem so hard anymore. It is the first proper festival of the year and is often seen as a time for the reunion of families. In this sense, it demonstrates strong cultural and familial values. It is not uncommon in India for young men to leave home, or the states or

Vendors sell flowers for the festival of Pongal at a market in Bangalore. (Dibyangshu Sarkar/AFP/Getty)

provinces where they were born, to go and work in the larger metropolitan cities where there are better job opportunities, and Pongal often sees them return home to spend time with their families.

Pongal is celebrated in many different forms depending where you are in India. In much of India the festival traditionally runs over four days, as explained below, while other regions focus on particular elements and the celebrations might just be one or two days, many of which replicate the festivities seen on the second day, known as Makar Sankranti.

The day before Pongal is celebrated as Lohri in Punjab and western Uttar Pradesh, and is a celebration of the passing of the winter solstice; it's an excuse for merriment, singing and dancing around bonfires. In both these regions, as well as in West Bengal, bathing in a river or sacred place in the early hours of Makar Sankranti (known as Maghi) is important, and the Punjabis dance their famous bhangra dance, before sitting down to a feast – a common feature of this festival wherever it is celebrated!

The first day of Pongal is when families traditionally have a clear out and discard old things, as this festival is a chance to focus on the new, hoping for change and transformation. At dawn, people light symbolic bonfires and burn old clothes to mark the end of the old and the emergence of the new. The burning of unwanted physical possessions represents the throwing off of old habits and vices and the chance to start again. Sweets are often prepared and shared, and gifts of food, clothes and money might be given.

The second day is a chance for people to wear new clothes and pray as well as making offerings of traditional foods to those who have died. Beautiful *rangoli* patterns are often designed out of chalk or flour in front of people's homes and decorated with flowers and bright colours.

On the third day, the animal kingdom is celebrated, particularly cattle as they are a symbol of prosperity (some regions see bull fighting or taming taking place throughout the festival), while on the fourth day people, particularly farmers, offer prayers to the elements – rain, fire, earth – for helping in the harvest.

One of the things that Pongal is most famous for is the flying of kites, called *patang*, and in every town and city people gather and the sky is filled with beautiful colourful kites. This is particularly seen in Gujarat.

The food during Pongal varies from region to region, however it often features seasonal delicacies in celebration of a good harvest. I remember breakfast on Sankranti always used to be a meal of soaked rice flakes, yoghurt and some sugar or jaggery. And that was it – as simple as that, no cooking involved. Then lunch always had to be *kichri*; rice, lentils and whatever vegetables you had, plus perhaps a little burnt aubergine relish with mustard oil (see page 24). This simple meal was the basis of Sankranti for me, every single year. And no matter what, it was always vegetarian. In fact, in many regions, the first three days of Pongal are strictly vegetarian, with meat only eaten on the last day.

Opposite page: Women draw colourful patterns outside their homes to celebrate Pongal. (Sebastian D'Souza/AFP/Getty)

This page, top: Pongal traditions include the boiling of rice in milk, and when the pot spills over the festivities can really begin. (IndiaPictures/UIG via Getty)

This page, bottom: Bull-wrestling is often seen during Pongal, where decorated bulls run into a crowd of men who try to catch and ride the animals. It is very dangerous. (Palani Mohan/Getty)

In the evening, often *litti* (see page 14) would be made on a small fire made by burning cow pat. These little dough balls filled with a roasted lentil mixture are a favourite of mine, enjoyed with potato crush and burnt aubergine relish. Sweets made from sesame and boiled sugar have always proved very popular with the kids, as well as grown ups! Sesame features widely in many sweets, such as *til gajak*, coated in sugar syrup (see page 28).

Litti Chokha

Rustic Doughballs with Roasted Yellow Lentil Relish

If I ever had to pick just one, this probably would be my inheritance recipe –
baked dough balls filled with spiced chickpeas and raisins, served with burnt
aubergine crush with mustard oil (see page 24). During Makar Sankranti or north
Indian Pongal, this is often cooked in the late afternoon/early evening, and the
fire serves the dual purpose of a bonfire and the equivalent of a barbecue in the
western world.

The rather spicy relish that forms the filling is extremely versatile and can
be used as an accompaniment to a simple meal of steamed rice and vegetables
or as a filling for bread. It's quite commonly made and served in parts of eastern
Uttar Pradesh, Rajasthan and Bihar. It's generally great for dry and arid heat,
as it helps water retention in the body.

This rather basic rustic meal from eastern Uttar Pradesh was often cooked by
my dad when we were growing up. As I have often said, my mother cooked three
meals a day for the five of us, 364 days a year, and we hardly took any notice
of her efforts, whereas my dad cooked one meal a year and it stuck with me!
Think of this al fresco experience as similar to a BBQ in the west – men cooking
man food.

Makes 15 dough balls

For the dough
500g chapati flour
½ teaspoon salt
1 teaspoon carom seeds
25ml vegetable oil
3 tablespoons ghee, for tossing the litti
   (dough balls)

For the filling
400g roasted chana dal, ground
75ml mustard oil, or oil from hot
   mango pickle
2 red onions, finely chopped
4 garlic cloves, finely chopped
4 green chillies, finely chopped
2.5cm piece of ginger, finely chopped
1½ teaspoons carom seeds
1½ teaspoons nigella seeds
1 tablespoon salt
1 tablespoon sugar
3 tablespoons freshly chopped
   coriander
4 tablespoons raisins

To make the dough, mix the flour, salt, carom seeds and vegetable oil together
in a bowl with 225ml of water. Knead until smooth, then set aside to rest for
10 minutes.

To make the filling, mix together all the ingredients and keep refrigerated. It
keeps really well and may be stored in an airtight container for up to a week.
If you wish, add more oil to the mix to get it to hold together better.

Divide the dough into 15 balls, each of about 50g. Flatten each dough ball
slightly, then make an indentation with your thumb to create a cavity which
is slightly thicker at the bottom and thinner at the sides. The cavity should be
big enough to accommodate 40–50g of the lentil filling. Place the filling in the
cavity, then pull the dough from the sides to cover the filling and set aside.

Preheat the oven to 200°C/180°C Fan/Gas Mark 6.

Lay the dough balls on a wire rack and bake in the preheated oven for 15–18
minutes, turning once if needed. Some parts of the dough balls may begin to
blister and crack but that's OK. Remove from the oven and toss the litti with
ghee when they are still warm.

Serve with aubergine relish with mustard oil and garlic (see page 24).

Madras Sambar

Tamil Sambar with Mixed Vegetables

This is a favourite meal for most Tamilians at Pongal. The Tamil *sambar* is different from other versions as it doesn't use coconut, which is otherwise seen in Andhra and sometimes Kerala. Don't worry if you can't find some of the vegetables listed – just use what you can and increase quantities to suit. It's quite a flexible dish in that sense.

Serves 4

100g toor lentils, washed in 2 changes of water and soaked in water for 20 minutes
2 teaspoons ground turmeric
4 teaspoons salt
2 sprigs of fresh curry leaves
50ml vegetable oil
1 whole dried red chilli
2 teaspoons black mustard seeds
½ teaspoon fenugreek seeds
1 teaspoon white urad dal
¼ teaspoon asafoetida
100g shallots, sliced
200g tomatoes, finely chopped
2 small aubergines (about 90g in total), stalk discarded and flesh diced
50g white pumpkin, peeled and diced into 2cm cubes
50g drumstick, cut into 2cm long pieces (optional)
1 small mango, seed removed, peeled and diced into 1cm cubes
120ml tamarind pulp
10g jaggery or molasses, grated
1 tablespoon freshly chopped coriander leaves

For the Tamil sambar masala
1 teaspoon toor dal
1 teaspoon cumin seeds
1 teaspoon chana dal
1 teaspoon peppercorns
1 tablespoon coriander seeds
a sprig of fresh curry leaves
2 dried whole red chillies, broken, stalk removed

Place the drained lentils in a pan with the turmeric, ½ teaspoon of the salt, 1 sprig of the curry leaves and 1 litre of water. Bring to the boil and cook for 50 minutes or until thoroughly cooked, then set aside (no need to drain).

Dry roast the ingredients for the sambar masala in a shallow frying pan for 2–3 minutes over a medium heat until they give off a roasted aroma. Let them cool, then grind to a fine powder using a mortar and pestle or a blender.

Heat the oil in a pan, add the dried red chilli and stir for 30 seconds or until it changes colour and becomes dark red and blistered in parts. Immediately add the mustard seeds, fenugreek seeds and urad dal and stir for 15 seconds until they crackle and pop and the lentils change colour and become darker brown. Add the asafoetida, the remaining curry leaves and the sliced shallots and sauté well for 5–6 minutes. When the shallots have softened, add all the remaining vegetables, drumstick (if using) and the mango and stir to mix well. Cook over a high heat for 3–4 minutes, then add the remaining salt and the sambar masala. Mix well, add 350ml of water and the tamarind pulp, and boil for 10 minutes, then add the jaggery and cook for another couple of minutes. Add the boiled lentils and cook over a low heat for a further 10 minutes.

Check the seasoning and finish with fresh coriander. Serve with plain rice.

Top right: Litti Chokha (page 14)
Bottom left: Baingan ka Chokha (page 24)

Top right: Chivda Mutter (page 25)
Middle: Andhra Til Chutney (page 28)
Bottom right: Achari Kaddu ki Subzi (page 18)

Achari Kaddu ki Subzi

Pumpkin Curry with Pickle Spices

This is an adaptation of my mother's recipe for sweet pumpkin chutney and as a child I was a great fan of this rich, sweet and spicy dish with strong flavours. In its intense chutney form, it was fantastic with parathas and could also be used as a spread in sandwiches or wraps. As good as it is as a chutney, this curry is the real thing and a brilliant way to enjoy pumpkin in all its glory. Serve with either plain boiled rice or simple bread.

I remember as a child we lived for some time in our small colliery town, and the nearest market was a few miles away so food shopping wasn't easy. My mum was reliant on either my dad or his driver to bring back the shopping. During those days, once or twice a week a vegetable seller would come to the colliery in the afternoons, selling vegetables from a basket carried over his head. From time to time my mum would buy vegetables from him, particularly if he had a pumpkin for sale. She would always tell me 'It's probably the heaviest of all the things he is carrying and he will be happy to lose the load off his head'. That I loved her pumpkin dishes more than any other vegetable is beside the point!

Serves 4

4 tablespoons vegetable oil
½ teaspoon fenugreek seeds
1 teaspoon nigella seeds
4 dried red chillies, each broken in 2–3 pieces
1kg pumpkin, peeled, seeds and fibre removed, diced into 2.5cm cubes
1 teaspoon ground turmeric
2 teaspoons salt
2 teaspoons red chilli powder
4 tablespoons sugar
2 teaspoons dried mango powder or mango chutney (optional)
2 tablespoons freshly chopped coriander

Heat the oil in a pan, add the fenugreek seeds, nigella seeds and dried red chillies and allow them to pop. Add the pumpkin and stir over a high heat for 4–5 minutes. Add the turmeric, salt, red chilli powder and sugar, and stir for 2 minutes, then add 500ml of water, reduce the heat to medium, and cook for 8–10 minutes until the pumpkin is tender and but still retains its shape. If the curry appears thin, simply mash a few pieces of the pumpkin with a spoon or ladle to thicken the sauce.

Finish with the dried mango powder or a couple of teaspoons of mango chutney, sprinkle with chopped coriander and serve with rice or bread of your choice.

This pumpkin curry makes an excellent accompaniment for game dishes, such as grouse or deer, too.

Padavalanga Kootu

Snake Gourd Stew

This is a delicious recipe using snake gourd – a vegetable frequently used in south Indian cooking. Although it's becoming increasingly available in supermarkets and good Asian stores in the UK, if you can't find it, feel free to replace with aubergine or bottle gourd (*doodhi*), or even courgettes. They taste delicious cooked like this.

Serves 6

75g chana dal, washed and soaked in
   water for 20 minutes
100g moong dal, washed and soaked
   in water for 20 minutes
2 teaspoons ground turmeric
1 tablespoon salt
2 sprigs of fresh curry leaves
50ml vegetable oil
200g shallots, thinly sliced
2 green chillies, slit lengthways
7 small garlic cloves, thinly sliced
400g snake gourd, peeled and sliced
   in half lengthways, then into 5mm
   thick pieces
200g tomatoes, finely chopped
2 tablespoons freshly chopped
   coriander leaves
juice of ½ lemon (optional)

For the coconut spice mix
½ teaspoon black peppercorns
1 teaspoon cumin seeds
20g desiccated coconut

For the tempering
20g ghee
1 whole red chilli
2 teaspoons black mustard seeds
2 teaspoons white urad dal
a sprig of fresh curry leaves
½ teaspoon asafoetida

Dry roast the 3 spice mix ingredients in a pan until golden in colour, then cool and grind coarsely.

Drain the lentils and mix together in a pan, add 1.75 litres of water, 1 teaspoon of the turmeric, 1 teaspoon of the salt and 1 sprig of the curry leaves. Bring to the boil, cover and boil for 30–40 minutes until the lentils are cooked. Drain and set aside.

Heat the oil in a pan, then add the shallots, green chillies, garlic, the remaining curry leaves and the remaining salt and cook over a medium-low heat for 5 minutes. When the shallots have softened, add the remaining turmeric and the snake gourd and sauté for 3–4 minutes. Add the tomatoes and cook over a low heat for 10 minutes, then add the cooked lentils and coconut spice mix, mix well and cook for another 10–15 minutes.

For the tempering, heat the ghee in a pan and add the whole red chilli and mustard seeds. When the mustard seeds splutter, add the urad dal, curry leaves and asafoetida. Pour the hot mixture into the pan with the gourd and lentils, then finish with the coriander leaves and lemon juice.

Kichri

Kedgeree with Cauliflower, Carrots and Peas

Kedgeree, or *kichri* as it is known in India, is a humble dish perfectly suited to cold, rainy days. When it is combined with crunchy, caramelised, spicy cauliflower, carrots and peas, there is a fascinating interaction of textures and flavours.

Serves 4

2 tablespoons vegetable or corn oil
1 teaspoon cumin seeds
½ teaspoon black onion seeds
½ teaspoon fennel seeds
2.5cm piece of fresh ginger, finely chopped
3 green chillies, slit and finely chopped
½ cauliflower head, cut into 1cm florets
1 carrot, diced into 1cm cubes
150g petits pois or green peas
1 teaspoon salt
pinch of ground turmeric
½ teaspoon sugar
2 tablespoons white vinegar or cider vinegar (optional)
50g fresh coriander, chopped

For the kichri
150g split yellow moong lentils, washed in 2–3 changes of water and soaked for 20 minutes
50g basmati rice, washed in 2–3 changes of water and soaked for 20 minutes
1½ teaspoons salt
a pinch of ground turmeric
3 tablespoons ghee or clarified butter
1 teaspoon cumin seeds
4 garlic cloves, finely chopped
1 large onion, finely chopped
1cm piece of fresh ginger, finely chopped
2–3 green chillies, finely chopped
2 tablespoons freshly chopped coriander
juice of 1 lemon

Start by making the kichri. Place the drained lentils and rice in a heavy-based pan with the salt, turmeric and 1 litre of water. Bring to the boil and skim any scum from the surface of the water. Lower the heat, partially cover and cook for 25–30 minutes until the lentils and rice are cooked thoroughly. Remove from the heat and set aside.

Meanwhile, get on with the vegetables. Heat the oil in a frying pan, add the cumin seeds and let them crackle. Add the onion seeds, fennel seeds, ginger and chillies, and then the cauliflower, carrot and peas. Stir over a high heat for 1–2 minutes, then add the salt, turmeric, sugar and vinegar. Stir to mix, then cover with a lid, reduce the heat and allow the vegetables to cook in their own steam for 2–3 minutes. Remove the lid, add the coriander and heat through, then remove from the heat and keep warm.

Back to the kichri – heat 2 tablespoons of the ghee or butter in a pan, add the cumin seeds and garlic and cook gently until golden. Add the onion and sauté until it begins to colour, then stir in the ginger and green chillies and cook for 1 minute. Stir in the cooked rice and lentils plus any cooking liquid and the coriander and stir over a low heat for 3–4 minutes. If the kichri appears too thick or gloopy, add boiling water to water it down a little (the dish is meant to be quite wet and will continue to thicken after cooking). Correct the seasoning as required and finish with the remaining tablespoon of ghee or butter and the lemon juice. Remove from the heat and keep warm.

Divide the kedgeree among 4 plates and serve with the vegetable stir-fry on top.

Left: Padavalanga Kootu (page 19)
Right: Madras Sambar (page 15)

Baingan ka Chokha

Aubergine Relish with Mustard Oil and Garlic

A *chokha* is the ultimate pairing for the humble *kichri* served up at Makar Sankranti in Uttar Pradesh. This simple but very effective aubergine crush is an excellent accompaniment to grilled meats and fish. It is also very versatile, and can be served as a filling for wraps too. The aubergines can be either roasted in an oven or charred on a very hot grill, or even burnt on an open flame. Akin to roasting peppers to remove the skin, this imparts a wonderful smokiness to the dish. Unlike a north Indian aubergine crush where the aubergines are cooked further with onions, tomatoes and spices after being roasted, this version is eastern Indian in influence.

Serves 4 as a generous accompaniment

2 large aubergines
4 garlic cloves, each cut into half
5 tablespoons mustard oil (optional, feel free to substitute olive oil)
3 green chillies, finely chopped
2 red onions, finely chopped
2 tablespoons freshly chopped coriander
juice of 2 limes
sea salt

Preheat the oven to 200°C/180°C Fan/Gas Mark 6.

Prick the aubergines using a sharp pointed knife and stuff the halved garlic cloves into them. Smear each aubergine with ½ tablespoon of the oil, place on a baking tray and bake in the preheated oven for 30–40 minutes until the aubergines are roasted and completely cooked. Don't worry if the skin is charred – you actually want that to happen. Alternatively, you can cook them on a barbecue or the flame of a gas hob, which allows the skin to become properly burnt. This adds smokiness and umami to the finished dish.

Allow the aubergines to cool, then peel and discard the skin and stem. Chop up the aubergine pulp and mix with the green chillies, onions, coriander, lime juice and the remaining oil. Add sea salt to taste.

Chivda Mutter

Crisp Rice Flake Stir-fry with Fresh Peas

I remember my mother would make this every day from the day after Makar Sankranti (14th January) until around Holi for my dad's evening snack when he returned from work. If the rice flakes (*pawa*) you are using are the thick variety, then it is advisable to deep fry the rice flakes in very hot oil. If they are the thin variety, they can be slow roasted or shallow fried in a wide pan for 10–15 minutes with continuous stirring.

Serves 6 as a snack

For the rice flakes
50ml vegetable oil
½ red onion, thinly sliced
1 green chilli, slit lengthways
100g pressed rice flakes
½ teaspoon salt
½ teaspoon ground turmeric (optional)
¼ teaspoon red chilli powder (optional)

For the peas
1 tablespoon ghee
1 teaspoon cumin seeds
1 tablespoon garlic chives or spring onion greens, finely chopped
100g shelled peas or petits pois (frozen is fine)
½ teaspoon salt

Start with the rice flakes. Heat the oil in a pan, add the sliced onion and green chilli and stir for 1 minute. Next add the pressed rice flakes and continue cooking over a low-medium heat, stirring constantly for 8–10 minutes until the rice flakes are roasted and turn almost brown and the onion becomes crisp. Sprinkle in the salt, turmeric and chilli powder, if using, and stir for another 2–3 minutes. Remove from the heat and let the mixture cool.

In the meantime, heat the ghee in a separate pan, add the cumin seeds and let them crackle for 30 seconds. Add the garlic chives or spring onions, then add the peas and cook over a high heat for 4–5 minutes until cooked and soft. Season with salt.

Divide the crisp rice flakes among individual plates, top with the cooked peas and serve immediately for the perfect evening or mid-morning snack.

Panchamruth

Temple Nectar

Amruth literally means 'immortal nectar'. This is a mixture of five (*panch*) ingredients that are considered to have health benefits. The combination of these ingredients is often used as a *prasad*, distributed in very small quantities to devotees at the end of a veneration or *puja*. Here we are suggesting serving slightly larger portions, almost like a *lassi* or a milkshake.

Serves 4

1 banana
200ml milk
120ml yoghurt
20g caster sugar
20ml honey
2 sprigs of holy basil, leaves torn (optional)

Blend all the ingredients and chill for 30 minutes. Serve as a lassi in a small cup or bowl, either straight up or over ice.

Top left: Til Gajak (page 28)
Bottom left: Kheer (page 29)
Top right: Panchamruth (page 25)
Bottom right: Moong dal Payasam (page 29)

Andhra Til Chutney

Ginger, Sesame and Jaggery Chutney

The deep, spicy, warm heat of ginger combined with the richness of sesame and the sweet-sour of jaggery and tamarind makes this a rather special chutney. It will keep well even outside the fridge for a couple of days.

Makes about 220ml

100g ginger
1 tablespoon vegetable or
  sesame oil
2 small dried red chillies
2 garlic cloves, finely
  chopped
1 tablespoon urad dal
1½ tablespoons chana dal
2 tablespoons sesame
  seeds
2 tablespoons jaggery or
brown sugar
2 tablespoons tamarind
  pulp
½ teaspoon salt

For the tempering
2 teaspoons vegetable or
  sesame oil
½ teaspoon black or brown
  mustard seeds
a small sprig of fresh curry
  leaves

Peel the ginger and chop it roughly into pieces 5mm x 1cm. Set aside.

Heat ½ tablespoon of the oil in a pan, add the red chillies and garlic and stir for a few minutes until the garlic turns golden brown. Tip out of the pan and set aside.

Add both types of lentils to the same pan and stir for 2 minutes over a medium heat until golden brown. Add the sesame seeds and roast for another minute or so until the sesame seeds begin to pop, turn brown and smell roasted. Remove from the pan.

Heat the remaining ½ tablespoon of oil in the pan oil, add the ginger and sauté for 3–4 minutes until nicely browned, then set aside.

Mix all the cooked ingredients together and let them cool. Add the jaggery and tamarind, then grind coarsely in a blender or food processor. Add just enough water to make a paste in the blender and mix in the salt. Transfer to a bowl.

Heat the oil for the tempering in a pan, add the mustard seeds and curry leaves and let them crackle for 30 seconds or so, then pour over the chutney.

Til Gajak

Sesame and Jaggery Snaps

As a child, these were some of my favourite boiled sweets during Sankranti. When I was growing up they weren't available all year round – only during January – but no one ever made them at home. They were almost always bought in. It took me a few goes to get this right, but do try them. They're great to offer to kids and to serve with coffee at the end of a meal.

Makes 16–20 4cm squares

100g sesame seeds
75g jaggery or brown sugar
½ teaspoon ground
  cardamom
2 tablespoons ghee

Dry roast the sesame seeds in a pan over a medium heat, stirring continuously to avoid them spluttering out of the pan, until the seeds are golden and give off a roasted aroma.

Dissolve the jaggery in a pan with 60ml of water, then bring to the boil and cook to soft crack stage on a sugar thermometer (approximately 132–143ºC). Check its consistency by putting a drop of the syrup in a dish of cold water. If the drop stays firm, the consistency is right.

Add the roasted sesame seeds and ground cardamom to the syrup. Grease an 18cm square metal tray with a film of the ghee and spread out the sesame–jaggery mixture to an even thickness.

Apply some more ghee to a flat spoon and press to flatten the mixture to a thickness of approximately 5mm. When the mixture has cooled down enough to handle, cut it into square pieces. Let it cool completely and store in an airtight container.

Kheer

Rice Pudding with Cardamom

Rice *kheer* is considered to be the simplest and purest of all foods in Hinduism. *Kheer* is often offered to gods during veneration and religious ceremonies, and then distributed among the devotees as *bhog* or *prasadam*, or a blessing, afterwards.

It is one of the few dishes that are made all over the country, from the north to the south and the east to the west, and much like most other recipes, there are thousands of variations! The addition of dried fruit, nuts, raisins or coconut − all these are affectations as the basis of this food of the gods is only three ingredients: milk, sugar and rice.

Serves 4

25g basmati rice
1.3 litres whole milk
6 green cardamom pods
45g sugar
1 tablespoon raisins

1 tablespoon coarsely chopped cashew nuts or almonds
1 teaspoon blanched and coarsely chopped pistachios

Wash the rice in cold running water, then soak in 250ml of water for 15 minutes.

Bring the milk to the boil with the cardamom and sugar, then reduce the heat and simmer until it is about 850ml in volume. Add the drained rice and cook over a low heat for 25−30 minutes, simmering and stirring occasionally until the rice is soft and the grains begin to break up. Add the raisins, cashews or almonds and pistachios and simmer for 3−4 minutes. Remove from the heat and allow it to cool slightly before serving.

Kheer can be served hot or cold, although most commonly it is served at room temperature.

Moong dal Payasam

Moong Lentil Kheer

Most of the nation uses rice to make *kheer* or *payasam*, but this Tamil version with roasted moong lentils is an excellent alternative at Pongal.

Serves 6

200g moong lentils
250g jaggery
50g coconut milk powder, mixed with 100ml warm water

½ teaspoon ground cardamom
40g ghee
30g cashew nuts
20g raisins
20g desiccated coconut

Dry-roast the moong lentils in a frying pan over a low heat for 8−10 minutes, until they change colour, smell roasted and get brown specks in parts. Soak the lentils in 1.25 litres of water for 20 minutes, then drain. Place in a pan and add 1.25 litres of fresh water, bring to the boil and then simmer over a low heat for around 45 minutes, until almost all the water has gone and the lentils are mushy, like porridge.

In a separate pan, make a syrup by dissolving the jaggery in 125ml of water and bring to the boil. Boil just until the jaggery has dissolved and no lumps remain.

When the moong lentils are cooked, add the jaggery syrup and coconut milk to the pan, cook over a medium heat for another 5 minutes, then add the ground cardamom.

Heat the ghee in another small pan, add the cashew nuts and raisins and fry over a low heat for a minute or so until the cashews are golden and the raisins puff up, then add the desiccated coconut and cook over a low heat until they all turn golden. Pour over the lentil kheer, mix and serve hot.

Holi

There are several stories in Hindu mythology about the origins of Holi, but my favourite one is that of Krishna, known for his playfulness and mischief. As naughty and popular as he was in the village, the one thing he couldn't come to terms with was why everybody else in the village was of a fair complexion. Radha, his girlfriend, was especially fair. He often asked his mother Yashoda, 'why is it that I am so dark and Radha so fair?' Tired of Krishna's frequent lamenting and complaining about his complexion, Yashoda gave him a plate of several colours, and said 'You can colour Radha in whichever colours you like.' And so they say began Holi, often known as the festival of love!

Holi is an Indian festival of colours celebrated to announce the arrival of spring and the passing of winter. According to Indian mythology it is a festival celebrating the victory of good over evil. It is also a festival of letting go of what has already passed, traditionally a time to end conflicts and forget past mistakes and move on, and awaken new hopes and strengthen our ties with our friends and loved ones.

Holi festivities at Bankey Bihari Temple in Vrindavan. (Majid Saeedi/Getty)

Holi is a festival unlike anything anywhere else in the
world. Most of the other festivals in this book are about
sharing, remembering, sacrificing or abstinence, but Holi
is also a festival of fun, frolics, pranks and good food. It is
about friends and not taking oneself too seriously.

The only rule about Holi is that there are no rules. For
a hierarchical society like India, where there is a lot of
emphasis on traditions, rituals and rules about not doing
things in certain ways, Holi is the one festival that doesn't
have any rules. This festival bridges social gaps and brings
people together; old and young, men and women, teachers
and students, it's about letting your hair down, having fun,
letting go and celebrating friendships.

Holi is infamously known for its free-for-all carnival
of colours and the iconic paint fights – the way that people
'play Holi' by chasing each other with *gulal* (coloured
powdered paints), wet paints or water. Everyone is
involved, from young to old, and rich to poor, and the riots
of colours are seen in all open spaces, but it is a generally
accepted rule that only dry powder is used inside homes
or in doorways. Before this day of fun begins, however,
people often spend time collecting wood or materials to
build a big bonfire which is lit the night before Holi to
symbolise the victory of good over evil. The festivities
begin with people gathered together and dancing
around the fire.

As a child this was probably my favourite festival. Partly
because there were no formalities, nor any rules, and
partly because what a rowdy riot of a party it could end up
being! It was a public holiday, which meant the coal mine
was shut and all the families in the community had a rare
day off. The entire community, about 300 families, would
play Holi amongst their friends and eventually would all
end up in this massive playground in front of the house.
There would be music, singing, dancing, food and drink,
generally lots of fun!

When we were younger we used to play Holi at different
stages and different levels of intensity. The start of the
day used to be the most hard core, which was playing
Holi with mud and slush; frankly, not very pleasant. The
second stage was with wet colours, whilst the third stage
was with dry colours. Over the years I have dropped the

'hard' Holi way and just play with colours now! The arrival of spring also meant that the weather was much kinder and there was a generally good spirit all around.

Fast forward to modern day life and Holi is being embraced all over the world by people of all backgrounds and faiths. This is one of those festivals that has transcended the bounds of religion and gone on to become a true modern day festival of pure fun. Today there is so much more awareness and interest around what used to be a pretty niche festival when I was growing up, showing how society has evolved and how people are so much more interested in other people's cultures and discovering new experiences.

Dozens of Holi celebrations have cropped up in the UK, most notably being The Cinnamon Kitchen's House of Holi that we are so proud of. I absolutely love the look on people's faces when they walk past a rather austere and formal looking city square in a predictable grey suit, seeing other people throw paints at each other like there's no tomorrow. And they just can't resist the temptation of jumping in and joining in the fun.

Much like the festival, the food itself has very few rules; it's one of the few Indian festivals where it's okay to serve and eat meat. Whether it's a meal or nibbles, snacks, savouries or sweets, just about everything goes.

Top row, left to right: Palak Pakoda Chaat (page 175); Papdi (for Papdi Chaat, page 36); Lentil dumplings (for Dahi Vada, page 40); Mutter Jeera Tikiya Chaat (page 38), Papdi Chaat (page 36); Golgappa (page 52).
Middle row, left to right: Dahi Vada (page 40); Samosa (page 37); Dhaniyey ki Hari Chutney (page 51) and Jodhpuri Mirchi Vada (page 39); curried chickpeas.
Bottom row, left to right: Mutter Jeera Tikiya Chaat (page 38) and curried chickpeas; Imli ki Chutney (page 51); Dahi ka Ghol (page 51).

Papdi Chaat

Crisp Wheat Biscuits with Spiced Potato and Chutneys

Short, crisp discs made with wheat, dipped in tart-sweet tamarind chutney, loaded with spiced potato, more fresh zingy coriander and cooling yoghurt – *papdi chaat* is, for many people, the Prince of Chaats.

Serves 4

oil, for deep frying
2 tablespoons green coriander chutney (see page 51)
50g sev (chickpea vermicelli, available online and in good Asian stores), to garnish
50g pomegranate seeds, to garnish

For the papdi dough
250g plain flour
3 tablespoons ghee
½ teaspoon carom seeds
½ teaspoon salt

For the yoghurt dressing
250ml plain yoghurt
1 teaspoon salt
2 teaspoons sugar
250ml chilled water

For the potato chaat
2 potatoes, boiled in their skins, peeled and diced into 5mm cubes
1 red onion, finely chopped
2 green chillies, chopped
1cm piece of ginger, finely chopped
1 teaspoon chaat masala (see page 261)
1 teaspoon red chilli powder
1 teaspoon cumin seeds, dry roasted in a hot pan for 1 minute and coarsely crushed
1 tablespoon freshly chopped coriander
2 tablespoons tamarind chutney (see page 51)

To make the papdi dough, place all the ingredients in a mixing bowl with 125ml of water and mix to a stiff dough without kneading too much. Set aside for 20 minutes at room temperature.

To make the yoghurt dressing, mix all the ingredients together and refrigerate until required.

Using a rolling pin, roll out the dough to a sheet about 2mm thick. Prick it with a fork to prevent shrinkage. Cut out the dough into circles about 4cm in diameter using a cutter. Deep fry in batches in hot oil at 150–160°C for 6–7 minutes until golden brown. Remove from the oil and spread out on kitchen paper to remove the excess oil. Divide the papdi between 4 plates.

Place all the ingredients for the chaat in a mixing bowl, mix well and spoon it over the papdi. Drizzle the yoghurt dressing and green coriander chutney over and sprinkle sev and pomegranate seeds on top.

Samosa

Punjabi-style Samosas

A samosa is a deep-fried snack sold and eaten on streets all across north India. It is a triangular pastry shell stuffed with either spiced vegetables or meat. The filling can be made from potatoes, onions, peas and lamb (or paneer) with spices. It is commonly served with tamarind-date chutney and coriander chutney or mint chutney and sometimes with ketchup. The real deal with Punjabi samosas is the technique involved in shaping them. Properly made dough and well-folded samosas sit like proud 3D pyramids, much like the proud Punjabi!

Makes 24 samosas

For the filling
2 tablespoons vegetable oil
½ onion, finely chopped
200g lamb mince
1 teaspoon ground cumin
½ teaspoon ground turmeric
½ teaspoon red chilli powder
1 teaspoon salt
1 teaspoon sugar
2 tablespoons cashew nuts, chopped
1 tablespoon raisins
1 medium potato, boiled and grated
125g green peas or petits pois
2 green chillies, finely chopped
1cm piece of ginger, finely chopped
2 tablespoons freshly chopped mint leaves
juice of ½ lemon

For the pastry
130g plain flour
½ teaspoon ajwain or carom seeds
½ teaspoon nigella seeds
¼ teaspoon salt
2 tablespoons vegetable oil, plus extra for deep frying

To make the filling, heat the oil in a pan over a medium heat. Add the onion and sauté until it turns a light golden colour. Add the lamb and cook over a high heat for 2–3 minutes, stirring continuously, then add the ground cumin, turmeric, red chilli powder and salt and cook for a minute or so. Next add the sugar, cashew nuts and raisins and cook for 1 minute, then add the grated potato, peas, chillies and ginger. Cook, stirring well, for 3–4 minutes over a medium heat until well mixed. Finally, sprinkle the chopped mint in and squeeze the lemon juice over. Turn off the heat and let the mixture cool, then divide into 24 equal portions.

To make the pastry, mix the flour, spices and salt in a bowl. Add the oil and rub with your fingers until the oil is incorporated into the flour and you have a crumbly texture. Slowly add 60ml of water and knead into a smooth ball of dough (do not add all the water at once). Rub some oil over the dough ball and cover it with clingfilm. Set aside to rest for 10 minutes.

Roll the dough into a long cylinder and cut with a knife into 12 equal parts. Roll each portion between your palms and press into a circle. Using a rolling pin, roll it gently into a flat circle about 7.5–10cm in diameter. (Do not dust your work surface with flour – if the dough is sticking, use some oil.)

Cut each rolled circle in half to make 2 equal semi-circles. Apply a dab of water to the straight edge and make a cone shape by joining and slightly overlapping the straight edge. Press gently on the join to seal.

Fill the cone with a portion of the cooled stuffing, then apply a little more water on the outer edge and seal the samosa completely. Repeat the same process until all the pastry and filling are used.

Heat the oil for deep frying in a deep pan over a medium heat. Once hot, add a few samosas at a time and deep fry until golden brown. You need to cook over a low-medium heat to allow the pastry shell to cook through, otherwise it will remain dough-like. Fry all the samosas in batches and drain on kitchen paper.

Serve hot with green coriander chutney, mint chutney and tamarind chutney.

Mutter Jeera Tikiya Chaat

Green Pea and Potato Cakes

Pretty much every square in every town has a chaat vendor that people will flock to day and night to sample their range of chaats. During the winter green peas get added but if they're not available, these cakes can be made with just plain boiled potatoes too.

Makes 8

250g green peas, fresh or frozen
2.5cm piece of ginger, peeled and roughly chopped
4 green chillies, roughly chopped
¼ bunch of coriander stalks, washed and roughly cut

5 medium boiled potatoes, peeled and grated
2 teaspoons roasted cumin seeds, crushed
50g cornflour
2 teaspoons salt
35g roasted peanuts, crushed (optional)
vegetable oil, for shallow frying

Place the green peas, ginger, green chillies and coriander stalks in a food processor and coarsely grind them. Place the grated potatoes in a mixing bowl; add the ground green pea mixture and the cumin seeds, cornflour, salt and peanuts. Mix evenly.

Make 8 equal-sized patties and shallow fry them in a medium-hot frying pan for 2–3 minutes on each side until they turn a golden colour on both sides and become crisp. Serve hot with curried chickpeas and tamarind and green coriander chutneys and yoghurt dressing (see page 51).

Makhana

Puffed Lotus Seeds

I remember my dad preparing trays of lotus seeds, chopped nuts and dried fruits to welcome guests during Holi. For some reason, lotus seeds were only offered in our household to guests during Holi or in emergency situations when my mother had run out of virtually everything else in her cupboard! Usually they are served straight up along with chopped dried fruits and nuts, but I prefer the roasted version when they have been sautéed with ghee over a low heat and sprinkled with salt and chaat masala. Then, to add another dimension, I caramelise half of them and mix them back in with the salted version – it's an amazing snack for kids and grown-ups alike.

Serves 6–8

50g ghee
100g puffed lotus seeds (available in good Asian stores and health food shops)
½ teaspoon ground turmeric
½ teaspoon salt

1 teaspoon sugar
2 tablespoons chopped coriander
½ teaspoon chaat masala (see page 261)

For the sweet lotus seeds
100g sugar

Heat the ghee in a pan over a medium heat. Add both types of lotus seeds and roast over a medium heat for 6–8 minutes, stirring constantly. When they start to smell roasted and begin to colour in parts, remove half and then add the turmeric, salt, sugar, coriander and chaat masala to the pan. Mix well and remove from the heat. (If you don't have a pan large enough to hold all the lotus seeds at once, then cook in 2 batches.)

The salted version is ready to serve, and the second part can now be caramelised.

To make the sweet lotus seeds, place the sugar in a large deep frying pan and add 50ml of water. Bring the sugar and water solution to the boil. When it boils, reduce it until it turns into a golden caramel, which will take about 5–6 minutes. Add the reserved roasted lotus seeds, stir to mix evenly, remove and cool on a tray.

Mix the 2 types together and store in an airtight container until ready to serve.

Jodhpuri Mirchi Vada

Spiced Potato-filled Chilli Fritters

Even though the name suggests this dish comes from Jodhpur, these snacks
are popular all over northern India, especially during the winter and at Holi.
It's not uncommon to see young men compete to see how many *mirchi vadas*
they can have during Holi. Men will be men, no matter which part of the world
they live in – I suppose with a few drinks down, bravado kicks in! Contrary to
how it may appear, depending upon the choice of chilli being used, the dish
doesn't have to be 'blow your head off' hot.

Serves 6

300g or 25–30 mild banana chillies,
   Padron peppers or jalapeño peppers
vegetable oil, for deep frying

For the stuffing
4 medium potatoes
1 green chilli, finely chopped
2 tablespoons freshly chopped
   coriander
½ teaspoon fennel seeds, crushed
½ teaspoon ground coriander
1 teaspoon dried mango powder (or
   juice of ½ lemon)
½ teaspoon ground cumin
½ teaspoon red chilli powder

For the batter
120g chickpea flour
¼ teaspoon red chilli powder
1 teaspoon carom seeds
pinch of asafoetida
½ teaspoon salt
pinch of baking soda (optional)

Using the tip of a sharp knife, slit each chilli down one side, taking care to
leave the stalk intact. Slit from the top and keep about 5–10mm uncut at the
bottom. Remove the seeds.

To make the filling, steam or boil the potatoes in their skins until they are
cooked and soft. While the potatoes are still warm, peel and mash them. Add
the remaining stuffing ingredients and mix well. Stuff each slit green chilli with
the potato mixture and set aside.

To make the batter, place the chickpea flour in a bowl with the chilli powder,
carom seeds, asafoetida, salt and baking soda, if using. Add 120ml of water and
mix well to make a medium-thick batter – it should be thick enough to coat
the chillies.

Heat the oil in a deep fryer to 160–170°C.

Dip the stuffed chillies in the batter and coat well. Fry the chillies in batches
in the hot oil for 5–6 minutes or until they are golden. When golden and crisp,
remove from the oil and drain on kitchen paper to remove the excess oil. Serve
hot with tamarind chutney (see page 51) or tomato ketchup.

Dahi Vada

Chilled Lentil Dumplings

These chilled lentil dumplings are perfect as an anytime snack and are
often served on hot summer afternoons or balmy evenings in India. Feel free
to sprinkle some Bombay mix or crushed nuts on top for that extra texture.

Serves 6

For the lentil dumplings
200g white urad dal
1½ teaspoons salt
1 teaspoon black peppercorns,
    coarsely crushed
1 tablespoon golden raisins
2 tablespoons semolina
vegetable oil, for frying

For the yoghurt mixture
600ml plain yoghurt
2.5cm piece of fresh ginger, finely
    chopped
2 green chillies, finely chopped
2 tablespoons freshly chopped
    coriander
½ teaspoon asafoetida
2 teaspoons cumin seeds, roasted and
    coarsely crushed
1 teaspoon red chilli powder
1 teaspoon salt
1 teaspoon sugar

To garnish
tamarind chutney (see page 51)
green coriander chutney (see page 51)
2 tablespoons pomegranate seeds
micro cress (optional)

Rinse the lentils in cold running water and soak in water overnight. Drain
the lentils and blend, adding just enough water to blend to a mixture slightly
thicker than double cream. Add the salt, black peppercorns, raisins and
semolina. Whip together with a spoon until the batter is light and fluffy.

Heat the oil in a deep pan. Divide the batter into 12 round balls of equal size
and deep fry them until golden brown in colour. Remove from the oil with a
slotted spoon and soak the fried dumplings in a bowl of lukewarm water for 20
minutes until soft. Squeeze out the excess water and place them in a deep dish.

Beat the yoghurt with a whisk until smooth (add some water if required).
Add the remaining ingredients and pour over the dumplings, covering them
entirely. Place in the fridge for 30 minutes to chill.

Serve the lentil dumplings garnished with tamarind chutney, green coriander
chutney and pomegranate seeds. Garnish with micro cress, if using, and
serve chilled.

Kathal ki Subzi

Jackfruit Curry

One of the most underrated of all Indian fruits, as well as being the largest tree-borne fruit on the planet, jackfruit isn't the most desirable of fruits in its ripened form. But in its raw (i.e. unripened) form, it is commonly used across India and is highly prized. This dish is a speciality in northern India during Holi. Raw jackfruit curry has a texture similar to meat in this curry.

Serves 4

500g raw jackfruit (available in Indian/ Asian supermarkets; alternatively use two 500–600g cans of tinned jackfruit, drained)
2 tablespoons mustard oil
½ teaspoon cumin seeds
½ teaspoon panch phoron
2 bay leaves
2 dried red chillies
1 green chilli, chopped
3 onions, finely chopped
2 tomatoes, finely chopped
½ teaspoon ground turmeric
1 teaspoon red chilli powder
½ teaspoon ground cumin
1 teaspoon ground coriander
1 teaspoon salt
1 large potato, boiled, peeled and diced into 2.5cm cubes
½ teaspoon garam masala (see page 251)

Peel the jackfruit, remove the seeds and dice into 2.5cm cubes. Place them in a pan with enough water to cover, bring to the boil and cook for 30–40 minutes or until tender. Alternatively, boil them for 10 minutes in a pressure cooker (2 whistles). Drain and set aside.

Heat the mustard oil in a frying pan to smoking point. Add the cumin seeds, panch phoron, bay leaves, dried red chillies and green chilli in that order. Cover and leave for 3–4 minutes. As soon as the red chillies turn dark red, add the chopped onions. Cook over a low heat for 7–8 minutes until the onions are translucent.

Add the chopped tomatoes to the pan. Follow with the turmeric, red chilli powder, cumin, coriander and salt. Stir well and add the jackfruit cubes and boiled potato cubes. Cook over a low heat, covered, for 5–7 minutes, then add the garam masala, cook for another minute and then remove from the heat.

Serve with boiled rice.

Top: Subz Mutter Pulao (page 44)
Bottom left: Khad Murgh (page 48)
Bottom right: Aloo–Gobhi (page 45)

Subz Mutter Pulao

Mixed Vegetable Pilau

In northern India, this vegetable pilau is a firm fixture on most menus at Holi. These are the vegetables that are in season at that time in India, but feel free to replace with whatever seasonal root vegetables you may be able to find. It's just as flexible with a choice of dried fruits and nuts. My mother nearly always makes this dish when she's entertaining, and she always serves it at Holi.

Serves 6–8

400g basmati rice
75g ghee
1 cinnamon stick
3 bay leaves
4 black cardamom pods
½ teaspoon cloves
1 teaspoon cumin seeds
2 red onions, finely sliced
100g cauliflower, cut into 1cm florets
1 carrot, diced into 1cm cubes
1 teaspoon ground turmeric
4 teaspoons salt
1 teaspoon sugar
4 green chillies, slit lengthways
100g frozen petits pois or garden peas
2 tablespoons ready-to-eat raisins
2 tablespoons freshly chopped coriander
2 tablespoons freshly chopped mint leaves
50g cashew nuts, deep fried and coarsely chopped

Wash the rice under cold running water, then soak in a bowl of water for 10 minutes. (Soaking the rice reduces its cooking time and helps to prevent the grains breaking up while cooking.)

Heat the ghee in a heavy-based pan. Add the cinnamon stick, bay leaves, cardamom and cloves and allow them to crackle for a minute or so, then add the cumin seeds. As they start to splutter, immediately add the sliced onions and sauté for 3–5 minutes until they begin to change colour. Add the cauliflower and carrot and stir to mix well, then reduce the heat and sweat for 2–3 minutes. Add the turmeric, salt, sugar and green chillies, and cook for another minute until the turmeric is thoroughly mixed in.

Add the drained rice and carefully stir to mix all the ingredients together. Be careful not to overwork the rice as the grains may break. After a minute or so, mix in the peas and raisins.

(At this stage, you could remove the rice from the heat and let it cool, then store in a refrigerator for a couple of days if you want to get ahead but not finish the pilau just yet.)

To finish the pilau, in a separate pan bring 900ml of water to the boil, keeping the pan covered with a lid. When the water is boiling, add it to the sautéed rice and vegetable mixture and bring back to the boil. Gently stir over a medium-high heat, remembering that too much handling may break the rice grains.

When the water is nearly absorbed and you can see small holes on the surface of the rice in the casserole, sprinkle over the coriander and mint, cover the pan with a tight-fitting lid and reduce the heat to low for 8–10 minutes (alternatively, place in the oven at 120°C/100°C Fan/Gas Mark ½ for 10 minutes for the rice to finish cooking). Sprinkle with the fried cashew nuts before serving.

Another method of cooking is to follow the recipe up to the stage of adding peas and raisins, then pour the 900ml of water over the rice in the container, sprinkle with coriander and mint, cover with clingfilm, prick a few holes in the film and place in a microwave (800W) for 15 minutes. Allow the rice to rest for 5 minutes before serving.

Aloo-Gobhi Gajjar Mutter Tamatar ki Subzi

Vegetable Curry with Potatoes, Cauliflower, Carrots, Peas and Tomatoes

This simple vegetable curry is a firm fixture on the menu at Holi in most of north India. Thinking about it, it's not only served at Holi but at most parties and celebrations. Maincrop potatoes, cauliflower, tomatoes and carrots are in season during Holi in India, but this dish can be made with turnips instead of the vegetables listed below, for example, or served with plenty of sauce to accompany rice. If the quantity of water is reduced, this semi-dry dish goes well with poories – my preference is for the drier version, as the flavours are more pronounced.

Serves 4

3 tablespoons vegetable or corn oil
2 bay leaves
1 teaspoon cumin seeds
3 onions, finely chopped
2 carrots, diced into 1cm cubes
1 large potato, peeled and diced into 1cm cubes
3 ripe tomatoes, blended to a purée or very finely chopped
2 green chillies, halved lengthways
2.5cm piece of fresh ginger, finely chopped
½ teaspoon ground turmeric
½ teaspoon red chilli powder
2 teaspoons ground coriander
2 teaspoons salt
1 cauliflower, cut into 1cm florets
200g frozen peas or petits pois
4 black cardamom pods, seeds only
juice of 1 lemon
½ teaspoon garam masala (see page 261)
2 tablespoons chopped fresh coriander and/or dill

Heat the oil in a heavy-based pan, add the bay leaves and cumin seeds and let them crackle. Add the chopped onions and cook over a fairly high heat for 10–12 minutes until light golden brown.

Now add the carrots and potatoes and stir for 3–4 minutes. Stir in the puréed tomatoes, green chillies, ginger, spices and salt and cook for 8–10 minutes, until the oil begins to separate from the mixture at the sides of the pan. Add the cauliflower and cook, stirring, for 2 minutes, then add the peas and cook for a further 3 minutes.

Pour in 450ml of water and cook until the vegetables are tender but still retain a little bite. Add the black cardamom seeds and check the seasoning, then stir in the lemon juice and garam masala and sprinkle with the chopped herbs. Cover and leave for 3–4 minutes, then serve hot with poories or any flatbread of your choice.

Jhinga 65

Shrimp Stir Fry with Curry Leaf and Mustard Seeds

Strictly speaking, this dish isn't a Holi tradition but it's increasingly making appearances on Holi party menus across the country. This is what most of south India ate in the 1980s before we discovered the joys of Indo-Chinese chilli shrimp. This recipe has been adapted from a military officer's favourite Chicken 65. It's proving just as popular made with prawns.

Serves 6–8 as a snack

400g small prawns
vegetable oil, for deep frying
1 tablespoon freshly chopped
  coriander

For the first marinade
2.5cm piece of ginger, chopped
2 garlic cloves, chopped
3 teaspoons red chilli powder
1 teaspoon salt
2 tablespoons yoghurt

For the second marinade
1 tablespoon ginger-garlic paste (see
  page 260)
2 tablespoons cornflour
½ teaspoon sugar
1 egg
juice of ½ lemon

For the tempering
3 tablespoons vegetable oil
1 teaspoon black mustard seeds
10 curry leaves
50g spring onions, chopped, or ½ red
  onion, chopped
2.5cm piece of ginger, chopped
3 garlic cloves, chopped
1 green chilli, finely chopped
½ teaspoon salt
a pinch of sugar
juice of ½ lemon

Mix together all the ingredients for the first marinade in a large bowl, add the prawns and set aside for 10 minutes.

Mix together all the ingredients for the second marinade, dip the prawn pieces in, then deep fry for 3–4 minutes at 160–170°C until cooked and crisp. Drain on kitchen paper and keep warm.

Heat the tempering oil in a wok, add the mustard seeds and let them crackle for 30 seconds or so. Then add the curry leaves, onions, ginger, garlic and green chilli and sauté over a high heat for 1 minute.

Add the prawns to the pan and toss until the prawns hold all the tempering ingredients. Add the salt and sugar and cook over a high heat, stirring, for another 1–2 minutes until the sugar begins to caramelise but not burn. Keep the heat high and finish with a squeeze of lemon, correct the seasoning and serve immediately.

Garnish with finely chopped coriander and you'll be mobbed in no time.

Murgi Lollipops

Chilli Chicken Wings

When I worked at The Oberoi in New Delhi, we would make huge quantities
of these chicken lollipops (as we called them) for the coffee-shop menu. Coated
in a spiced cornflour batter and deep fried, I find these the best for entertaining
large numbers of guests. I like the way these become really crisp when fried,
and they're still easy enough to eat in spite of messy hands.

Serves 4

1kg chicken wings, skin on (preferably
 use only the one joint from the
 shoulder to the next joint)
100g cornflour
60g rice flour
½ teaspoon red chilli powder
½ teaspoon chicken bouillon
 seasoning (optional)
vegetable oil, for deep frying
50g fresh coriander, chopped
barbecue sauce or hot garlic sauce, to
 serve

For the marinade
1½ teaspoons sea salt
1 teaspoon black peppercorns,
 coarsely cracked
4 garlic cloves, finely chopped
1 teaspoon crushed red chilli flakes
1 teaspoon crushed cumin seeds
1 teaspoon crushed coriander seeds
2 tablespoons dark soya sauce
juice of 1 lemon

Mix the marinade ingredients together in a bowl. Add the chicken wings,
mixing well, and set aside for at least an hour or overnight if possible.

Mix together the cornflour, rice flour, red chilli powder and chicken seasoning,
if using, and set aside in a bowl.

Preheat the oil in the deep fryer to 170°C.

Just before frying, mix the coriander into the marinated wings, then drop them
into the cornflour mix, a few at a time, and roll them so they are dusted evenly
and coated with the flour mix.

Deep fry in the hot oil for 7–8 minutes until the wings are cooked. Fry in small
batches so the fryer isn't crowded, repeating the process until all the chicken is
fried, then drain on kitchen paper and serve with barbecue sauce or hot garlic
sauce on the side.

Khad Murgh

Chicken Tikka Wrapped in Handkerchief Bread

This dish is inspired by how the nomadic tribes would cook chicken in the deserts of Rajasthan – tender marinated chicken wrapped in thin bread, baked for a few hours in a pit dug in the ground and covered with wood and cowpat and then devoured at the end of the day's expedition. This would be an ideal barbecue dish as the smokiness from the charcoal brings out the flavour of the marinade.

Roomali refers to the bread's resemblance to a handkerchief, so thin and so large, and is traditionally cooked on an inverted wok. The technique of making this is similar to that of making a pizza; just toss it in the air and watch it grow!

Serves 4 as a starter

500g boneless chicken legs, diced
    into 2.5cm cubes
8 bamboo skewers, soaked in water

For the first marinade
1 tablespoon ginger-garlic paste (see
    page 260)
½ teaspoon red chilli powder
1 teaspoon ground turmeric
1 teaspoon salt
juice of 1 lemon
2.5cm piece of green papaya, finely
    grated (or use 2 tablespoons freshly
    grated pineapple or juice)

For the second marinade
100ml Greek yoghurt
2 tablespoons wholegrain mustard
1 tablespoon honey
1 teaspoon garam masala
2 green chillies, finely chopped
1 tablespoon freshly chopped
    coriander
2 tablespoons mustard oil
    (alternatively use vegetable oil mixed
    with 1 teaspoon English mustard)

For the roomali bread
150g chapati flour (fine ground
    wholemeal flour)
100g plain flour, plus extra for dusting
½ teaspoon salt

Mix together all the ingredients for the first marinade and rub it onto the chicken legs, massaging it well into the meat. Set aside.

Now mix together all the ingredients for the second marinade and add it to the chicken. Marinate for an hour or so in the fridge (you could marinate it overnight too).

Thread the chicken pieces onto skewers and cook on a hot barbecue for 10–15 minutes, turning regularly. Alternatively, preheat the oven to 180°C/160°C Fan/Gas Mark 4, place the chicken skewers on a baking tray and cook in the oven for 18–20 minutes, turning them regularly. If the chicken cooks but does not take colour, place under a very hot grill for a couple of minutes.

Meanwhile, make the bread. Mix together the 2 flours, salt and 125ml of water and knead to a soft smooth dough. (If you wish, you could use 120ml of spinach purée instead of the water to give a bright green bread.) Let the dough rest for 15 minutes, then divide it into 6 equal balls, cover them with clingfilm and let them rest for 5 minutes.

Dust your work surface with flour. Roll the dough in thin pancakes about 15cm in diameter, then enlarge the pancakes by tossing like a pizza base. This requires some practice – you usually get plenty of fails, but on the whole, it's very entertaining! This recipe makes enough dough for 6 pancakes – allowing you a couple of practice runs if necessary!

Once the dough is as thin as you can possibly manage, turn it out onto an inverted wok if you have one or just lay it on a flat griddle over a high heat, and the bread cooks in a matter of seconds!

Preheat the oven to 180°C/160°C Fan/Gas Mark 4. Wrap a portion of cooked chicken in the thin bread to make a parcel, then wrap the entire thing in foil and bake for about 20 minutes until the bread is crisp. This is great served with pickled onions and a kachumbar salad (roughly chop onion, carrot and cucumber and mix together).

Khela Kalia

Holiday Meat Curry

This is a kind of celebration meat dish that can be prepared on any holiday, be it on account of Holi, Dussehra, any Bank Holiday or even a Sunday! In my ancestral village in Ballia, it is called *Khela Kalia* and in Bengal, there is a similar recipe that goes by the name Sunday Special Meat Curry (*Robibarer Mangsho*).

Serves 6

1kg goat meat, diced into 2.5cm
    cubes (usually on the bone)
6 tablespoons plain yoghurt
2 tablespoons mustard oil (optional)
1½ teaspoons cumin seeds
4–5 hot green chillies
60ml vegetable or corn oil
4 potatoes, peeled and halved
4 red onions, finely chopped
6 bay leaves
2 tablespoons ginger-garlic paste (see
    page 260)
1 tablespoon ground coriander
1 tablespoon ground turmeric
2 teaspoons red chilli powder
2 teaspoons salt
2 tablespoons ghee
2 tablespoons freshly chopped
    coriander leaves

For the rustic garam masala
16 green cardamom pods
2 x 5cm cinnamon sticks
24 cloves
2 tablespoons black peppercorns

Start by marinating the meat with the yoghurt and mustard oil, if using, and set aside for about 30 minutes.

Make the rustic garam masala by grinding the spices together.

Blend the cumin seeds and green chillies together in a mortar and pestle to make a coarse paste.

Heat the oil in a large heavy-based pan, add the potatoes and gently fry for 3–5 minutes until coloured on the outside. Remove from the pan and set aside.

Add the chopped onions and the bay leaves to the same pan and sauté for 8–10 minutes until the onions start changing colour, then add the ginger-garlic paste and the cumin-chilli paste. Fry them with the onions for 3–5 minutes and when you see the oil separating, add the ground spices, red chilli powder and 2 tablespoons of the rustic garam masala. Continue to cook over a low heat, stirring continuously to make sure the spices do not burn.

When the oil starts to separate, add the marinated meat and salt. Slightly increase the heat and continue to *bhunno* (i.e. to sauté well, to heat the spices sufficiently so the oils are released from them) the meat for about 15–20 minutes until the meat appears browned at the edges and the juices have evaporated.

At this point, either transfer the meat to a pressure cooker or continue cooking in the same pan. Either way, add the potatoes, the remaining tablespoon of garam masala and the ghee, then stir to mix. Add 475ml of water if cooking in a pressure cooker, or 1 litre of water if cooking in the pan. Reduce the heat and cook until the meat is tender and the potatoes cooked through; this should take 15 minutes in a pressure cooker, or 45 minutes in a pan. Reduce the heat and simmer until the gravy is thick and rich.

Check the seasoning and serve immediately with either pulao or poories, and garnish with the chopped coriander leaves.

Clockwise from top left:
Thandai (page 52); Shikanji
(page 53); Makhana (page
38); Jinga 65 (page 46); Murgi
Lollipops (page 47)

Imli ki Chutney

Tamarind Chutney

Makes 450ml

350ml tamarind pulp
1½ teaspoons red chilli powder
½ teaspoon salt
100g jaggery or brown sugar
50g pitted dates, chopped (optional)
½ teaspoon ground ginger

Mix all the ingredients together in a pan with 200ml of water. Bring to the boil, then lower the heat and simmer for 15 minutes, skimming intermittently to remove any scum that rises to the top. Cook until the sauce is thick and glossy, then allow to cool. Serve with samosas. This chutney keeps for a week in the fridge.

Dhaniyey ki Hari Chutney

Green Coriander Chutney

Makes 280ml

200g coriander leaves and stalks
40g mint leaves, stalks removed (optional)
6 garlic cloves
4 Thai green chillies, stalks removed
5 tablespoons vegetable oil
2 teaspoons salt
1 teaspoon sugar
juice of 1 lemon

Blend together the herbs, garlic and chillies until a soft, spoonable consistency. Cover with the oil and store in the fridge until required.

To use, mix with the salt, sugar and lemon juice, check the seasoning and use as needed.

This chutney will keep in the fridge for 2–3 days, but once salt and lemon have been added, it is best used straight away. It can be served with chaats, or even kebabs from the tandoor.

Dahi ka Ghol

Yoghurt Dressing

Makes 320ml

250ml plain yoghurt
1 teaspoon sugar
½ teaspoon salt
½ teaspoon cumin seeds, roasted and then crushed

Mix the ingredients together with 75ml of water. Most chaats are served with a mélange of the 3 chutneys – yoghurt, tamarind and green coriander – in proportions suited to your individual preference.

Golgappa

Crisp Pastry, Spiced Potatoes and Chutneys

These *golgappa* or *pani puris* are possibly the most popular and recognised of all street food in India. The explosion of flavours when the semolina shell bursts in your mouth and the spiced liquid fills the space is an experience everyone should have at least once in their lives!

Serves 4

32 ready-made puris or golgappa (available online or in good Asian stores)
1 onion, finely chopped
50g sev
100g tamarind chutney (see page 51) (optional)

For the tangy green water
30g mint leaves, chopped
60g coriander leaves, chopped
2 green chillies, chopped
1cm piece of fresh ginger
juice of 1½ lemons
3 tablespoons sugar
1 teaspoon chaat masala

(see page 261)
¼ teaspoon black salt
1 teaspoon salt (optional)

For the filling
200g boiled, peeled potatoes (approx. 3 medium potatoes)
75g boiled black chickpeas
½ teaspoon red chilli powder
½ teaspoon roasted ground cumin
¼ teaspoon ground chaat masala
2 tablespoons finely chopped coriander leaves, optional
1 teaspoon salt

To make the tangy green water, place the mint, coriander, green chillies, ginger and lemon juice in a grinder. Grind until it makes a smooth paste (if required, add 120ml of water while grinding). Transfer the mixture to a large bowl and add the sugar, chaat masala, black salt and 900ml of water. Stir with a large spoon to mix. Taste for the salt and add as required. Place the spiced water in a refrigerator for at least 1 hour before serving – it tastes best chilled.

To make the filling, mash the potatoes with half of the chickpeas, then season with the remaining filling ingredients. Mix through the remaining whole chickpeas and refrigerate to chill.

To assemble, take each puri and gently make a large hole in the centre of its top side. Stuff with the filling, sprinkle the chopped onion and sev over it and drizzle with a drop of tamarind chutney, if using. Dip each shell in the green water and pop into your mouth! Alternatively, fill the shells and serve with the chilled water in a jug on the side.

Thandhai

Spiced Milk Cooler

This is the base for the quintessential Holi drink *bhaang*. Originally supposed to be spiked with a paste of cannabis leaves, it is believed to be Shiva's preferred drink. Without the cannabis, *thandhai* is still a great refreshing drink to be enjoyed on any hot day.

Serves 8–10

150g sugar
2 tablespoons ground almonds
1 tablespoon melon seeds
½ tablespoon fennel seeds
½ tablespoon white poppy seeds
1 teaspoon black peppercorns
40g dried rose petals
250ml milk
½ teaspoon ground cardamom
½ teaspoon rose water

Dissolve the sugar in 500ml of water and set aside.

Mix all the other ingredients, except the milk, cardamom and rose water, together and soak in 500ml of water. Keep aside for 2 hours.

Grind all soaked ingredients to a very fine paste using a mortar and pestle or electric blender.

Add another 500ml of water to the paste and pass it through a fine sieve or muslin to extract all the liquid. Add the sugar solution, milk, cardamom and rose water to the extracted liquid. Keep refrigerated and serve over cubes of ice.

Shikanji

Still Indian Lemonade

This cooling Indian drink is made during the summer. The salt and sugar help keep the body hydrated in the intense heat, and the mint and lemon add extra freshness and zing. You could use sparkling water if you prefer, for a not-so-still lemonade.

Serves 4–6

juice of 3 large lemons
20 mint leaves, crushed, plus a few whole leaves reserved to garnish

2 teaspoons roasted cumin, crushed in a mortar and pestle
75g sugar
1 teaspoon rock salt
ice cubes, to serve

In a bowl mix together the lemon juice, crushed mint leaves, crushed roasted cumin, sugar and salt and stir until the sugar dissolves. Pour over 750ml of water and mix well. Leave to infuse for 30 minutes, then strain through a fine sieve and refrigerate until chilled.

When you're ready to serve, place a few ice cubes in each glass, scatter some mint leaves on top and divide the lemon drink between the glasses. If you like, top the drinks with soda water or fizzy water.

Malpua

Deep-fried Indian Pancakes

Pua (short for malpua) is something my mum makes each year at Holi, and whenever she is feeling happy! Commercially sold malpuas have reduced milk, cream and many such luxury ingredients to make them tasty, but I still much prefer this homely version over the shop-bought ones. I have an early memory of a very large *kadhai* of oil being used for frying both poories and malpuas for a very large gathering at Holi. Sometimes the cooks would accidentally drain off the malpuas in the tray for poories... This was quite a happy accident for those sitting down to eat at that time, as they would receive sweet malpuas instead of plain poories! This is such a simple recipe, ready in literally no time, so give this a go.

Serves 4–6

250g plain flour
200g sugar
enough milk to make a smooth pouring batter (about 500ml)

½ teaspoon green cardamom powder
2 tablespoons golden raisins
½ banana, mashed (optional)
vegetable oil, for deep frying

Mix together all the ingredients (except the oil) to make a smooth batter, then set aside in the fridge for 2–3 hours to allow the flavours to develop.

Pour the oil in a wok to the depth of around 5cm and heat to medium-hot.

Mix the batter using a spoon, then pour a small ladle full of the batter into medium-hot oil to fry for 3–4 minutes until the edges are crisp and the middle of the pancake is still soft. Turn over halfway through the cooking when the underside is golden and crisp. Drain, using a slotted spoon. Let it cool for a minute or so, and then serve with ice cream of your choice or on its own.

This mixture will make approximately 20 pancakes.

Easter

Easter is one of the most significant festivals in the Christian calendar, celebrating the resurrection of Jesus Christ which is at the heart of the religion. Although Christians constitute just 3 per cent of the total population in India, Easter is celebrated with full pomp and show especially in the largest Christian communities such as Goa, Maharashtra, Kerala and Mangalore. Church services and vibrant carnivals are part of the festivities, decorated Easter eggs, flowers and colourful lanterns are exchanged as gifts, and plays, songs and dances are staged.

A traditional Palm Sunday procession, similar to that seen all over the world, is often undertaken by communities the week before the main celebration, and further processions also take place on Good Friday, often with re-enactments of the Bible story taking place in the streets. Midnight vigils are also held to commemorate the death of Christ.

I have many memories of Easter from my time in Asansol where I attended St Patrick's School, which is an Irish brothers' Christian school. Asansol was a massive industrial town due to its steel and coal resources – it was probably the biggest industrial town after Calcutta (now Kolkata) in West Bengal – and had a very big Anglo-Indian community, which meant that there were dozens of Christian schools. I suppose as a young boy I didn't quite understand what Easter was about, or the sombre nature of its origins, but what I do remember is that the boys would go out singing and dancing at night after the

Christians carry palm fronds during a Palm Sunday procession, marking the beginning of Holy Week and the last week of lent. (Mujeeb Faruqui/Hindustan Times/Getty)

Midnight Mass (it was a good excuse to be outdoors late at night!), and we would all end up at a friend's house.

The kind of food that was served at Easter was very recognisable to us Bengali and Indian boys but often had an Anglo influence. For example, dishes like duck roast would be served – although they'd be called duck roast but were barely a roast, rather duck in a sauce or curry – or things like Lady Kenny's very dark *gulab jamuns* were enjoyed, which were like any other *gulab jamuns*, just much darker and slightly more caramelised. It was and is an incredible example of how these very different influences come together to create something rather wonderful and new.

One of the places where Easter is most celebrated in India is Goa, which was a Portuguese colony pre-independence. In this small western state, Easter celebrations are vibrant and energetic, with plays, music and dances being performed in the street. In Goa traditional Easter recipes reflect the legacies left by the Portuguese in India; sweet treats are baked and Portuguese and Indian ingredients are combined to create a fiery Easter lunch with dishes such as prawn *balchao*, chicken *cafreal* and fish peri peri.

In India the food cooked around the time of Easter varies from region to region due to the diversity in the lifestyle and culture. Although Easter is not as popular as Christmas in India, or celebrated as widely, Christians ensure that the resurrection of Jesus Christ is celebrated with great enthusiasm. To serve the purpose, many people have adopted the popular tradition of hosting lavish lunch, dinner and Easter parties. Interesting games are arranged to keep up the festive spirits. You can see small children making beautiful crafts for the festival. All in all, Easter is another wonderful festival that embraces fun and feasting.

Balchao

Prawn Balchao

This is yet another example of playing the hits – a *balchao* appears at several celebrations, including weddings and at Easter. Although traditionally this is a pickle, meant to be enjoyed for days after it's been made, it tastes just as delicious fresh and hot! As a celebration dish or even cooked simply on a barbecue, this is and will always be a show-stopper.

You may find the portions slightly small for a main course on its own, but the dish works well served along with a few others and on its own may be a bit too spicy and full-on for a balanced meal. Try to combine this with a mild and saucy curry.

Serves 4

4 tablespoons vegetable or corn oil
3 red onions, finely chopped
10 fresh curry leaves
2 tablespoons ginger-garlic paste (see page 260)
3 green chillies, chopped
½ teaspoon ground turmeric
1½ teaspoons salt
1 teaspoon sugar
3 tablespoons malt vinegar
15–18 large king prawns, head on, slit open and left on the shell
juice of 1 lime
2 tablespoons freshly chopped coriander

For the spice mix
1 tablespoon cumin seeds, dry roasted in a pan
1 teaspoon black peppercorns
1 teaspoon red chilli powder

For the spice mix, mix together the roasted cumin seeds, peppercorns and red chilli powder in a food processor until fine.

Heat the oil in a large frying pan, add the onions and curry leaves and stir over a medium heat until golden brown. Add the ginger-garlic paste and green chillies and stir for 1 minute. Add the turmeric, followed by the spice mix and sauté for 3–4 minutes until the spices are cooked. Add the salt, sugar and malt vinegar and continue cooking until the oil separates (less than 5 minutes).

Remove and cool the mixture. If making for later, transfer to an airtight container and refrigerate.

If using immediately, smear the cooked paste on to the king prawns on the flesh side and marinate for 20 minutes while you get your grill or barbecue hot. Simply cook for 3–4 minutes on each side, and serve immediately squeezed with lime and sprinkled with coriander.

Top left: Wak Me-A-Mesang Pura (page 72)
Bottom left: Kabri Fish (page 63)
Top right: Galinha Cafreal (page 64)
Bottom right: Caldinho di Peixe (page 62)

Caldinho de Peixe

Fish in a Light Coconut Milk Curry

This fresh and lightly spiced fish curry is one of several dishes laid out on a Goan family table during Easter but you can also serve this on its own with rice for a perfectly acceptable midweek dinner. Ask your fishmonger to cut the fish into darnes for you (you can, of course, just use fillets, but the flavour and shapes are much better with the bone left in).

Serves 4

250g grated coconut (frozen is fine)
1 teaspoon ground turmeric
2 teaspoons cumin seeds
1½ tablespoons coriander seeds
2 tablespoons uncooked rice
6 garlic cloves, peeled
2 medium white onions, 1 chopped
   and 1 thinly sliced
3 green chillies, 1 finely chopped and
   2 slit open
2 whole trout (or pomfret), heads
   removed and cut into darnes on the
   bone, approx. 2.5cm thick
1½ teaspoons salt
2 tablespoons vegetable oil
1 teaspoon sugar
1½ tablespoons white wine vinegar

Grind the coconut with 200ml of warm water, the turmeric, cumin and coriander seeds, rice, garlic, chopped onion and chopped green chilli in a blender to obtain a thick, spicy coconut extract.

Pass the extract through a sieve, pressing to extract as much liquid as possible (this is the first thick coconut/spice extract). Blend the spices and coconut husk left in the sieve again with 300ml of warm water and pass through the sieve again to obtain a second thin extract. Keep the 2 extracts separate. Discard anything still left in the sieve.

Season the fish with 1 teaspoon of the salt and set aside.

Heat the vegetable oil in a pan wide enough to accommodate the fish and add the sliced onions. Sauté over a medium heat for 3–4 minutes until the onions are soft. Add the thin (second) coconut extract and reduce the heat, add the remaining salt and sugar and simmer for 6–8 minutes until the spices are cooked and don't taste raw.

Add the fish and the slit green chillies, cover the pan with a lid and cook for 6–8 minutes over a medium heat. Move the pan around to spread the heat evenly but avoid stirring as you don't want the fish to break up.

Add the vinegar and check the seasoning, adjusting the salt and chilli to your taste and adding more if necessary. Finally, add the thick coconut extract and cook over a medium heat for 2 minutes, covered. Do not let the sauce boil vigorously after adding the thick extract as it will lose its shine and richness. Remove from the heat and serve with rice.

Kabri Fish

Fish Curry with Milk and Butter

This off-beat recipe – a sort of hybrid between European fish and béchamel bake and a mild curry for kids – isn't an everyday dish. Anglo-Indian families in Asansol (the mining cum railway town that I grew up in) would serve this at Easter.

Serves 4–6

1kg boneless fillet of large white fish, such as monkfish, or halibut, cut into 4cm cubes
1½ teaspoons salt
200ml vegetable oil
1 tablespoon cornflour
500ml milk
5cm piece of cinnamon
6 green cardamom pods
5 bay leaves
1 tablespoon ginger paste (see page 260)
6 green chillies, slit lengthways
60g cold butter
1 tablespoon freshly chopped coriander or parsley

Season the fish with ½ teaspoon of the salt. Heat the oil in a wok and fry the fish in 2 or 3 batches. Set aside.

Dissolve the cornflour in 2 tablespoons of the milk to make a loose paste.

Pound the cinnamon and cardamom together.

Heat the remaining milk in a large pan with the pounded cinnamon–cardamom and bay leaves and boil for 2–3 minutes. Remove the skin from the boiled milk, then stir in the cornflour mixture and cook the milk until it has reduced by a third.

Add the ginger paste, green chillies, fried fish and remaining salt to the pan. Cook for a couple of minutes until the sauce has thickened considerably, then add the cold butter and stir to mix until the butter just melts. Add the coriander or parsley and serve immediately.

Galinha Cafreal

Chicken Cafreal

This is the type of dish where anything goes! I've seen people make this as a curry, as a grilled chicken on a barbecue, with or without skin, fried and even as a roast in the oven. I prefer a grilled or roasted version, leaving a little gravy to dunk pieces of bread into. Use spring chicken which has been spatchcocked and grill it on a barbecue, or just use chicken legs.

Serves 2 as a main, or 4–6 as an accompaniment

2 free-range poussins, cut into 4 lengthways (ask your butcher to do this if you wish) or spatchcocked
1 teaspoon red chilli powder
½ teaspoon ground turmeric
1 teaspoon salt
juice of 1 lime
1 tablespoon freshly chopped coriander

For the spice paste
2.5cm piece of cinnamon stick
4 cloves
2 green cardamom pods
2 star anise
½ teaspoon black peppercorns
5cm piece of ginger, cleaned
4 garlic cloves, peeled
5 green chillies
1 white onion, roughly chopped
70g freshly chopped coriander stems
35g freshly grated coconut
1 teaspoon salt
1 teaspoon sugar
4 tablespoons peanut or vegetable oil
1 tablespoon Worcestershire sauce

Place the poussins in a baking dish and prick them with the tip of a sharp knife. Mix together the chilli powder, turmeric and salt and rub over the poussins. Set aside for 15 minutes.

In the meantime, make the spice paste. Pound together the cinnamon, cloves, cardamom, star anise and peppercorns into a coarse powder, then blend to a fine paste with the ginger, garlic, green chillies and onion. Add the chopped coriander, coconut, salt, sugar, peanut or vegetable oil and Worcestershire sauce and check the seasoning.

Rub the spice paste over the poussins, inside and out, pushing some of the spices between the skin and the flesh, taking care not to rip the skin off. Set aside for 30 minutes in the fridge.

Preheat the oven to 180°C/160°C Fan/Gas Mark 4.

Cook the poussins in the preheated oven for 20 minutes or until the juices run clear. Remove from the oven and rest for 15–20 minutes. To achieve a golden, crispy skin, finish the poussins under a hot grill or on the barbecue.

Reserve the juices and gravy in a pan. Add 100ml of water, then reduce over a medium heat to make gravy. Adjust the seasoning and finish with lime juice, simmering for 10 minutes.

Sprinkle the fresh coriander on top of the poussins, and serve with hunks of baguette or similar bread.

Baffado de Galinha

Chicken in Coconut Gravy

This is yet another of several dishes that would feature on the menu at a Goan family feast. The technique of using a little raw rice while grinding the spice paste slowly brings natural thickening and shine to the sauce as the rice cooks.

Serves 4

5 tablespoons vegetable oil
3 white onions, finely sliced
1 whole medium chicken, skin off, jointed into 10–12 pieces on the bone
2 green chillies, slit lengthways
2 teaspoons salt
240ml coconut milk
3 tablespoons malt vinegar

For the spice paste
6–8 dried whole red chillies, broken, seeds discarded
1 tablespoon coriander seeds
1 teaspoon cumin seeds
8 black peppercorns
2.5cm piece of cinnamon stick
5 cloves
½ teaspoon uncooked rice
½ teaspoon ground turmeric
2 tablespoons ginger-garlic paste (see page 260)

Grind together all the spice paste ingredients using as little water as possible to make a smooth paste (about 2 tablespoons of water should suffice).

Heat the oil in a heavy-based casserole, add the onions and sauté over a high heat for 6–8 minutes or until golden. Reduce the heat to medium, add the spice paste and cook for 4–5 minutes, stirring continuously to prevent it sticking to the bottom of the pan. Increase the heat to high, add the jointed chicken and fry for 5–6 minutes. Add the chillies, salt and coconut milk, lower the heat and simmer for 20 minutes or so, partially covered.

Preheat the oven to 160°C/140°C Fan/Gas Mark 3.

Transfer the casserole dish to the preheated oven and cook, covered with a lid, for 20–25 minutes until the chicken is cooked through (alternatively, you can continue to cook on the hob). Add the vinegar, check the seasoning and serve.

Bhoona Gahori Chaap

Roast Pork Chops

Pork was not used much in Indian cooking until the late eighteenth century. Although most of the country was Hindu and consumption of pork was not barred in Hinduism, a large proportion of the population was vegetarian and pork did not feature much in cooking, except in Anglo-Indian dishes and the cooking of the hills in the eastern part of the country.

This recipe originates from Assam and was very popular with the British when they lived on the tea plantations. The term *bhoona* refers to 'roast' – this was a dish bearing some resemblance to an English roast but using spices to coat the pork chops when the dish was finished. This now frequently makes an appearance on Easter tables of the Anglo-Indian households as a celebratory dish.

Serves 4

6 pork chops, approx. 200g each, excess fat trimmed
1 teaspoon salt
1 teaspoon red chilli powder
1 tablespoon corn oil

For the masala
1½ tablespoons mild chilli powder
1 teaspoon ground turmeric
2 tablespoons ginger-garlic paste (see page 260)
3 tomatoes, finely chopped
60ml corn oil
½ teaspoon fenugreek seeds
20 curry leaves
2 large onions, finely sliced
2 tablespoons tomato ketchup
1 teaspoon salt
1 teaspoon sugar
1 teaspoon garam masala

To garnish
2 large potatoes, peeled and cut lengthways
½ teaspoon salt
½ teaspoon ground turmeric
2 tablespoons corn oil
2 tablespoons freshly chopped coriander

Preheat the oven to 160°C/140°C Fan/Gas Mark 3.

Sprinkle the pork chops on both sides with the salt and red chilli. Heat the oil in a large, heavy ovenproof pan and sear the chops for 2 minutes on each side until they are coloured on the outside. Remove from the pan and set aside.

To make the masala, mix together the chilli powder, turmeric, ginger-garlic paste and finely chopped tomatoes in a bowl and set aside. Heat the oil in the pan used to sear the chops, add the fenugreek seeds and stir for 1 minute. As the seeds begin to brown, add the curry leaves and sliced onions and sauté for 6–8 minutes until the onions begin to turn golden brown in colour. Add the mix of tomatoes and spices to the onions and sauté for another 3–5 minutes until the spices are fragrant. Add 200ml of water and continue cooking until the water has been absorbed.

Return the seared chops to the pan, add the tomato ketchup, salt and sugar and stir until the spices coat the chops evenly. Place the pan in the preheated oven for 8–10 minutes or until the pork juices run clear.

Meanwhile, make the garnish. Boil the potatoes in 500ml of water with the salt and turmeric added to the pan for 6–8 minutes until cooked al dente, then drain. Heat the oil in another pan and colour the potatoes until they are crisp on the outside and golden in colour.

Remove the chops from the oven and sprinkle over the garam masala.

To serve, arrange the pork chops on a platter and pour the thick gravy over the top. Arrange the crisp potatoes on the outside and sprinkle with the freshly chopped coriander.

Vindalho de Carne de Porco

Pork Vindaloo

Vindalho is the Portuguese influence of cooking with garlic and vinegar, although you will come across several mentions of *aloo* or potatoes in recipes all over the world. This is a dish that has travelled far and wide and is seen on Indian restaurant menus all over the world. In the UK it has transcended into an entire genre of its own, but this is the original recipe as cooked in Goan households at Easter.

Serves 4–6

1kg pork, preferably from the neck, diced into 2.5cm cubes
4 tablespoons vegetable oil
4 onions, finely sliced
2 green chillies, slit lengthways

For the spice paste
10–12 dried whole Kashmiri chillies, broken, stalks and seeds removed
½ teaspoon black peppercorns
2.5cm piece of cinnamon stick
6 cloves
1 teaspoon cumin seeds
½ teaspoon mustard seeds
1 teaspoon ground turmeric
2 tablespoons ginger-garlic paste (see page 260)
2 teaspoons salt
1 teaspoon sugar
5 tablespoons malt vinegar, plus extra for seasoning

Crush the chillies, whole spices and seeds, then blend to a paste with the turmeric, ginger-garlic paste, salt, sugar and vinegar.

Mix the pork with the spice paste and marinate in the fridge for 12 hours.

Heat the oil in a heavy-based pan and sauté the onions for 12 minutes until golden. Add the marinated pork and cook over a high heat for 7–8 minutes until browned at the edges. Add 750ml of water and simmer, half covered, for 45–75 minutes until the gravy is thick and the pork is tender and cooked through. Add the green chillies, check the seasoning, adjust the vinegar and sugar as required and set aside.

It can be eaten on the same day, but this dish tastes much better reheated the next day. Serve with crusty bread or rice.

Sarapatel

Spicy Pork and Liver Curry

Sarapatel, or *Sorpotel* as it's often referred to, is a brilliant example of Portuguese influences adapted with Indian spicing and a resulting dish that combines the best of both worlds. Part curry, part pickle and part stew, this is a good example of using more than just the best parts of an animal. If you don't like liver, simply omit it and replace it with more pork. Much like any other pickle, this dish also tastes better two days after it has been made, when the vinegar has had a chance to work as the flavours improve with maturing. As a part of the Easter spread, it's handy that this can be prepared a day or two in advance.

Serves 4–6

750g pork shoulder or leg, diced into 2.5cm cubes
200g pork liver, diced into 2.5cm cubes
10 dried whole red chillies, broken, seeds discarded
10 whole black peppercorns
1 teaspoon cumin seeds
2.5cm piece of cinnamon stick
5 cloves
½ teaspoon ground turmeric
2 tablespoons garlic paste (see page 260)
1 tablespoon ginger paste (see page 260)
150ml white wine vinegar
120ml vegetable oil
3 onions, finely chopped
2 teaspoons salt
1 teaspoon sugar
2 green chillies, slit lengthways

Place the pork and liver in a large pan with just enough water to cover, bring to the boil, then simmer for 12–15 minutes. Strain the meat from the cooking liquid, reserving the liquid. Allow the meat to cool.

Meanwhile, blend together the dried chillies, peppercorns, cumin seeds, cinnamon stick, cloves and turmeric with half the garlic and half the ginger pastes and approximately 100ml of the vinegar to obtain as fine a paste as possible. Set aside.

In a wide pan, heat 1 tablespoon of oil at a time and fry a quarter of the boiled meats to get an even brown colour on all sides (cooking in batches avoids overcrowding the pan, which means the meat will brown rather than steam). Repeat until all the pork and liver is browned. Set all the meat aside once browned.

Next, add the remaining oil to the pan over a medium heat. Add the chopped onions and cook for 6–8 minutes until the onions are golden brown. Add the remaining ginger and garlic pastes and sauté for another minute or so, stirring continuously to prevent them from sticking and burning. Add the spice paste, and continue to cook, stirring, for about 5 minutes until the spices begin to turn fragrant.

Now add the pork and liver and the salt to the pan and mix well. Add about 475ml of the reserved stock and bring the mixture to the boil. Reduce the heat, cover and simmer for about 30–40 minutes until the pork is tender.

Add the remaining vinegar, the sugar and the green chillies to the pan. Add more stock or water if the mixture seems a little dry and simmer for another 5 minutes. Use only as much liquid as you need to keep the curry semi-thick. The longer you wish to keep this, the drier the mixture can be (i.e. more like a pickle), or the more people you're feeding, the wetter this can be (i.e. more like a stew or curry).

This dish can be served with rice or sannas (steamed rice and toddy dumplings, see page 78).

Top left: Sanna (page 78)
Bottom left: Sarapatel (page 69)
Middle: Baffado de Galinha (page 65)
Top right: Kenny Memsaab ke Kaaley Jaam (page 77)
Bottom right: Mutton Xacuti (page 76)

Wak Me-A-Mesang Pura

Pork and Fermented Bamboo Shoots

Several tribal communities in the north-eastern Indian states have converted to Christianity over the years and now cook this dish at Easter and during other celebrations. Feel free to replace fermented bamboo shoots with regular tinned bamboo shoots if you wish.

Serves 4–6

1 tablespoon vegetable oil
1kg pork, from neck or leg, skin and
    fat removed, diced into 2.5cm cubes
1½ teaspoons salt
500g tin of fermented bamboo shoots,
    drained, sliced 3mm thick
4 green chillies, chopped
5cm piece of ginger, finely chopped
½ teaspoon ground turmeric
20g ground raw rice or rice flour
    (optional)

Heat the oil in a heavy pan over a low heat, add the pork and cook uncovered for 30–40 minutes without adding any water. Stir occasionally and add the salt after 25 minutes, cooking until all the juices have been absorbed and the meat begins to turn brown.

Add the bamboo shoots to the pan and stir for 5 minutes. Add the green chillies, ginger and turmeric and stir, cook for another 5 minutes, then add 700ml of water and simmer over a low heat for 15 minutes until the pork is cooked.

If you wish, you can add the ground rice flour and cook for another 10 minutes until the sauce is thick and glossy. Check the seasoning and serve immediately.

Bhoona Soovar

Whole Roast Pork Loin with Garlic and Chilli

This dish is wheeled out at most celebrations as long as you can fit the beast in your oven! This can be done with smaller cuts of meat – you can use just the loin or neck for example. If you can get your butcher to debone and tie up the entire piglet, go for it. If not, make do with a boned and rolled loin of pork.

Serves 8–10

1.6kg pork loin, skin removed, boned
   and rolled
1 tablespoon black peppercorns
6 cloves
5cm piece of cinnamon stick
6 green cardamom pods
120ml vegetable oil
2 large white onions, finely sliced
1 tablespoon salt
1½ teaspoons plain flour

For the paste
2 teaspoons brown mustard seeds
1 teaspoon fenugreek seeds
1 head of garlic, peeled and chopped
1½ tablespoons red chilli powder
5cm piece of ginger, peeled and finely
   chopped
2 shallots, finely chopped
5 tablespoons malt vinegar
2 teaspoons sugar
1 teaspoon salt

To make the paste, dry roast the mustard seeds and fenugreek seeds in a medium–hot frying pan for 30–60 seconds until they begin to pop, then blend with the remaining ingredients to make a smooth paste.

Apply the paste all over the pork loin. If you're rolling the loin yourself, even better – apply the spice paste on all sides, then roll the loin up using butcher's twine or cooking bands to hold in place. Leave to marinate in the fridge for 3 hours or, better still, overnight.

Preheat the oven to 160°C/140°C Fan/Gas Mark 3.

Pound the peppercorns, cloves, cinnamon and cardamom coarsely using a mortar and pestle.

Heat a roasting tray and add 80ml of the oil. Wipe away the excess marinade from the outside surface of the loin and reserve. Add the loin to the hot pan and sear for 3–5 minutes, moving the pork around to get an even colouring on all sides. Add the excess marinade to the pan and stir fry for 2–3 minutes, then add 950ml of water and the pounded spices and mix well.

Cover the roasting tray with foil and cook in the preheated oven for 35–40 minutes. Remove from the oven and let the loin rest for 15–20 minutes, keeping it warm.

Reserve the juices and drippings from the pan, pass through a strainer and discard the whole spices.

In the meantime, in a separate pan, heat the remaining oil. Add the onions and salt and cook over a medium heat for 12–14 minutes until golden brown. Add the flour and stir well, cooking for a minute or so until the flour is well roasted and then pour in the strained juices from the pork. Reduce the heat and simmer for 1 minute. Check the seasoning and correct as required. The sauce should taste hot, sharp and sweet all at the same time. Add more sugar, salt or vinegar to balance as required.

Slice the rested pork loin and serve on a platter with the sauce either simply poured over or on the side.

Buttakh Moile

East Indian Duck Moile

Bombay's rise to prominence under British rule in the eighteenth century should have been good news for the local Christians, who were well positioned to work with the British rulers. But they were less than pleased to find that the city's prosperity started attracting migrants from all over the country, and especially Goa, who were soon competing for the same jobs. To differentiate themselves, the locals decided to adopt a new name and the name they chose was East Indians, to demonstrate a closer relationship with the East India Company. The fact that this made them East Indians in western India didn't seem to matter much to them. Regardless, our East Indians from Mumbai and the western coast of Maharashtra have been practising Christianity since the mid-sixteenth century and this is one of the dishes they would always make at Easter.

Serves 4

1 medium duck, cut into 8–10 pieces (sauté cut – ask your butcher to do this for you)
1½ teaspoons salt
1 tablespoon black peppercorns
4 bay leaves
5 tablespoons ghee
2 teaspoons sugar
4 white onions, cut into rings 5mm thick
2.5cm piece of ginger, peeled and cut into matchsticks
5–6 garlic cloves, cut into thin slivers
6 green chillies, slit and deseeded
15 curry leaves
4 tablespoons botal (bottle) masala (see page 262)
2 tablespoons white vinegar

Preheat the oven to 180°C / 160°C Fan / Gas Mark 4.

Put the duck pieces in a large ovenproof dish with the salt, peppercorns and bay leaves. Add 2–2.5 litres of cold water to cover and bring to the boil. Skim off any scum which appears on the surface, then transfer the dish to the preheated oven. Cook for 1¼ hours or until the duck is tender (the leg pieces will take longer to cook than the breast).

Remove the duck pieces and set aside, then reduce the gravy until around 500ml remains. Strain the gravy and set aside.

Heat the ghee in a separate pan, add the duck pieces and fry until almost browned. Add the sugar and stir, then remove the duck from the pan. The meat will be tender but not falling off the bone.

In the same pan, fry the onions for 12–15 minutes over a gentle heat until golden brown. Add the ginger, garlic, chillies and curry leaves and fry for 2 minutes. Add the botal masala and fry gently for a minute or so. Add 1 or 2 spoons of water if the pan is too dry at this stage – this will prevent the spices from burning. Add the reduced gravy and vinegar, then return the duck to the pan and simmer over a low heat for 4–5 minutes.

Serve with rice or home-made potato chips.

Mutton Xacuti

Goan Mutton Curry with Roasted Coconut and Spices

Xacuti (pronounced 'shakuti') is a classic Goan dish that is not for the faint of heart. Fiery and loaded with flavour, it can be absolutely delicious if one takes the time to roast all the components separately and follow the sequence correctly. As they say, there are no shortcuts to anywhere nice and it's certainly true for the Goan way of life.

Serves 6–8

1.5kg mutton, diced from the leg
2 teaspoons salt
2 tablespoons ginger-garlic paste (see page 260)
2 tablespoons vegetable oil
1 onion, finely chopped
3 potatoes, peeled, and diced into 2.5cm cubes
3 tablespoons tamarind purée
½ teaspoon sugar
5 fresh curry leaves, to garnish

For the spice paste (to roast and grind)

5cm piece of cinnamon stick, broken into small pieces
1 star anise
2 blades of mace
6 cardamom pods
6 cloves
8–10 dried whole red chillies, broken into small pieces
¾ teaspoon peppercorns
1 teaspoon cumin seeds
½ teaspoon royal cumin seeds
2 teaspoons poppy seeds
3 tablespoons coriander seeds
1 teaspoon coconut oil
75g desiccated coconut
½ teaspoon ground turmeric
2 tablespoons vegetable oil
7 garlic cloves
2 onions, finely chopped
½ teaspoon salt

Place the mutton in a bowl with the salt and ginger-garlic paste, stir well to coat the mutton and set aside in the fridge to marinate for an hour.

In the meantime, dry roast the spices in a non-stick pan over a medium heat. Do not let the spices burn or it will make the curry taste bitter. Start with the dried whole spices first, adding the larger spices first and stirring for a few seconds before adding the next spice, until all the spices have been added. Keep stirring constantly until the spices turn toasted and fragrant. Remove the spices from the pan.

Roast the coconut next. Add the coconut oil to the desiccated coconut in the pan and stir. Once the coconut starts to brown, add the turmeric to it. Stir for 10 seconds and remove from the pan. Next add 2 tablespoons of vegetable oil and shallow fry the whole garlic cloves until golden, then add the chopped onions and salt. Stir continuously until brown, but do not let them burn.

Grind the roasted spices to a thick, smooth paste with the coconut mixture, garlic and onions and 120ml of water. Set aside.

Place the marinated mutton in a pan with 1.4 litres of water, bring to the boil, then reduce the heat, skim the scum off the top, cover and simmer for 20–25 minutes until about 80–85 per cent cooked. Remove the meat from the stock and set aside. Do not discard the stock once the meat is cooked as it will be used later.

Heat the oil in a large pan and sauté the chopped onion in it for 6–8 minutes. Once the onion turns translucent, add the diced potatoes and cook over a high heat for 2–3 minutes until they turn golden. Next add the ground spice paste to the pan. Fry over a medium heat for a few minutes. You will notice the paste darkening as it fries. Once it starts to dry and oil begins to leave the sides of the pan, add 950ml of the stock to the pan. Mix well and let it come to the boil, then cook over a medium heat for about 8 minutes until the potatoes are almost cooked through. Add the cooked mutton to the pan with the tamarind purée and bring the curry back to the boil, adding more stock if necessary. Cook for 15–20 minutes or until the mutton is tender. Taste for salt and add a pinch or two of sugar to the curry before turning off the heat. Keep warm until ready to serve. Garnish with the curry leaves.

Kenny Memsaab ke Kaaley Jaam

Lady Kenny's Very Dark Gulab Jamuns

This dessert, it is said, was a favourite of Lady Kenny, the lady of the house at a tea plantation in the hills of Assam. She would insist on this being a part of the meal at Easter. The recipe uses *khoya* – these are milk solids made by cooking and slowly evaporating the moisture from the milk. They are available from specialist Asian shops.

Makes 16 (serve 2 per person)

250g paneer
250g khoya
50–70g semolina
50ml full-fat milk
¼ teaspoon baking powder
16 shelled pistachios
500g sugar
juice of ½ lemon
½ teaspoon green cardamom powder
vegetable oil, for frying
chopped nuts, to serve (optional)

Grate the paneer using the fine side of a grater. Mix together with the khoya, 50g of the semolina, milk and baking powder (it is easiest to rub everything together using the heel of your palm) and knead to a smooth dough. If the dough isn't coming together, add the remaining semolina to the dough. Divide into 16 balls, push a pistachio into the centre of each ball and roll back into a smooth ball without any cracks.

Place the sugar in a pan with 250ml of water and boil for 5–6 minutes until the mixture reaches 105°C. Then add the lemon juice and shake the pan gently to mix (do not stir). Skim the impurities off the top as they rise. Stir in the cardamom powder and keep warm.

Heat the vegetable oil in a wok or a deep fryer to medium-hot (160–170°C). Add the dough balls and fry for 6–8 minutes or until very dark chocolate brown. Drain them on kitchen paper, then immediately add them to the syrup while they are hot (don't let the balls go cold before adding into the syrup or they won't absorb the syrup properly).

Let the fried balls soak in the syrup for 5–6 minutes, but do not stir the jamuns too much when they are in the syrup. Then remove from the syrup and serve warm with custard or ice cream, and chopped nuts if you wish.

Sanna

Steamed Rice Dumplings with Toddy

These toddy-flavoured rice dumplings are light and soft pillowy delights. A bit like *idlis*, these have a faint sourness and a depth of flavour that makes them very interesting. They are one of the local delicacies from Goa and makes for an excellent accompaniment to most Goan dishes, but Sarapatel in particular (see page 69).

Makes about 16

300g basmati rice
50g freshly grated coconut
100g palm toddy or white wine
3 tablespoons sugar
100ml coconut milk, warmed
15g fresh yeast
1½ teaspoons salt
40ml white distilled vinegar
2 tablespoons vegetable oil

Wash the rice and soak it in water for an hour or so, then drain and grind it to a fine paste with the grated coconut and toddy (if you can't find palm toddy, feel free to replace it with any cheap white wine).

To activate the yeast, mix 1 teaspoon of the sugar with the warm coconut milk in a bowl and sprinkle the yeast over. Leave for 10–15 minutes for the yeast to dissolve and come to life.

Mix the yeast mixture into the rice and coconut paste, add the remaining sugar and the salt and add a little water if required to make a thick but spoonable batter. Stir in the vinegar. Cover and rest in a warm place for 4 hours or until the mixture doubles in volume.

Grease small idli steamers or ramekins with the vegetable oil. Half-fill the moulds with the batter. Place the moulds in a bamboo steamer set over a pan of simmering water with a lid on top and steam for 15 minutes or until cooked but still fluffy. To test if they are done, pierce a dumpling with a wooden skewer – it should come out clean.

Biscut

Easter Biscuits

In Goa at Easter they make chocolate marzipan sweets coated with coconut and various biscuits, and sometimes fruit custard too, but in Bengal where I grew up, these cookies would form the bulk of snacks prepared for the late-night revelries.

Makes 10–15 biscuits, depending on size

120g whole wheat flour
150g semolina
¾ teaspoon ground nutmeg
⅔ teaspoon baking powder
100g raisins
80g salted butter, softened, plus extra for greasing
150g caster sugar
2 eggs, beaten

Sift the flour, semolina, nutmeg and baking powder together into a bowl, then stir in the raisins.

Cream together the butter and sugar in another bowl, then add the beaten eggs. Mix in, then add the dry ingredients. Mix together, adding 2 tablespoons of water to help the dough bind together. Rest the dough for 30 minutes in the fridge.

Preheat the oven to 150°C/130°C Fan/Gas Mark 2.

Divide the dough into 10–15 balls. Place on a greased baking tray and press each ball down lightly, until they are about 1cm thick. Bake in the preheated oven for 15–20 minutes or until golden. Remove from the oven and transfer to a wire cooling rack.

Vaisakhi

Vaisakhi is the harvest festival of the Punjab region, and also known as Baisakhi. Vaisakhi marks the New Year for Sikhs, and for all in the Punjab, standing out more than any other celebration, possibly because of the colour, verve and vigour of the Punjabi folk – they are just up for any kind of celebration!

Celebrated on the 13th or 14th April, Vaisakhi also commemorates the year 1699 when Sikhism was born as a collective faith, and the founding of the Sikh community, otherwise known as the Khalsa.

At the time of Vaisakhi, the weather is still very good in the north, and so much of the partying happens outdoors. You mostly see Vaisakhi celebrations in rural communities (it's much less significant in urban areas, although there is a growing population of city dwellers). Bonfires are lit, people sing and dance around them, and traditional folk dance performances like *giddha* and *bhangra* are popular. People wear yellow (the colour of harvest) and red (an auspicious colour). This form of celebration in the community demonstrates the vitality, fun and exuberance of Punjabi life. Other rituals on the day include going to the Gurdwara to pay respects, and attending a community lunch held at the Gurdwara, which is served to the public by volunteers.

Devotees gather at the Golden Temple to celebrate Vaisakhi. (Sameer Sehgai/Hindustan Times via Getty)

Although most of India would mark this occasion with rather austere or serious religious offerings to the gods, and preparing largely vegetarian food, Vaisakhi in the Sikh universe and in Punjab is just like any other party, and they wouldn't think twice about preparing meat and non-vegetarian food to extend the celebration, which is part of the appeal.

It's also an important date in the Hindu calendar. In the Punjab region, Vaisakhi is the beginning of the solar New Year. In addition, it's believed that it is the time that the Goddess Ganga descended to earth. There is a huge gathering of Hindus along the River Ganges in north India and Tamil Nadu for ritual baths.

In India, the main celebration takes place at Talwindi Sabo, where Guru Gobind Singh stayed for nine months and completed the recompilation of Guru Granth Sahib – the Sikh scripture. Major celebrations also take place in the Gurdwara at Anandpur Sahib and at the Golden Temple in Amritsar.

Possibly due to the contributions of the Sikh community in different parts of the world, Vaisakhi is widely celebrated by people outside of the Sikh community as a mark of respect and recognition of the good work that the Sikhs do in all walks of life, whether it's business, military or any other industry. Processions in London called *Nagar Kirtans* or 'street hymn singing' of 50,000 people take place – the largest procession for this outside India. And no matter which government is in power in the UK, each year the British Prime Minister's office organises a Vaisakhi Party at 10 Downing Street to celebrate the festival and acknowledge the community!

Top left: Makki di Roti (page 97)
Bottom left: Sarson ka Saag (page 86)
Top and bottom centre and top right:
    Kadha Prasad (page 97)
Middle: Mutter Paneer (page 87)
Bottom right: Achaari Gobhi (page 90)

Sarson ka Saag

Punjabi Mustard Greens

This rustic north Indian Punjabi dish is a firm favourite in the winter months when the fields of Punjab are filled with mustard and their greens are aplenty. The very mention of this rich purée of mustard served with dollops of freshly churned, home-made butter, jaggery and cornmeal bread brings tears to grown-up Punjabi men's eyes! Ignore the calorie counter if you're tempted to try this recipe! This dish can be served in different guises, as small canapés or as spreads or dips for finger food.

Serves 4 as an accompaniment

1 tablespoon vegetable oil
½ onion, sliced
1 turnip, roughly diced
½ carrot, roughly diced
2.5cm piece of ginger, grated
2 garlic cloves, crushed
4 green chillies, slit lengthways
300g mustard greens, roughly chopped
100g spinach, roughly chopped
1 teaspoon salt
½ teaspoon sugar

For the tempering
4 tablespoons mustard or vegetable oil
½ teaspoon cloves
6 garlic cloves, chopped
1 onion, chopped
1 tablespoon cornmeal
50g unsalted butter
½ teaspoon garam masala (see page 261)
juice of ½ lime

Heat the oil in a heavy-based pan with a lid, add the onion and sweat over a low heat with the lid on until soft. Add the turnip and carrot and sweat for 3–4 minutes until half cooked. Add the ginger, garlic and green chillies and cook for another 3–4 minutes. Now add the mustard greens and spinach to the pot. Sprinkle with 2 tablespoons of water, add the salt and sugar, cover and cook for 10–15 minutes until the vegetables are completely cooked in their own steam.

Remove the pan from the heat and blend the mixture to a smooth purée.

To prepare the tempering, heat the oil in a pan, add the cloves and fry for 30 seconds until they pop. Add the garlic and then the onion, stir quickly and sauté until the onions turn golden. Add the purée and stir over a medium heat for 4–5 minutes until the onions and purée are well mixed and the oil is just about to start to separate. Sprinkle over the cornmeal, mix it in well and cook for another 3–4 minutes to get rid of any rawness. Add the butter and garam masala and mix them thoroughly. Squeeze the lime juice over and remove from the heat.

Serve hot with chickpea bread, fresh butter and crushed molasses.

Mutter Paneer

Paneer and Pea Curry

Even though this dish is made all over the country from north to south, from humble homes to fancy hotels, there isn't one set recipe for it. It's a must-have dish on your menu for most celebrations but for Vaisakhi in particular, it's an easy go-to dish to cater for kids too. This dish will be served in most Indian homes – every family has its own recipe and mine is full of my own tweaks. Paneer is now available in most supermarkets in the UK, but you can use tofu or halloumi cheese instead if you wish.

Serves 4

5 tomatoes
4 tablespoons vegetable oil
3 green cardamom pods
½ teaspoon cloves
2 bay leaves
1 teaspoon cumin seeds
2 large white onions, finely chopped
½ teaspoon ground turmeric
1 teaspoon red chilli powder
1 teaspoon ground coriander
1 teaspoon salt
2 green chillies, finely chopped
2.5cm piece of ginger, finely chopped
300g paneer, diced into 1cm cubes
200g frozen petits pois or green peas, thawed
1 teaspoon sugar
½ teaspoon garam masala (see page 261)
3 tablespoons single cream (optional)
2 tablespoons salted butter (optional)
freshly ground black pepper
1 teaspoon dried fenugreek leaves, crumbled between fingertips
2 tablespoons freshly chopped coriander
juice of ½ lemon

Cut the tomatoes into quarters, and purée in a blender.

Heat the oil in a frying pan, add the cardamom, cloves and bay leaves and let them sizzle and pop for a minute or so, then add the cumin seeds and as they crackle, stir to mix evenly. After 20–30 seconds, add the chopped onions and cook for 10–12 minutes until golden brown, stirring constantly so they colour evenly.

Add the turmeric, chilli powder, ground coriander and salt. Stir, mixing well, and cook for a minute or so. Add the chopped green chillies and ginger, sauté for 1 minute, then add the tomato purée. Reduce the heat, cover with a lid and cook the tomatoes down for 2–3 minutes until the onions and tomatoes come together. Add the diced paneer and cook for 2–3 minutes, mixing well, then add the petits pois.

Simmer for 1 minute, then sprinkle with the sugar and garam masala. Stir in the cream and butter, if using. Add a couple of twists of ground black pepper, then stir in the fenugreek and coriander. Finish with squeeze of lemon juice. Serve hot with your choice of parathas, poories or chapatis.

Top: Pindi Chaney (page 89)
Bottom: Bhaturey (page 98)

Pindi Chaney

Village-style Chickpea Curry

This classic Punjabi dish is also prepared with small variations in Pakistan, Delhi and almost all of north India. Traditionally eaten with deep-fried leavened breads called *bhaturey*, this is just as good with steamed rice or served with tamarind chutney as a part of chaats.

Pind is a Punjabi word for village and in big weddings and other celebrations, copious quantities of chickpeas would often be boiled in old oil tins which, in part, impart the dark colour that is associated with this dish. At home, the dark colour can be achieved by throwing a couple of teabags into the boiling liquid. I like the sourness provided by the dried pomegranate seeds, which serve the dual purpose of flavour as well as texture, but feel free to substitute tamarind pulp if you struggle to find dried pomegranate seeds.

Serves 6

200g white chickpeas, soaked in plenty of water overnight (or use canned cooked chickpeas)
1 teabag
a pinch of bicarbonate of soda (optional)
6 tablespoons vegetable oil
2 black cardamom pods
½ teaspoon cloves
2 bay leaves
1 teaspoon cumin seeds
½ teaspoon asafoetida
2 onions, finely chopped
2 tablespoons ginger-garlic paste (see page 260)
3 tomatoes, finely chopped
3 green chillies, chopped
2 teaspoons salt
2 teaspoons red chilli powder
1 tablespoon ground coriander
1 teaspoon dried mango powder
1 tablespoon pomegranate seeds (anardana), pounded coarsely (or 2 tablespoons tamarind pulp)
1 teaspoon sugar
juice of 1 lemon
2 tablespoons freshly chopped coriander leaves
1.5cm piece of ginger, cut into matchsticks

Drain the chickpeas from their soaking water and place in a heavy-based pan with 2.5 litres of water and a teabag. Boil for 40–50 minutes, covered, or until they are soft and give way when pressed between two fingers. If you wish, add a pinch of bicarbonate of soda to reduce the cooking time. Drain and set aside, reserving the water. If using canned chickpeas, simply rinse and drain.

In a separate pan, heat the oil, then add the cardamom, cloves and bay leaves and stir for 30 seconds. Add the cumin seeds and asafoetida and fry for 30–60 seconds until the seeds crackle. Add the onions and sauté for 8–10 minutes until golden brown. Reduce the heat to medium, then add the ginger-garlic paste and sauté for another 1–2 minutes. (This spits quite violently due to the amount of oil and water in the paste so I suggest using a high-sided pan.)

Add the tomatoes, chopped chillies and salt and stir fry over a high heat for 3 minutes. Add the chilli powder and ground coriander and continue cooking until the mixture turns dark and the oil starts to separate from the sides.

Pour in the boiled chickpeas and blend by mashing a few chickpeas with the back of a wooden spoon to thicken the sauce. If the mixture is too thick, add some of the reserved liquid. Once it is thick and all the spices are mixed together, add the dried mango powder and crushed pomegranate seeds.

Check and correct the seasoning if necessary, add the sugar and lemon juice and garnish with the chopped coriander leaves and ginger. Serve hot with either steamed rice or fried/baked bread.

Achaari Gobhi

Chargrilled Cauliflower Florets with Pickling Spices

This combination of cauliflower and pickling spices is often seen as a curry or a vegetable dish, but I like it marinated and cooked in a tandoor or on a grill or barbecue. The piquant pickle spices and the smokiness from the grill add a delightful complexity to the dish. It's light and healthy, yet packs a punch.

Serves 4

6 tablespoons white vinegar
1 teaspoon ground turmeric
1 teaspoon salt
1 teaspoon sugar
2 bay leaves
1 large cauliflower, cut into 3cm florets
bamboo skewers, soaked in water

For the chickpea roux
1 tablespoon vegetable oil
1 teaspoon carom seeds
½ teaspoon nigella seeds
4 garlic cloves, finely chopped
½ teaspoon ground turmeric
1 teaspoon crushed chilli flakes
2 tablespoons chickpea flour
2 green chillies, finely chopped

For the marinade
100g thick Greek yoghurt
2 tablespoons ginger-garlic paste (see page 260)
juice of 1 lemon
1 teaspoon salt
½ teaspoon sugar
½ tablespoon pickling spices mix (1 part mustard seeds, 1 part black onion seeds, 1 part cumin seeds, ½ part fenugreek seeds, 2 parts fennel seeds)
2.5cm piece of ginger, peeled and finely chopped
½ teaspoon garam masala (optional)
1 tablespoon freshly chopped coriander
2 tablespoons mustard oil

Place the vinegar, turmeric, salt, sugar and bay leaves in a pan with 1 litre of water, bring to the boil, then simmer for 5–6 minutes. Add the cauliflower florets, cover and cook for 2–3 minutes or so until the florets are cooked but still retain a bite. Drain in a colander and let them cool.

To make the roux, heat the vegetable oil in a small pan, add the carom and nigella seeds and let them splutter for 30 seconds or so. Add the chopped garlic and cook for a minute or so until golden, then add the turmeric and chilli flakes and stir to mix. Next add the chickpea flour and cook for 2–3 minutes until the mixture resembles the consistency of sand and gives off a roasted aroma. Add the chopped green chillies, mix and remove from the heat. Transfer to a bowl and let it cool.

For the marinade, mix the yoghurt in a large bowl with the ginger-garlic paste, lemon juice, salt, sugar, pickling spices, chickpea roux, chopped ginger, garam masala and chopped coriander. Check the seasoning and into this mix add the blanched cauliflower florets and let it marinate for 30 minutes (or if possible overnight). Drizzle the mustard oil over.

Preheat the grill to very hot. Thread the cauliflower onto the bamboo skewers, and cook under the preheated grill for 7–8 minutes, turning once, or until the cauliflower is well charred.

Serve either as snacks or as a main for vegetarians. You can also cook the skewers on a barbecue if you have one going.

Saag Meat

Spinach and Lamb Curry

No Vaisakhi celebration is complete without this curry. Lamb, goat or mutton is preferred, but it can also be made with chicken if you wish. It's a simple and easy dish to prepare and is quite forgiving so it's well worth giving it a go. It's a good option to make in advance and is great reheated, too.

Serves 4

4 tablespoons vegetable oil
4 garlic cloves, chopped
4 large onions, chopped
1½ teaspoons red chilli powder
1 teaspoon ground turmeric
1½ teaspoons salt
1½ teaspoons cumin seeds
750g boned leg or shoulder of lamb, diced into 2.5cm cubes
3 tomatoes, seeded and finely chopped
500g fresh spinach leaves or drained frozen spinach
½ nutmeg, grated
4 green chillies, finely chopped
2.5cm piece of ginger, finely chopped

Heat the oil in a heavy-based casserole, add the garlic and onions and cook over a medium heat for 6–8 minutes until the onions start changing colour to light golden. Add the chilli powder, turmeric, salt and cumin seeds and cook for 2–3 minutes, stirring constantly to prevent the spices from catching. Add a splash of water if you need to cook the spices well. Cook until the oil begins to separate.

Add the lamb and cook for 10–12 minutes until the lamb is seared on all sides and starts to turn brown at the edges. Add the tomatoes and cook for another 5 minutes, then add approximately 750ml of water. Reduce the heat, cover with a lid and cook for about 30 minutes until the lamb is 85–90 per cent cooked.

Add the spinach and cook for 10–15 minutes until the lamb is tender and the excess liquid has evaporated, leaving a thickish sauce. Check the seasoning and correct if necessary.

Add the grated nutmeg and sprinkle with the chopped green chillies and ginger. Serve with rice or bread of your choice.

Top left: Achaari Gosht (page 96)
Bottom left: Peele Chawal (page 98)
Right: Saag Meat (page 91)

Top left: Lassi (page 99)
Top right: Dhaniyey ki Hari Chutney (page 51)
Bottom: Tandoori Murgh (page 95)

Tandoori Murgh

Tandoori Chicken

No Punjabi celebration can be complete without tandoori chicken and Vaisakhi is no different. This is the sort of dish you could just as well cook on a barbecue if you don't have a tandoor. It can also be cooked in an oven, but the smokiness from the barbecue or a tandoor is something else. Young chickens are perfect for this dish, ideally cut in half lengthways and cooked on bamboo or metal skewers.

I recently read that domesticating chicken for human consumption first started in India! And even though the tandoor arrived much later, only in around the eleventh century in India, this dish caught on very well in Punjab as it was a quick thing to cook, and easy to share, as well as quick to eat, compared to lamb, for example.

Serves 4

2 spring chickens, 750–800g each
juice of ½ lemon
1 tablespoon finely chopped coriander
    stalks
2 tablespoons butter, melted
½ teaspoon chaat masala (see page
    261)
bamboo skewers, soaked in water

For the marinade
juice of ½ lemon
2 tablespoons vegetable oil
2 tablespoons red chilli powder
2 tablespoons ginger-garlic paste (see
    page 260)
1 tablespoon ground roasted cumin
215ml plain yoghurt
1½ teaspoons salt
1 teaspoon ground garam masala
1 teaspoon crushed dried fenugreek
    leaves
1 teaspoon sugar

For the salad garnish
2 red onions, thinly sliced
1 tomato, deseeded and sliced
1 green chilli, finely chopped
1 tablespoon white vinegar

Skin the chicken by literally peeling off the skin and separating it from the carcass. (This is done for all tandoori cooking and it helps the marinade to penetrate the meat better. Most halaal butchers are able to do this easily, or just ask your butcher nicely to do this for you!) Cut the chicken in half lengthways or spatchcock it, then wash and dry it using kitchen paper. Prick the breasts and legs with the tip of a knife – these incisions help the chicken to retain flavours and cook evenly.

Mix all the marinade ingredients together in a large bowl. Thread the chicken onto pre-soaked bamboo skewers or metal skewers, place in the marinade and chill in the refrigerator for at least 30 minutes.

Mix together all the salad ingredients and set aside for 10–15 minutes for the flavours to develop.

Preheat the grill to 180°C and grill the marinated chicken for 12 minutes on each side until it is coloured and the juices run clear when the chicken is pricked with a knife.

Squeeze the lemon juice over the cooked chicken, scatter over the chopped coriander and brush with butter. Sprinkle with chaat masala and serve immediately with salad.

Achaari Gosht

Mutton Curry with Pickling Spices

Punjabis love chicken but it's more of an everyday ingredient. At special
feasts and banquets, they love richly spiced mutton or lamb dishes. This one
in particular has a deep flavour from the use of mustard oil and spices used in
an *achaar* or pickle. The addition of jaggery rounds the dish off nicely.

Serves 4

750g lamb from leg, diced into 2.5cm
   pieces (ask your butcher to include
   some pieces with the bone too, as
   it's nicer)
1½ teaspoons salt
1 teaspoon ground turmeric
80ml mustard oil
6–8 dried whole red chillies (or 12–15 if
   you're feeling brave)
½ teaspoon brown mustard seeds
½ teaspoon fenugreek seeds
1 teaspoon fennel seeds
2 teaspoons cumin seeds
5 cloves
¼ teaspoon asafoetida (optional)
20 curry leaves
1 large white onion, finely chopped
2 tablespoons ginger-garlic paste (see
   page 260)
½ teaspoon ground red chilli powder
1 teaspoon nigella seeds
1 tablespoon jaggery or brown sugar
250ml plain yoghurt, whisked
1 teaspoon chickpea flour (optional)
juice of 1 lemon
2 tablespoons freshly chopped
   coriander

Place the lamb in a high-sided, heavy-based pan. Add 1 teaspoon of the salt,
the turmeric and just enough water to cover the lamb, and bring to the boil.
Once it boils, skim the surface to remove any scum that rises to the top, reduce
the heat to low, cover and cook for 35–40 minutes or until the lamb is 90 per
cent cooked through but still retains a bite. Drain the meat, reserve the liquid
and let the meat cool down.

Meanwhile, in a large separate pan, bring the mustard oil to smoking point,
then let it cool down. Next, add the red chillies and heat again for 30–60
seconds until the chillies turn dark. Remove the chillies from the oil (if you
wish, keep them aside to use as a garnish).

Add the mustard seeds, fenugreek seeds, fennel seeds, cumin seeds and cloves
to the chilli-flavoured oil and stir. Let the spices crackle and pop for a minute
or so, then add the asafoetida and curry leaves in quick succession. Add the
chopped onion and cook for 8–10 minutes, stirring frequently, until the onions
are softened and turn golden brown. Add a splash of water if they get
too coloured.

Next add the boiled meat, ginger-garlic paste, chilli powder, nigella seeds,
jaggery and the remaining salt and cook over a medium heat until the meat
begins to brown slightly. Add half the reserved liquid from boiling the meat
and reduce it down for 6–8 minutes.

Reduce the heat to low. Whisk the yoghurt with the chickpea flour, then stir
the mixture into the pan. Cook for 5–6 minutes or until the oil begins to rise
to the surface, stirring continuously. Finish with the lemon juice and chopped
coriander. If you wish, garnish with some of the reserved red chillies. Feast!

Makki di Roti

Cornmeal Bread

The world-famous Punjabi cornmeal bread is almost always mentioned in the same breath as *sarson ka saag*, a wintery vegetable preparation made of mustard greens (see page 86).

Serves 4

300g cornmeal or maize
  flour
1 teaspoon carom seeds
½ teaspoon salt
1 tablespoon chopped
  coriander
4 tablespoons ghee

Mix the cornmeal, carom seeds, salt and coriander together in a bowl.

Bring 150ml of water to the boil, then let it cool to a temperature that can be handled. Pour into the bowl of dry ingredients and knead into a firm dough.

Divide the dough into 8 equal-sized balls. Place 1 ball of dough between 2 plastic sheets and carefully roll the dough to a thickness of 3–4mm (rolling between plastic makes the dough easier to handle, as it can crack easily due to its lack of gluten).

Heat a dry frying pan over a medium heat and roast the disc for 2–3 minutes until slightly coloured on the base. Turn over and brush the cooked side with ghee, cook for 2–3 minutes, then turn over. Brush the second side with ghee and repeat the same process until it is cooked on both sides. Repeat until all the dough has been used up.

Top the cornmeal bread with more butter and serve hot with mustard greens.

Kadha Prasad

Wheat Halwa from the Gurdwara

No matter which Gurdwara you go to, you are offered a meal if you arrive at mealtimes. On a Sunday morning when we visit the Gurdwara, the entire place is filled with a sweet smell of *kadha prasad*. The volunteers in the kitchen prepare this by stirring it continuously and singing hymns in praise of Waheguru. After the prayer ceremony, this halwa is distributed by volunteers and all the attendees receive it seated with their hands cupped and arms extended in gratitude. One can try one's best at replicating the recipe, but it is hard to match the wonderful aroma and taste of the Gurdwara's halwa. I put this down to the scale of cooking. Somehow the large quantity of halwa being cooked has an impact on the way the halwa roasts, sweetens and cooks, but this adapted recipe works on a smaller scale.

Serves 6

50g ghee
150g wheat flour
150g sugar
1 teaspoon ground green
  cardamon
a few slivered almonds, to
  garnish (optional)

Melt the ghee in a pan, then add wheat flour and stir over a medium heat. Keep stirring for 7–9 minutes until the colour changes from pale brown to very dark brown.

Meanwhile, combine the sugar with 450ml of water and mix until the sugar is thoroughly dissolved.

Reduce the heat to low and, while stirring, mix in the sugar water. Stir in the ground green cardamom and mix well. Keep stirring continuously, mixing well to avoid lumps. The texture will change from soft to semi-soft and then to semi-solid in a couple of minutes. The halwa is ready when it starts leaving the sides of the pan and comes together in one large lump. Transfer to a serving bowl, garnish with slivered almonds and serve hot.

Bhaturey

Deep-fried Bread from Punjab

Most Punjabis will swear by the combination of curried chickpeas and deep-fried bread, known as *choley-bhaturey*, as their favourite breakfast ever. Unlikely as it may sound, it's true! No celebration, festival, funfair or even wedding these days is complete if *choley-bhaturey* aren't served at some point.

Makes 16 pieces

500g plain white flour, plus extra for kneading
10g baking powder
1½ teaspoons salt
25ml plain yoghurt
25g sugar
2 tablespoons vegetable oil for kneading, plus extra for frying

Sift together the flour, baking powder and salt.

Mix the yoghurt and sugar with 220ml of water and whisk well.

Add the yoghurt mixture to the flour mixture and mix together to form a soft dough. Transfer to a floured work surface, then knead well for 5 minutes, adding the oil to obtain a smooth dough. Place in a bowl, cover with a damp cloth and rest in a warm place for 10 minutes.

Divide the dough into 16 equal pieces. Lightly oil your palms and flatten the balls on an oiled work surface to get circles roughly 12.5cm in diameter. Fry in hot oil at 200°C for a minute or so until the bread puffs up. Flip over and cook the other side. Fry 1 or 2 at a time and repeat the process until all the dough is used up.

Tips

Frying the bhaturey so that they all puff up and colour evenly is a bit of a skill. If the oil is very hot, it helps to have the dough spread very thin. If the dough is slightly thick, then it helps to fry in slightly less hot oil. However, it comes down to a flick of the wrist while dropping the dough in the oil, as this makes the dough swirl in hot oil and puff up! Don't lose heart if they don't all puff up – it takes a few goes and most importantly they taste just as good as long as they're cooked!

Peele Chawal

Sweet Yellow Rice

Yellow is considered an auspicious colour in most of the Indian subcontinent, whether it's through the use of saffron or turmeric or, these days, increasingly through the use of food colouring. Yellow also is the colour associated with prosperity and hope, and sugar is symbolic of the sweetness that everyone desires in their lives. This simple sweet rice dish is an expression of the simplicity, hope and vibrancy of the Punjabi way of life.

Serves 6–8

3 tablespoons ghee
1 teaspoon fennel seeds
a generous pinch of saffron
4 green cardamom pods, bruised
150g sugar
300g basmati rice, washed and soaked in water for 20 minutes
75g mixed nuts and dried fruits (such as broken cashews, almonds, pistachios, golden raisins and dried cranberries)

Heat 2 tablespoons of the ghee in a pan with the fennel seeds. Add the saffron, cardamom, sugar and 475ml of water. Bring to the boil, then add the drained rice. Cover the pan and bring back to the boil, then lower the heat and cook for 7–8 minutes.

Heat the remaining ghee in a separate small saucepan and sauté the mixed nuts and raisins until they turn pink and give off a roasted aroma.

Stir the rice gently and add the sautéed nuts and dried fruit. Cover and let it cook for another 5–7 minutes until the rice is tender. Serve hot.

Lassi

Chilled Yoghurt Drink

This popular drink, often served as an aperitif in Indian restaurants, is very versatile and comes in various guises. It can be served sweet or salted, thick (as a nourishing drink) or thin (as a summer cooler). It can be flavoured with ripe mango or dried fruits, or salted and served with cumin and asafoetida. The Punjabi-style *lassi* comes either sweet or salted in tall stainless steel glasses and is more of a meal on its own.

Serves 4

700ml plain yoghurt
300ml iced water
4 tablespoons sugar
a few drops of rose water

Blend everything together until light and frothy and serve in tall glasses. (At Punjabi weddings they would often make these in a top-loading washing machine!)

Chaas

Salted and Spiced Chilled Yoghurt Cooler

Chaas is a thinner, lighter, spicier, homely version of *lassi*, often offered as an accompaniment to other rich dishes.

Serves 4

500ml plain yoghurt
500ml iced water
1cm piece of ginger, finely chopped
½ tablespoon finely chopped coriander
1 teaspoon crushed roasted cumin seeds
2 teaspoons salt

Mix all the ingredients together, then refrigerate to chill. Stir just before serving to mix well and serve chilled.

Eid al-Fitr

Eid al-Fitr is a great celebration and a time of thanksgiving, signifying the successful completion of the holy month of Ramadan, during which Muslims fast between the hours of sunrise and sunset. It is a special month for Muslims the world over, as a time of spiritual reflection, self-accountability and giving to charity. It is one of the most important months in the Islamic calendar as it is believed to be when the holy book – the Qur'an – was revealed to the Prophet Muhammed.

The word *Eid* means festivity in Arabic, and *Fitr* comes from the word *fatar* which means breaking, which therefore references the breaking of fasts in Ramadan, and a celebration of an end of this fasting. Following the month-long period of fasting, Eid al-Fitr becomes a great occasion to thank God for giving believers the willpower and endurance to observe the fast. It's also a time to renew one's faith and seek God's blessings.

Eid is celebrated much like an open-house event for everyone in the community to interact with one another as a reminder of God's grace in each other's lives. Therefore, 'sharing and caring' is the principal of Eid and what Islam as a religion emphasises. I remember there would always be people outside mosques distributing food to the whole community. The act of celebrating was all-encompassing, and everyone would get involved. If there happened to be a mosque, market or a fun fair in your area, it didn't matter what caste, creed or religion you were, as a child it was fun to get involved in all of the celebrations

A Muslim prepares the food prior to breaking fast during Ramadan, the completion of which culminates in Eid al-Fitr. (Noah Seelam/AFP/Getty)

and you were welcomed. For everybody we knew who was observing Ramadan and Eid, we would make the effort to visit and greet them, and likewise they would send something to our home.

Today, there are over 500 million Muslims throughout the Indian subcontinent, making it one of the largest population centres of Muslims in the world. As a result, Islamic festivals are prominent in the Indian calendar, and are a well-established part of the social fabric. In India, all communities join Muslims in celebrating Eid al-Fitr. You see markets and fun fairs popping up, selling toys, gifts, sweets and snacks. Hindus, Sikhs and Christians greet their Muslim friends on this day, and if you didn't meet someone until a week after Eid al-Fitr, you would still wish them a Happy Eid! The celebration truly brings out the cosmopolitan nature of both the festival and India, and shows how it transcends boundaries of pure religion, becoming a social occasion.

What I like about Eid, and the community that celebrates it, is that it's not simply a party, but also a time for giving thanks, as well as evoking a sense of sharing, community, being with family and giving to those less fortunate. Even in the run up to Eid al-Fitr, during the nights of Ramadan, *iftar* parties would be held so that people in the community could congregate to break their fast together. There is a sense of excitement around this occasion and everyone helps with the preparation; and before you've even broken your fast, you would share some food with your neighbour, whether they were fasting or not. These parties provide a real feeling of community; the President of India even organises an *iftar* party for MPs, and his lead is picked up by leaders of business and industry, civil servants, chief justices and MDs of companies, right down to small towns and villages, where people and families of prominence throw parties to acknowledge the role of Muslim colleagues. I remember my dad being out several nights a week attending one *iftar* party after the other! Much like most other festivals, regardless of and completely separate from faith, the number of invitations you had to the *iftar* parties was an indication of how active one's social life was.

Traditions and ways of celebrating Eid al-Fitr include waking up early, eating something sweet before going to Eid prayer at the mosque, visiting the graves of passed loved ones, giving money to charity, wearing your new or best clothes and wearing perfume. As with most of the festivals in this book, it is also common to exchange gifts.

As a child, even though we weren't fasting, it was absolutely acceptable for us to ask for a token gift from our elders. I didn't have much engagement in the religious aspect, but the joy one felt when embracing one another, and being wished happy Eid, was truly memorable. And of course, who doesn't like receiving something for nothing – whether it was just dates, dried fruits or maybe a bowl of vermicelli or biryani, or even sometimes more substantial gifts, such as embroidered handkerchiefs with a small perfume.

One of the main Eid traditions, though, is enjoying a meal together. The feasts begin literally at the doorstep of the mosque, where miraculously, street markets spring up in the days leading up to Eid al-Fitr, selling sweet rice, vermicelli, *phirni* (see page 116) and other boiled sweets I loved as a child. Other stalls sell kebabs, a few may sell biryani, others bangles, toys, paan, perfume, flowers, incense – you name it and it is likely to be there!

The meal itself is mostly celebrated at home with family and will traditionally comprise a couple of curries, a few kebabs, perhaps a biryani, *sheer khorma* – all of which you can find in this chapter.

Gucchi aur Murgh Kalia

Chicken and Morel Curry

In the mid-eighteenth century, competition between cooks and chefs (then known as *bawarchis* and *rakabdars*) increased in Lucknow, with each trying to out-do the others by creating different and more luxurious dishes than his rivals. The use of gold leaf to finish a dish, either as decoration or by incorporating it into the sauce, was one such attempt as gold leaf is symbolic of the ultimate luxury. This is a dish to stand out – the *piéce de résistance* and a great example of Lucknow's sophistication and culinary development.

Serves 4–6

50g large dried morels – the largest you can find! (Dried morels are expensive, so you could substitute a variety of dried wild mushrooms such as oyster, shiitake or maitake)
100g ghee or vegetable oil
1 teaspoon black or royal cumin seeds
a blade of mace
4 green cardamom pods
½ teaspoon freshly ground black pepper
1 teaspoon allspice
1kg boneless chicken thighs, skinned and cut into two
4 tablespoons ginger-garlic paste (see page 260)
1½–2 tablespoons Kashmiri red chilli powder
2 teaspoons salt
250g plain yoghurt
250ml chicken stock
100ml single cream
a pinch of saffron
½ teaspoon garam masala
½ nutmeg, grated
a few drops of rose water (optional)
2 edible gold leaves (optional)

For the fried onion paste
4 onions, finely sliced
vegetable oil, for deep frying
50g plain yoghurt

Wash the morels thoroughly to remove any grit, then soak them in 200ml of water for 30 minutes. Drain the morels, reserving the liquid, and pat them dry on kitchen paper.

To make the onion paste, heat the vegetable oil in a pan and deep fry the onions until golden. Mix the onions with the yoghurt and 2 tablespoons of water and blend into a paste using a blender or food processor. Set aside.

Heat 1 tablespoon of the ghee in a heavy-based pan and add ½ teaspoon of the royal cumin seeds. As it crackles, add the morels and sauté for a couple of minutes until they soften and brown. Add the remaining royal cumin seeds, let them crackle for 1 minute or two, then remove from the pan and set aside.

Add the remaining ghee to the same pan, add the mace, cardamom, black pepper and allspice and stir for 1 minute or two, then add the chicken pieces and sauté for 2–3 minutes over a high heat. Add the ginger-garlic paste and the fried onion paste and mix together. Stir for another 2–3 minutes, then add the red chilli powder and salt and cook for another 2–3 minutes.

Add the yoghurt little by little over a high heat, stirring continuously to make sure that the yoghurt is thoroughly mixed into the dish and does not split. Bring the yoghurt to the boil, then turn the heat down and simmer for 5 minutes. Next, add the stock and the reserved soaking liquid from the morels. Reduce the heat to medium-low, cover and cook for about 10 minutes until the chicken is cooked through. Remove the chicken pieces from the sauce and pass the sauce through a strainer to remove the whole spices.

Return the sauce to the pan and bring back to the boil. Reduce to the desired consistency if required, then stir in the cream, saffron, garam masala and grated nutmeg, add the chicken pieces back to the sauce and simmer for a brief minute or so to heat up.

Just before serving, add the morels into the curry, finish with rose water if you wish and turn out onto a shallow dish. If you wish, decorate the dish with gold leaves.

Methi aur Murgh Biryani

Fenugreek-scented Chicken Biryani

This is an unusual dish in the sense that most celebratory biryanis are expected to use lamb, beef or mutton. I think this version brings a nice change to the norm and, most importantly, the use of fenugreek makes it light and irresistibly fragrant, too.

Serves 6

120ml vegetable oil
2 onions, finely sliced
2 tablespoons ginger-garlic paste (see page 260)
100g fresh fenugreek leaves, coarsely chopped
1½ teaspoons salt
½ teaspoon ground turmeric
1½ teaspoons red chilli powder
2 tomatoes, chopped
800g boneless, skinless chicken thighs
4 green chillies, slit lengthways
350ml chicken stock or water
1½ teaspoons garam masala
2 teaspoons dried fenugreek leaves

For the rice
400g basmati rice, rinsed, soaked in water for 20 minutes, then drained
½ teaspoon royal cumin seeds
1 tablespoon salt
2 black cardamom pods (or green if you can't find black)
2 bay leaves
juice of ½ lime

To serve
100ml milk
30ml single cream
50g butter
2 hard-boiled eggs, sliced (optional)

Start by cooking the rice. Pour 1.5 litres of water into a pan, add the royal cumin seeds, salt, cardamom pods and bay leaves. Bring to the boil, then add the rice and lime juice and cook for 6–7 minutes until the rice is two-thirds cooked. Drain it and let it cool on an open flat tray.

Start on the chicken next. Reserve 1 tablespoon of the oil and heat the rest in a heavy-based pan. Add the sliced onions and cook over a medium heat for 8–10 minutes until golden brown. Next add the ginger-garlic paste, stir for 1 minute, then add 2 tablespoons of the chopped fresh fenugreek leaves and stir. Next add the salt, turmeric and chilli powder and cook for a minute or so, sprinkling a little water on if the spices begin to stick or burn. Add the chopped tomatoes and cook for 2–3 minutes.

Add the chicken and slit green chillies and cook for 5–6 minutes, then add the chicken stock or water. Reduce the heat to low and cook for another 7–8 minutes until the chicken is cooked and about 350ml liquid remains in the pan. Add the garam masala and the remaining fenugreek leaves, both dried and fresh. Cover with a lid and set aside for a couple of minutes.

To assemble, take a wide pan with a tightly fitting lid and smear the remaining tablespoon of oil over the base. Spread half the cooked rice in the pan, then layer the chicken and gravy over. Cover with the remaining rice.

Sprinkle over the milk and cream and dot the rice with the butter. Place the lid on, and cook for 2–3 minutes over a medium heat, then reduce the heat to low and cook for 10 minutes until the rice is steaming. Leave to rest for 5 minutes more.

Uncover and serve garnished with sliced hard-boiled egg if you wish.

Raan

Whole Braised Leg of Lamb with Peppercorn and Nutmeg

This has to be the ultimate celebration dish to put on the menu for any feast laid out at Eid. A proper centrepiece, it's also very simple as far as the number of ingredients go, making this an absolute must try. Do give this a go. It's traditional to use leg of lamb, but the dish tastes just as good if you use shoulder.

Serves 6

1 leg of lamb, approx. 1.8kg (or if using spring lamb, use 2 shoulders)
3 bay leaves
3 cinnamon sticks
3 green or black cardamom pods
1 tablespoon butter
20g spring onion greens, thinly sliced

For the marinade
4 tablespoons ginger-garlic paste (see page 260)
1 tablespoon Kashmiri red chilli powder
2 teaspoons salt
200ml malt vinegar
100g crisp fried onions (see page 261)
1 teaspoon sugar

For the sauce
200ml tomato purée
1½ tablespoons black peppercorns, roasted in a dry frying pan for 30–60 seconds, then coarsely crushed
¼ nutmeg, grated
60ml single cream
salt
sugar, to taste
1 tablespoon butter
30ml rum (optional)

Remove the surface fat from the leg or shoulder of lamb and prick the leg thoroughly using the tip of a sharp knife or a trussing needle (you can ask your butcher to do this for you, if you wish).

Mix all the marinade ingredients together into a paste. Spread the paste all over the lamb and massage the spices in. Set aside to marinate for at least 30 minutes, or preferably for a few hours in the fridge.

Preheat the oven to 150°C/130°C Fan/Gas Mark 2.

Scatter the whole spices in a deep baking tray large enough to accommodate the leg, then place the marinated lamb on top. Pour over enough water to come three-quarters of the way up the lamb. Cover with foil and cook in the preheated oven for 2½–3 hours until the meat is soft and easily comes off the bone. Remove from the oven and let the leg cool, then drain and reserve the cooking liquor.

Once cool, make deep incisions into the leg and remove the meat from the bone. Cut the meat into 1cm thick slices and arrange on an ovenproof serving platter. Brush with the butter and heat in a warm oven; hold warm until ready to serve.

For the sauce, transfer the strained cooking juices to a pan, add the tomato purée and cook down slowly to a sauce consistency. Add the peppercorns, nutmeg and cream. Check the seasoning and add salt and sugar to taste. Whisk in the butter, remove from the heat and pour over the sliced raan. Sprinkle with spring onions. If using rum, pour it into a ladle and heat it until flaming, then pour over the lamb and bring to the table as the show-stopper.

Top left: Elaichi Paratha (page 116)
Bottom left: Haleem (page 113)
Middle: Gucchi aur Murgh Kalia (page 104)
Top right: Methi aur Murgh Biryani (page 105)
Bottom right: Mughlai Paratha (page 110)

Mughlai Paratha

Paratha Stuffed with Minced Meat and Eggs

These parathas are a firm favourite on the street stalls that spring up outside the mosques during the month of Ramadan. In essence it's just a filled paratha, but the use of plain flour rather than whole wheat, the addition of eggs and mince, and the elaborate filling process make it suitable for most celebrations. Don't be put off by the lengthy process – it's well worth the effort!

Serves 8

For the dough
450g plain flour
½ teaspoon salt
a pinch of baking powder (optional)
2 tablespoons vegetable oil, plus extra
 for shallow frying
250ml warm water

For the minced meat filling
1 tablespoon vegetable oil
2 onions, finely chopped
450g minced lamb
1 tablespoon ginger-garlic paste (see
 page 260)
¼ teaspoon ground turmeric
1 teaspoon ground cumin
½ teaspoon Bengali garam masala
 (see page 261)
3 green chillies, finely chopped
1 teaspoon salt
½ teaspoon sugar (optional)
½ teaspoon red chilli powder
50g coriander, finely chopped
3 eggs, beaten with a pinch of salt

To serve
tomato ketchup
mustard sauce (kasundi)
lime wedges

To prepare the dough, sift together the flour, salt and baking powder, if using, in a large bowl. Make a well in the centre and add the oil. Using your fingers, bring the mixture together to form a dough, adding the warm water slowly and kneading to obtain a dough which is soft and pliable enough to be rolled out thinly. Cover the bowl with clingfilm and leave the dough to rest for 30 minutes.

Meanwhile, to make the filling, heat the oil in a pan and fry half the chopped onions over a high heat for 7–8 minutes until golden brown, then add the lamb and continue to cook over a high heat for another 4–5 minutes. Add the ginger-garlic paste, all the spices, half the green chillies, salt, sugar and chilli powder. Continue frying the mixture over a high heat for 4–5 minutes or until all the moisture from the meat has dried up. Check the seasoning, then lower the heat, cover and cook for 1 minute or until the meat is cooked thoroughly. Add a few spoonfuls of water if required to prevent the meat and spices burning. Add half the chopped coriander and mix it well. Leave the mixture to cool.

To assemble, divide the dough into 8 equal balls. Also divide the cooked mince and remaining onions, chillies and coriander into 8 separate portions. Grease a rolling pin and the work surface lightly with oil.

Roll a ball of dough into as thin a square as possible (but not thinner than 1-2 mm or it will not hold the stuffing well). Spread a teaspoon of beaten egg evenly on to the paratha, leaving the edges clear. Place the minced meat filling in the centre of the rolled dough, leaving enough space round the edges to fold the dough over. Sprinkle the chopped onions, chopped green chillies and coriander and 2 teaspoons of the egg mixture over the minced meat. Fold the dough over from the edges, enclosing the mince well.

Heat a shallow frying pan and place one paratha in the pan, folded side down first. Cook it over a medium heat for 2–3 minutes, then once it starts getting brown specks, flip it over and cook the other side for another 2 minutes. Brush the cooked side lightly with oil and flip over again. Cook for 30–60 seconds until crisp and golden. Brush the second side with oil and cook again in the same way.

Repeat until the dough and filling are used up. Serve or cut in to small pieces, with tomato ketchup, mustard for dipping and wedges of lime to squeeze over.

Kashmiri Biryani

Mutton Biryani with Dried Fruits and Kashmiri Spices

A biryani of some description is always a regulation dish at celebrations, but at Eid the Kashmiri version is often preferred as it is rich and made even more special by the use of dried fruit and nuts. Much as at all other celebrations where the dishes remain similar but the ingredients or their quality change with the status of the family, this dish is judged by both the quantity and the array of nuts and dried fruits included.

Serves 6–8

1kg mutton from leg or shoulder, on or
   off the bone, diced into 2.5cm cubes
150g ghee or vegetable oil
40g raisins
60g walnut halves
4 green cardamom pods
5cm piece of cinnamon stick
3 bay leaves
1 teaspoon royal cumin seeds
seeds from 2 black cardamom pods
2 teaspoons ground coriander
1 teaspoon ground garam masala (see
   page 261)
½ teaspoon saffron, soaked in 120ml
   warm milk or water
20g mint leaves
a few drops of rose water or kewra
   water
30g dried figs or apricots
30g dried cranberries

For the marinade
2 tablespoons ginger-garlic paste (see
   page 260)
430ml plain yoghurt, whisked
½ teaspoon ground turmeric
1 tablespoon red chilli powder
¼ nutmeg, grated
1 teaspoon sugar
1½ teaspoons salt
juice of 1 lemon

For the rice
500g basmati rice, rinsed and soaked
   in water for 20 minutes, then drained
juice of ½ lime
¾ tablespoon salt

Mix all the marinade ingredients together in a bowl, add the meat and stir to coat, then set aside to marinate for 30 minutes or, if possible, in the fridge overnight.

In the meantime, cook the rice. Bring 2.5 litres of water to the boil in a pan, add the drained rice, lime juice and salt and boil for 6 minutes, until the rice is two-thirds cooked. Drain the rice and immediately spread out on a tray to cool.

Next, start to cook the marinated meat. Heat 120g of the ghee in a wide heavy-based pan, add the raisins and fry for 30 seconds or so until they puff up, then remove them using a slotted spoon and drain. Next fry the walnuts for 30 seconds and remove these too.

Next, add the cardamom pods, cinnamon and bay leaves to the pan and crackle for 30–60 seconds, then add the royal cumin and black cardamom seeds. As they splutter, add the meat and the marinade and cook the meat for 10–12 minutes over a high heat. Add the ground coriander, garam masala and 250ml of water and cook, covered, over a medium heat for 30 minutes or so until the meat is almost cooked and about 235ml (or a cup) of gravy remains in the pan. If needed, add a little more water to make up the liquid.

Next, on to the assembly. Evenly spread the par-boiled rice over the cooked meat, sprinkle the saffron milk, rose water or kewra water, fried raisins, walnuts, figs/apricots, cranberries and mint over the rice and dot over the remaining ghee. Cover with a tightly fitting lid and cook over a medium-low heat for 12–15 minutes, turning the pot around every 3–4 minutes to prevent it catching, until the dish is hot and steaming. Set aside for another 5 minutes, then open the pot and serve.

Nihari

Spiced Lamb and Trotter Soup

Although difficult to imagine, this classic from Lucknow is served for breakfast. This hearty cross between soup and curry, made with trotters and served with saffron bread, is very popular during the month of Ramadan. The rich combination provides nourishment throughout the day. Instead of the combination of lamb trotters and diced lamb, you could also use four lamb shanks.

Serves 6–8

4 tablespoons ghee or vegetable oil
5 onions, thinly sliced
2 green cardamom pods
1 cinnamon stick
2 bay leaves
2.5cm piece of ginger, peeled and sliced into matchsticks
500g lamb trotters (or lamb shanks if you cannot find trotters)
500g diced lamb on the bone
2 tablespoons ginger–garlic paste (see page 260)
1 teaspoon garam masala
2 tablespoons fennel seeds, ground
1 teaspoon red chilli powder
¼ nutmeg, grated
½ teaspoon ground turmeric
170g plain yoghurt
2 teaspoons salt
1 tablespoon plain flour

To serve
20g fresh coriander, chopped
3 green chillies, cut into slivers
5cm piece of ginger, cut into small matchsticks

In a pan, heat 2 tablespoons of the ghee or oil. When hot, add the sliced onions. Reduce the heat to medium and fry the onions until golden brown. Remove from the oil and place the onions on kitchen paper to absorb any excess oil. Allow to cool, then crush the onions, divide into 2 bowls and set aside (one half will be used as a garnish).

Heat the remaining ghee or oil in the same pan and fry the cardamom pods, cinnamon, bay leaves and ginger for 30 seconds. Add all the meat and cook over a medium heat for 2–3 minutes, then add the ginger–garlic paste and continue cooking for 1–2 minutes, then add the ground spices. Cook, stirring continuously, for another 1–2 minutes. Now add the yoghurt carefully, little by little, stirring all the time so it doesn't split.

Once mixed in, add 2.5 litres water, the salt and the crushed onions. Bring to a simmer, cover and cook slowly for 1 hour, then remove the lid and cook uncovered for a further hour, stirring every 20–30 minutes.

Spoon off the ghee from the surface, place in a separate pan and bring to heat. Add in the flour and cook over a low heat to form a lightly roasted roux, then add back into the pot of simmering meat and stir to mix well. This should thicken the sauce and give it a nice glaze and body.

Garnish with the coriander leaves, green chillies, ginger and the reserved fried onions. Serve with sheermal bread (see page 168).

This dish could also be served as a soup. If so, do not add the flour at the end to thicken the soup – simply serve as it is.

Haleem

Spiced Lamb and Lentil Broth

This classic Muslim dish is a rich, rustic and hearty preparation with lentils and spiced lamb. During the month of Ramadan it's a very popular dish for breaking a fast, even though in Muslim parts of India, like Hyderabad and Old Delhi, and throughout Pakistan and Bangladesh it's sold in restaurants throughout the year. This is also great as a weekend brunch dish. If you are buying beef from a butcher, ask for the marrow bones to be chopped up and added in as well, as the marrow enriches the dish. It's easy enough to substitute beef for lamb if you prefer.

Serves 4

25g chana dal
50g bulgur or cracked wheat
60g ghee or clarified butter
3 green cardamom pods
6 cloves
2 x 2.5cm cinnamon sticks
2 bay leaves
3 red onions, sliced
1 tablespoon ginger-garlic paste (see page 260)
500g braising or chuck steak, diced into 2.5cm cubes
1 teaspoon red chilli powder
1 teaspoon ground turmeric
1½ teaspoons ground cumin
1½ teaspoons salt
1.4 litres boiling water
1½ teaspoons garam masala
2 tablespoons freshly chopped mint
juice of 1 lemon
3cm piece of ginger, peeled and cut into matchsticks
crisp fried onions (see page 261)

Rinse the chana dal in running water, then soak in a bowl of water for 30 minutes. Soak the bulgur wheat in another bowl of water for 30 minutes.

Reserving 1 tablespoon of ghee, heat the rest in a heavy-based pan. Add in the whole spices, bay leaf and sliced red onions and sauté for 8–10 minutes or until golden, then add the ginger-garlic paste and sauté for 30 seconds or so. Add the beef and cook over a high heat for 10 minutes, stirring, then add the chilli powder, turmeric, cumin and salt and cook for another 5 minutes.

Drain the soaked lentils and bulgur wheat and add to the pan. Let them cook in the meat juices for 5 minutes, stirring frequently to prevent the lentils and wheat catching. Reduce the heat to low, then add the boiling water and stir over a low heat. Cook over a low heat, covered, for 1–1½ hours until the meat, lentils and wheat are all thoroughly cooked. If the broth gets too thick, add more water – you are aiming for a consistency between soup and porridge.

Once cooked, remove the meat pieces from the pan. Transfer half the spicy lentil and wheat mixture to a blender and blend until smooth. Return the blended paste back into the pan and add back the pieces of meat.

Check the seasoning and correct as necessary while reheating over a low heat. Finish with the garam masala, half the mint and the juice of half the lemon, and stir in the remaining ghee.

Garnish with chopped ginger, the remaining mint, crisp fried onions and a last-minute squeeze of the remaining lemon. Serve with sheermal or a bread of your choice.

Top left: Phirni (page 116)
Bottom left: Sheer Korma (page 118)
Middle: Khajoor Biscut (page 117)
Top right: Parsi Sev (page 119)
Bottom right: Pista Kulfi (page 117)

Elaichi Paratha

Rich Cardamom Paratha

This slightly sweet and rich bread is a perfect foil for any gutsy and spicy *haleem*.

Makes about 25

500ml milk
75g sugar
2 pinches of saffron dissolved in 1 tablespoon milk OR 1 teaspoon turmeric mixed into ¼ cup water

1kg plain flour
35g salt
1 teaspoon ground green cardamom
150g ghee, plus extra for brushing

Heat the 500ml of milk in a pan to simmering point, then add the sugar and turmeric solution, if using, and stir until it dissolves completely. Allow to cool. If using saffron, add the saffron when it has cooled.

Place the flour in a mixing bowl with the salt, green cardamom and ghee and mix well until the ghee is evenly incorporated into the flour. Next add the milk and turmeric mixture and knead into a soft dough. Cover with cling film or a damp cloth and set aside for at least 15 minutes.

Divide the dough equally into 25 balls of about 60g in weight. Cover and set aside for another 10 minutes.

Roll the dough out into circles 15cm in diameter, then cook one at a time in a dry frying pan over a medium heat for 2–3 minutes until brown specks form on the side in contact with the pan. Turn over and repeat on the second side. While the second side is cooking, brush the first side with ghee and flip over again. Brush the second side too with ghee and cook for a minute or so, then remove from the heat. Repeat until all the dough has been used up, cover and keep warm until ready to serve.

Phirni

Ground Rice and Milk Pudding

Phirni is very similar to *kheer* in terms of its ingredients; however, the rice is ground for a *phirni*, whereas it's mostly added whole in a *kheer*. The other difference is that *kheer* can be served either hot or cold, whereas *phirni* is usually served chilled and is considered best served in earthenware bowls. The earthenware bowls help the *phirni* to set, as well as imparting a characteristic earthy flavour to the dish.

Serves 4–6

60g basmati rice
1.2 litres whole milk
6 green cardamom pods

60g sugar
30g pistachios, chopped
30g flaked almonds
a pinch of saffron, soaked in 1 tablespoon water

Soak the rice in water for 30 minutes.

Bring the milk to the boil, then reduce the heat, add 3 cardamom pods and simmer for 10–15 minutes. Add the sugar and continue to simmer the milk until it has reduced to about 750ml.

In the meantime, drain the rice, then grind with 150ml of water to get as smooth a paste as possible. Add the ground rice to the milk, stirring continuously to avoid any lumps, and cook for 10 minutes or until the rice is cooked and the milk is thick enough to coat the back of a spoon.

Crush the remaining cardamom pods to extract the seeds.

Pour the mixture into individual earthenware bowls if available or, if not, any serving bowl will do. Sprinkle with the pistachios, almonds and the remaining cardamom seeds, and dot with the drained saffron. Refrigerate until chilled, then serve.

Khajoor Biscut

Date Biscuits

Part cookie, part shortbread and part sticky date, these biscuits are a great thing to break the fast with. These are particularly popular with children. Grandparents often involve children in the shaping, rolling and baking of these biscuits, to keep them occupied and out of mischief! This recipe comes courtesy of Firdaus Takolia's family, and it's a firm fixture on their table at Eid.

Makes 30–35 biscuits

170g butter, softened, plus extra for greasing
100g caster sugar
50g cornflour
1 egg, separated
½ teaspoon vanilla extract
¾ teaspoon salt
1 teaspoon baking powder
⅛ teaspoon ground cardamom
180g plain flour, sieved
110 medjool dates, stoned and chopped into 6 pieces
50g desiccated coconut (buy the finest grain)

Preheat the oven to 155ºC/135ºC Fan/Gas Mark 2½. Grease a baking tray.

In a mixing bowl, beat together the butter and sugar until creamy and pale in colour. Add the cornflour and egg yolk and mix, then add the vanilla extract, salt and baking powder. Add the ground cardamom and flour to the bowl – you may need to add a little more flour to achieve a soft dough that is not too sticky, but not hard.

Pull off a piece of dough and flatten into an oval approximately 4 x 2cm. Place 3 pieces of date inside and roll up the dough so the dates are concealed inside. Repeat with the remaining dough to make 30–35 biscuits in total. Roll each biscuit lightly in beaten egg white, then coat on all sides with the desiccated coconut. Place on the greased baking tray.

Bake in the preheated oven for 20–25 minutes until lightly golden brown and firm to the touch.

Pista Kulfi

Pistachio Kulfi

We don't think twice about walking around with *kulfi* lollies during summer in Delhi today, but it must have been such hard work in the days of Emperor Akbar when teams were dispatched to the Himalayas to farm for ice. They would bring back cartloads of it to Agra so the most amazing frozen desserts could be fashioned out of seasonal fruits and reduced milk for the celebratory feasts and banquets the emperor would lay on for his guests. Thankfully it isn't anything like that now, and you can indulge in a treat every now and again without being an emperor.

Makes about 18

3 litres whole milk
200ml double cream
300g granulated sugar
8–10 green cardamom pods
150g shelled pistachio nuts

Place the milk, cream, sugar and cardamom in a large pan. Slowly bring to a simmer, stirring often. Reduce the liquid by about a third (to around 1.8 litres or so), again stirring often and scraping the sides of the pot – this will take about 35–40 minutes.

Preheat the oven to 160ºC/140ºC Fan/Gas Mark 3. Place the nuts on a baking tray and roast in the preheated oven for 5–6 minutes.

Remove the cardamom pods from the milk and add half the nuts. Blend with a hand blender, then place in an ice-cream maker to churn until it begins to freeze but is still pliable or spoonable. Chop the remaining pistachios. Mix the churned kulfi with the chopped pistachios and portion into metal containers or small glasses. Stick a bamboo stick in the centre of each and place in a freezer until frozen hard.

To serve as lollies, briefly dip the moulds in a hot water bath to help release the kulfis.

Sheer Khorma

Vermicelli Milk Pudding

Sheer Khorma is a favourite dessert for lots of people, young and old alike, during the festival of Eid al-Fitr. In its most basic form, it is vermicelli cooked in sweetened milk but during festivals it acquires a life of its own and the renditions are no less than an art form. The festival celebrations are an opportunity to use the best dried fruit and nuts possible, the best essences, colours and garnishes to make the most beautiful, the most delectable dessert in the community!

Some think of *sheer* as sugar, but it also refers to reduced milk. In Bengali language, *kheer* also implies reduced or evaporated milk.

This recipe comes courtesy of Habibur Rahman Khan, a longstanding chef friend of mine when we worked together at the Gharana restaurant in Kolkata in 1997. Habibur would often make this dessert for the team to break their fast during the month of Ramadan.

Serves 6

1.3 litres full-fat milk
2 tablespoons sugar or as required (the dates and raisins add a lot of sweetness to the milk, so add sugar accordingly)
1 tablespoon ghee
60g fine wholewheat vermicelli, broken
6 cashews, chopped coarsely
6 almonds, chopped coarsely
12 unsalted pistachios, chopped
8–9 dates, stoned and coarsely chopped
1 tablespoon golden raisins
seeds from 4 cardamom pods, crushed
½ teaspoon rose water

Serving suggestions

8 rose petals
a small pinch of saffron strands, soaked in milk
2–3 sheets of edible gold or silver leaf

Bring the milk to the boil in a pan, then add the sugar and simmer until reduced to about 700ml.

In a separate pan, heat ½ tablespoon of the ghee in a medium hot pan and roast the broken vermicelli until it is golden brown and evenly roasted. Remove from the pan and set aside to cool.

In the same pan heat the remaining ghee, add the chopped nuts and sauté for 3–4 minutes, stirring often, until the nuts are roasted and smell toasty. Then add the dates and raisins, stir in and remove from the heat.

Add the roasted vermicelli to the reduced milk and simmer for 6 minutes over a low heat until the vermicelli is cooked and has become soft. Add half of the dried fruit and nut mixture and the ground cardamom and stir in the rose water. Taste to see if more sugar is required.

Even though this can be served cold or at room temperature, its texture is best enjoyed hot. If serving hot, simply garnish with the remaining nuts and cardamom and serve in bowls. If serving cold, set in earthenware pots and serve garnished with rose petals, saffron strands, nuts, edible gold or silver leaf or anything else you fancy!

Parsi Sev

Dry Vermicelli with Rose, Nutmeg and Cardamom

In case you're wondering what a dish with a name like Parsi Sev is doing in this chapter, rest assured I haven't made a mistake. This is probably one of the hundreds of examples of the exchange of ideas, inspiration and rituals that exist in everyday India. Parsis too make vermicelli (*sev*) in their homes, but during Ramadan it's the Muslims who make it their own. This version is slightly different from Sheer Khorma (see page 118) in that this recipe doesn't use milk, only water to cook the vermicelli. I have several friends who swear by this recipe and it's the highlight of their Eid feast. I love it that they love it.

Serves 6–8

3 tablespoons ghee
50g flaked almonds
50g raisins, soaked in water for 30
    minutes, then drained
250g thin wheatflour vermicelli
    (available in most good Asian stores)
100g sugar
½ teaspoon ground green cardamom
¼ teaspoon grated nutmeg
1 teaspoon rose water

Mix the sugar in 575ml of water until the sugar is properly dissolved. Meanwhile heat 1 tablespoon of the ghee in a pan and fry the almonds and raisins for 30–60 seconds until the almonds are golden and the raisins puff up. Remove from the pan using a slotted spoon and set aside.

Into the same pan, add the remaining ghee and lightly roast the vermicelli over a medium heat for 4–5 minutes until it turns golden brown and smell roasted. Add the sugar solution and mix thoroughly, lower the heat and cook, covered, for 8–10 minutes until the liquid is absorbed and the vermicelli is cooked. If it still isn't completely cooked, sprinkle in 1–2 tablespoons of water, cover again and cook over a low heat for another 4–5 minutes. When done, sprinkle over the ground cardamom and nutmeg and mix.

Transfer to a serving plate, sprinkle with rose water and serve garnished with the fried almonds and raisins.

Navroze

Who are Parsis? My good friend Parizad Mody Katyal was often asked this by her children, who are growing up in Dubai and didn't understand their religion, its history or its rituals. Somewhat exasperated by the intrigue that surrounded the Parsis and their rituals, Parizad took it upon herself to learn the family way and the recipes, laying out a feast for her children at Navroze – a traditional Parsi festival – so she could explain it better to the kids.

Literally translated, Parsi means anyone from Persia, or all things Persian, but it is not so in this case. In India, Parsi or Parsee is a term colloquially applied only to those of Zoroastrian faith who are of Iranian descent but fled Iran from the fear of persecution when Islam was on the rise. As they were traders with India for years, and were familiar with the sea routes, the first boats arrived in Udwada in Gujarat. When the chief of the Parsis went to the local king, Jadhav Rana, asking for shelter, the Rana motioned to a bowl of milk full to the brim, symbolically suggesting that the kingdom was up to capacity and couldn't accommodate any more people. He expressed

After offering prayers at Navroze, a Parsi women walks by figures of knights outside a fire temple in Mumbai. (Indranil Mukherjee/AFP/Getty)

his regret and suggested the Parsis looked elsewhere. The Parsi chief respectfully asked for a spoon of sugar to be brought. When the sugar was presented, he slowly added the sugar to the milk and mixed it in. The milk didn't spill over, suggesting that just as the milk was sweetened with sugar but didn't spill over, the Parsis would sweeten the kingdom, and respectfully be absorbed in the land without necessarily being a burden on anyone. The Rana agreed to let the Parsis stay. This point in history is one of the greatest stories that deserves to be told. Particularly relevant today, this is a story of migration, of seeking refuge and of assimilation in society. It's also one of acceptance, of adapting and one of the best examples of successful integration anywhere in the world.

The three central principles of an ideal Parsi life are good thoughts, good words and good deeds.

The two most important Parsi festivals fall one after the other, and so we'll look at both together here. The first part of the prominent celebration is sometimes referred to as Navroz-I-Khas, Greater Noruz, namely the New Year or just Navroze.

Every year, just before the New Year, each Parsi family undertakes ten holy days full of prayers for the deceased. This period is called *Mukhtar*, a poignant time for most families, where they get together and pray for the souls they have lost, remembering them and their deeds and what they may have liked or not liked. During this period prayers are offered three times a day at the *Akhiyari* (fire temple) in remembrance of the deceased, and food is distributed amongst people who work in the *Akhiyari*. At this time, prayers are often said in thanksgiving too.

The last day of the ten days of *Mukhtar* is called *Pateti*, the day after this being New Year: the eleventh day, otherwise known as Navroze, which is a holy day for those in the Zoroastrian faith. Everyone showers, wears new clothes, houses are cleaned from top to bottom to symbolise purity of mind, body and environment and decorations are brought out. Houses are often decorated with jasmine and roses, with flower garlands swinging from doors, and *rangoli*, colourful chalk patterns, are drawn around houses. Tables are decorated and laid out with a copy of the *gathas*, a lit candle or lamp, ceramic plate with wheat

or beans, a small bowl with silver coins, flowers, painted eggs, sweets, rose water and a goldfish to symbolise prosperity, wealth, productivity, sweetness and happiness.

Having spent the last ten days remembering those that have passed away, Navroze is for enjoying blessings and looking ahead with optimism. People often make resolutions for the future – ways in which they can improve the lives of others and themselves. The day frequently culminates with people going to see a comedy play, and then gathering at someone's house for more food and to sing old Parsi songs.

Swiftly following on from Navroze, the Parsis celebrate Khordad Sal, the birth of the Prophet Zoroaster, founder of their faith in ancient Iran approximately 3,500 years ago. When the Parsis first landed in India, Jadhav Rana allowed them to stay in the country on a few conditions, one of which is that they would only marry within the faith. As a result, the Parsi community is very tight-knit and their celebrations bring families together. However, community is a central theme of Zoroastrianism, so guests are invited to participate in the celebrations. Any guest entering a home over Navroze or Khordad Sal will be greeted by a glass of *falooda*, a sweet and chilled vermicelli flavoured drink with rose essence.

Unlike most other religions which base their festivals, principles and celebrations on some kind of exercise of sacrifice, self-control or abstinence, the Parsi knows nothing of these things. If anything, Parsi celebrations are about unadulterated indulgence, hospitality and rejoicing. A true celebration of life and everything that is good about it.

A great feast is prepared to mark the occasion, and often features sweet treats (said to bring luck), such as *Parsi ravo* or *Parsi sev*. Food eaten at Khordad Sal is very similar to the dishes enjoyed at Navroze, and *dhan dar patio*, a simple yellow dal served with spicy pickle, is often seen on the table. As Parsis are non-vegetarian, the festival food is varied and includes meat and fish too.

Macchi Patia

Machhi Patia

Fish in Tomato Gravy

The Parsis believe in laying out a good spread and in the event that there isn't a great choice of ingredients available, they will often prepare the same ingredient in two or three different forms to offer a wide choice to their guests. They may have a steamed fish on the menu as well as a fish pulao, but it will not be considered too much to offer yet another fish curry. Just in case…

Serves 4–6

6 garlic cloves
1½ teaspoons red chilli powder
2 teaspoons cumin seeds
2 tablespoons white wine vinegar
750g pollack or cod fillet, skin removed and diced into 4cm cubes
juice of 1 lemon
1½ teaspoons salt
4 tablespoons sesame oil
6 white onions, finely chopped
1 teaspoon sugar
4 tablespoons tomato passata

Make a paste of the garlic, chilli powder, cumin seeds and vinegar either in a blender or using a mortar and pestle.

Marinate the fish with the lemon juice and half the salt for 10 minutes.

Meanwhile, heat the oil in a pan or wok, add the onions and sauté for 8–10 minutes until brown. Add the paste and remaining salt and cook while stirring for 2–3 minutes. Add the sugar and passata and simmer over a low heat for 5 minutes. Then add the marinated fish, cover and cook for 6–10 minutes until the fish is cooked. Check the seasoning and serve with steamed rice.

Machhi nu Pulao

Fish Pulao Cooked in Coconut Milk

This fish pulao is a celebratory dish served at the Parsi table for their new year celebrations. Traditionally pomfret would be used, but this dish could work just as well with monkfish or any other firm white fish.

Serves 6

400g basmati rice, washed in 2-3 changes of water
400g pomfret or monkfish fillets, diced into 2.5cm cubes
2 teaspoons salt
75g ghee or vegetable oil
4 white onions, sliced
500ml coconut milk
50g coriander, chopped
500ml hot water or fish stock

For the paste

2 teaspoons cumin seeds, lightly roasted in a dry frying pan
2.5cm piece of cinnamon stick
2 cloves
½ teaspoon ground turmeric
5 green cardamom pods
6 garlic cloves, peeled
6 dried whole red chillies, stalks removed, broken and seeds discarded
200g grated coconut (frozen is fine)

Rinse the rice under cold running water, then soak in water for 20 minutes.

Grind together all the paste ingredients using as little water as possible in a blender to get a thick, smooth paste.

Sprinkle the fish with 1 teaspoon of the salt and set aside to marinate for 5 minutes.

Heat the ghee or oil in a heavy-based pan, add the onions and sauté over a high heat for 8–10 minutes until brown, then add the ground paste and the remaining salt, and cook for another 2 minutes. Add the drained rice, coconut milk and half the chopped coriander and bring to the boil. Lower the heat and simmer for a few minutes, then add the hot water or stock. Cover and cook for 5 minutes and then add the fish and cook for a further 7–10 or so, covered, until the rice and fish are cooked.

Serve garnished with the remaining chopped coriander.

Top left: Dhansak (page 128)
Middle: Salli Boti (page 129)
Top right: Macchi nu Pulao (page 125)
Bottom right: straw potatoes (for Salli Boti, page 129)

Dhansak

Lamb Cooked with Mixed Lentils and Vegetables

Dhansak is very popular in Britain – it's a cornerstone of the institution that the curry houses are in British life. Although its known more as a 'genre' rather than a dish (lamb dhansak, chicken dhansak, prawn dhansak ... you get the drift), the original is made with lamb and is one of the few examples of dishes that use lentils, vegetables and meat all together in one dish. There is something for everyone here, and therefore *dhansak* appears on celebratory menus on most Parsi occasions.

Serves 6–8

25g red (masoor) lentils
120g toor (arhar) lentils
50g green whole moong lentils
25g chana lentils
1kg lamb leg or shoulder, diced into 2.5cm cubes
1 small or ½ large aubergine, diced into 1cm cubes
100g red pumpkin, peeled, seeds discarded and flesh diced into 1cm cubes
2 tomatoes, finely chopped
4 white onions, 3 finely chopped and 1 thinly sliced
1 small potato, peeled and diced into 1cm cubes
2 teaspoons salt
50ml vegetable oil
2 tablespoons ginger-garlic paste (see page 260)
2 tablespoons dhansak masala (see page 262)
1 teaspoon sugar (optional)
1 tablespoon dried fenugreek leaves (kasoori methi)
2 green chillies, slit lengthways

Rinse 4 types of lentils separately under cold running water and drain.

Place the lamb, all the lentils, aubergine, pumpkin, tomatoes, sliced onions, potato and salt in a large pressure cooker. Add 750ml of water and pressure cook for 10 minutes (4 whistles) or until the lamb is tender and the lentils and vegetables are cooked.

If you don't have a pressure cooker, use 1.5 litres water and cook for approximately 40 minutes in a large, lidded pan until the meat is tender and the lentils and vegetables are cooked and almost mashed.

In the meantime, heat the vegetable oil in a separate wok or pan. Add the chopped onions and cook for 8–10 minutes until they are browned but not burnt. Add the ginger-garlic paste and cook, stirring continuously, for 2 minutes, then add the dhansak masala and cook for another 2 minutes. Remove from the heat and set aside.

Once the lamb and lentils are cooked, remove the lamb pieces and set aside. Blend the lentils to make a smooth paste. If it's still thin, add to the pan with browned onions and spices and cook for another 5 minutes. Add the lamb back into the sauce and cook until the curry is thick and almost the consistency of porridge.

Correct the seasoning if required and finish with the sugar, fenugreek leaves and slit green chillies. It can be served with rice but is best eaten with chapatis.

Salli Boti

Lamb and Apricot Curry Garnished with Crisp Straw Potatoes

This rather unctuous, deep, rich and spicy curry can be made with either lamb or chicken. It is also one of the headline dishes that have come to represent the cooking of the community as well as an expression of their passion for flavour and texture. It's a hero dish in its own right, but even in a crowd of several others a good *salli boti* (or *salli murghi* if using chicken) is a standout dish.

Serves 4–6

4 tablespoons vegetable oil
3 white onions, thinly sliced
2 tablespoons ginger-garlic paste (see page 260)
800g lamb leg or shoulder, diced into 2.5cm cubes (or 1kg chicken, cut into 10–12 pieces on the bone)
2 teaspoons salt
4 tomatoes, finely chopped
8 dried apricots, soaked in warm water for 20 minutes
1 teaspoon jaggery or sugar
2 tablespoons freshly chopped coriander

For the spice paste
6 dried whole red chillies, stalks removed, broken and seeds discarded
2 teaspoons cumin seeds
2.5cm piece of cinnamon stick
6 cloves
6 green cardamom pods
2 teaspoons black peppercorns
2 tablespoons white wine vinegar

For the straw potatoes
2 floury potatoes, peeled, cut into matchsticks (approx. 2mm x 2mm x 6cm)
vegetable oil, for deep frying
salt
¼ teaspoon Kashmiri red chilli powder

Grind together all the paste ingredients in a mortar and pestle or a blender to make a smooth paste.

Heat the oil in a deep heavy-based pan, add the onions and ginger-garlic paste and cook over a medium heat for 2–3 minutes. As the onions soften (no colouring needed), add the lamb and cook over a high heat for 15–20 minutes or until the lamb turns brown and is coloured on the outside. Add the salt and the spice paste and cook for another 2–3 minutes, then add the tomatoes and cook for another 5 or so minutes.

Now lower the heat, add 350ml of water, cover and cook for 20 minutes until the lamb is tender. Cut the soaked apricots into 2 or 3 pieces each and add to the cooked lamb. Check the seasoning and finish with jaggery or sugar. Sprinkle over the coriander, remove from the heat and keep warm.

In the meantime, wash the matchstick potatoes in 2 changes of water to get rid of excess starch, then dry on kitchen paper. Heat the oil in a deep fryer or pan to 160–170°C and fry the potatoes until they are crisp and golden. Remove from the oil, drain on kitchen paper and sprinkle with salt and red chilli powder. Use to garnish the lamb and apricot curry.

Brown Chawal

Parsi Cinnamon Rice

This is the customary rice dish to be served at most celebrations, with vegetables, with kebabs or on its own.

Serves 6–8 as an accompaniment

2 tablespoons vegetable oil
5cm piece of cinnamon stick, broken into 3–4 pieces
2 tablespoons sugar
1½ teaspoons salt
400g basmati rice, rinsed in running water and soaked in water for 20 minutes
100g crisp fried onions (see page 261)

Heat the oil in a heavy-based pan, then add the cinnamon stick and sugar. Stir continuously over a low heat for 3–4 minutes or until the sugar caramelises but doesn't burn – a medium caramel is what you are looking for.

Next add the salt and 800ml of water and bring it to the boil. Add the drained rice, stir to mix and let it come to the boil again. When the water is mostly absorbed and you can see the bubbles breaking on the surface of rice, reduce the heat, give it one more stir, then cover with a lid and cook over a low heat for 10–12 minutes.

Remove the lid to check the rice is cooked. Fluff up the rice so the grains separate, then add the crisp fried onions to garnish generously and serve.

Falooda

Refreshing Rose Milk with Basil Seeds

The Parsis are very partial to a *falooda* – a chilled, sweet, perfumed, rose-flavoured milk with soaked basil seeds. The pretty pink drink may not be for everyone as one could be put off by the bright pink, but it is a firm favourite at most Parsi celebrations, especially with the children.

Serves 4

2 teaspoons basil seeds
500ml chilled whole milk
250g ice
3 tablespoons rose syrup
1 tablespoon caster sugar, or to taste (optional)
1 teaspoon rose water
1 teaspoon flaked almonds (optional)
a few rose petals (optional)

Soak the basil seeds in 120ml of water for 15–30 minutes, then strain and set aside.

Mix the chilled milk with the ice and rose syrup, stirring very well so that the rose syrup is completely dissolved in the milk. Add ½ tablespoon of the sugar and taste, adding more as required. Either way, sugar is optional and you may wish to omit it if the rose syrup is sweet enough.

Next, add the rose water. Finally add the drained basil seeds, stir again and pour the rose milk in to glasses. Serve garnished with flaked almonds and rose petals, if you wish.

Rava

Parsi Semolina Garnished with Dried Fruits

Although *rava* is a term loosely used to describe semolina all over the country, this is yet another of the hundreds of different versions of semolina halwa or *sooji halwa*. My mother also makes semolina halwa and it's a favourite of mine, but this Parsi version is as different from hers as anything can be! The use of dried fruits and nuts is a Persian influence, as is the use of aromatics like rose water.

Serves 6–8

180g ghee
60g flaked almonds
150g golden raisins
250g coarse semolina
180g sugar
4 eggs, lightly beaten
750ml whole milk
1 teaspoon ground green cardamom
¼ teaspoon ground nutmeg
2 teaspoons rose water

Heat 80g of the ghee in a wok and fry the almonds until they just start to turn golden; add the raisins and continue until the raisins puff up, then remove with a slotted spoon and drain. Set aside.

Add the semolina to the same pan and sauté over a low heat for 5–7 minutes until a roasted aroma emanates and the semolina resembles the consistency of sand, stirring constantly. Remove from the heat and stir in 125ml of water. Return to the heat and cook for 2–3 minutes, then add the sugar and cook for 2 minutes. Remove from the heat.

Mix together the eggs and milk and add to the semolina mix, stirring to mix well. Return to the heat and cook over a low heat for 3–4 minutes, stirring constantly to prevent the egg mixture curdling.

Slowly add the remaining ghee, a little at a time until it is incorporated and the mixture thickens. Mix in the ground cardamom, nutmeg and rose water.

Serve warm in a bowl garnished with the almonds and raisins.

Lagan nu Custard

Wedding Custard

Even though the name gives it away as being a favourite on Parsi wedding menus, this dessert is served at most celebratory meals and is the highlight of the meal for many, especially children.

Serves 6

2 tablespoons flaked almonds
750ml whole milk
180g sugar
2 eggs, beaten
3 yolks
1 teaspoon vanilla extract
1 teaspoon rose water
1 teaspoon ground green cardamom
½ teaspoon grated nutmeg

Preheat the oven to 150°C/130°C Fan/Gas Mark 2.

First roast the almond flakes under a grill or in a dry frying pan for 2–3 minutes over a medium heat, then let them cool.

Boil the milk and sugar in a pan over a low heat until reduced to about half of their original volume (approximately 575ml), then let it cool.

Add the beaten eggs and the 3 yolks, vanilla extract, rose water and green cardamom. Mix well and pour the mixture into a baking dish with a 25cm diameter. Sprinkle with the grated nutmeg and roasted almonds, then bake in the preheated oven for 20 minutes until the custard is set and the top is golden brown.

Remove from the oven, allow to cool and refrigerate until you are ready to serve. You can serve this whole at the table or cut into pieces and serve.

Top left: Lagan nu Custard (page 132)
Middle: Rava (page 131)

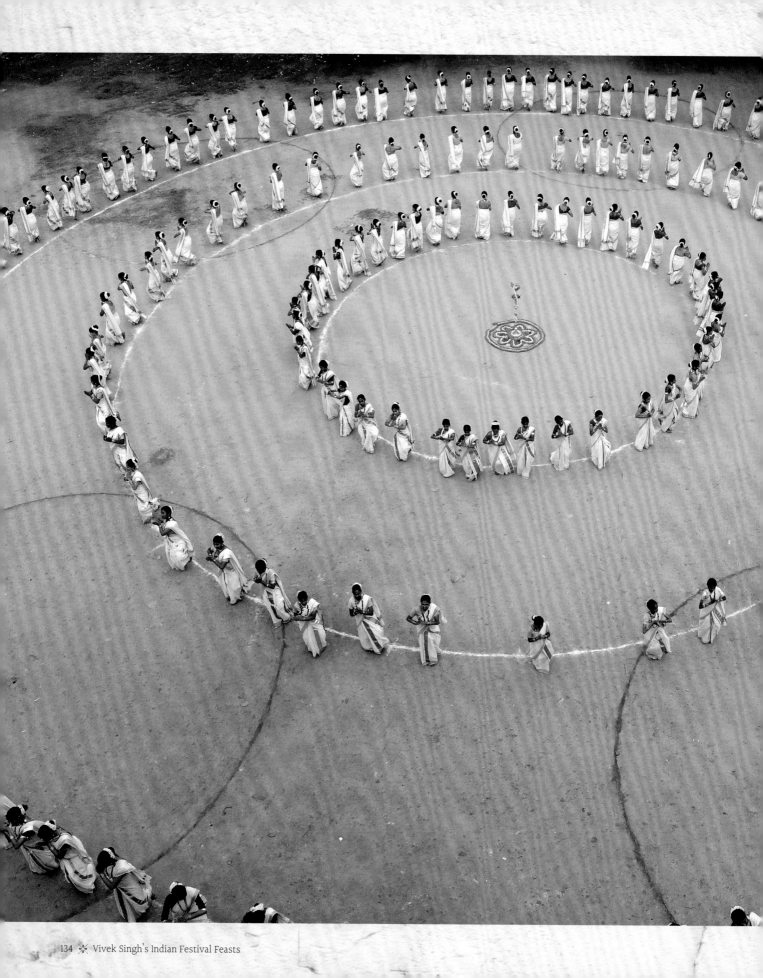

Onam

One of my very close friends, Rakesh Ravindran Nair, gave me an insight into the significance of Onam and how it is celebrated. The following is what he had to say:

Onam is a Hindu harvest festival celebrated all over Kerala and lasts for over ten days. It is celebrated specifically by Keralites to remember their agrarian past and as a way to thank God for their blessings. The rich cultural heritage of Kerala comes out in its best form and spirit during the festival, and always evokes happy memories as it is an occasion for everyone to return to their ancestral homes, meet friends and family, exchange gifts and have lots of fun and games. For expatriates like me, it is even considered rude and disrespectful to our parents and other family members if we do not make the effort to go back to meet them and take part in the festive activities! Unfortunately, with schools here in England reopening in September, it is not always possible to take children back home to celebrate Onam (if only the English education system realised how important Onam is!). The most important day of the festival is called *Thiruvonam* and is characterised by a big vegetarian feast or *sadya*, served on banana leaves.

Girls perfom a 'Thiruvathira kali' as part of the Onam celebrations. (Raveendran/ AFP/Getty)

The festival falls during the Malayalam month of Chingam (August to September) and marks the commemoration of Vamana Avatara of Vishnu and the homecoming of the mythical king Mahabali. Mahabali is said to return every year from the underworld to make sure that his subjects are thriving and living happily and he blesses them; a feast is thrown in his honour. I remember that my uncle, who used to live in a village a bit far away, once travelled in a bullock cart (in the late 1970's) overnight to bring rice and vegetables from his field to our ancestral home to use in the Onam feast! Even though both he and the driver were fast asleep when the cart reached us, the bullocks were wide awake and knew their way! There is even a famous Malayalam proverb 'kaanam vittum onam unnanam' which means one must enjoy the Onam feast even if one is forced to sell the last of one's property or possessions.

Onam is also celebrated through a number of rituals and traditions such as *talappanthukali*, a ball game for boys and men; *vadam vali*, a tug of war; *pookkalam*, in which children lay out floral carpets outside the front door of a house and they grow in size throughout the festival, with more added to the patterns each day; *onavillu*, a bow-shaped musical instrument which is played to accompany the *kummattikali*, a famous colourful masked dance, which sees the dancers go from house to house entertaining people and collecting small gifts; *thiruvathira kali*, a group dance performance by women in a circle around a lamp; *kaazhchakkula*, the offering of fruits; and *onakkodi*, the exchange or offering of gifts practiced by the adults as they give gifts to the younger ones.

As well as the rituals mentioned here, Onam is well known for the famous *vallam kali*, a snake boat race that is held on the River Pampa. One hundred oarsmen row huge and graceful snake boats throughout the day and people come from far and wide to watch them. One of the most iconic rituals is the *puli kali*, which sees performers painted like tigers and hunters parade and dance through the streets.

Traditionally the eldest member of the family presents gifts and new clothes to the other family members. Clothes are a special part of the festival, with women wearing traditional white saris with a gold border and men wear white *dhoti* with a golden or colourful border.

My earliest childhood memories of Onam are of the fun and games that I had with all the kids in the family and also from the neighbourhood. Boys usually played *talappanthukali* and the winner had all the bragging rights in front of girls. The girls used to collect flowers from the garden for *pookkalam* or played hide and seek. Both boys and girls took turns at the swing and the competition was always to see who could go the highest. For the kids, these were the next best thing to receiving gifts from the elders. These days, with the advances made in international tourism, you often see foreigners taking part in the festivities. I once saw an English lady, very efficiently, taking part in *thiruvathira kali* with the local ladies and also a rather large American gentleman playing the part of an overweight tiger in *puli kali*!

The Onam *sadya* (or feast) consists of rice and around twenty to thirty different accompaniments or dishes served in a particular sequence on a banana leaf and consumed in a specific order using lentil based dishes to begin with, and yoghurt based dishes to finish the meal. They can be broadly classified into eight types of dishes (fries, pickles or chutneys, stir-fries, stews, starch, lentils, soups and desserts). Water served with the meal is usually simmered with cumin, dried ginger or the bark of an acacia tree. The banana leaf is first placed in front of a person so that the tapering end always points to the left side. The *sadya* is served from the top left corner of the leaf and then continues to the upper half of the leaf, leaving the lower half for rice and a few fried accompaniments. Traditionally, the Onam *sadya* is served in at least eight courses. It starts with *parippu* served on rice followed by *sambar* and *rasam*, served with more rice. Then comes the dessert course of *payasam* followed by at least two *pradhamans*. Rice makes an appearance again and this time is served with *pulissery* and then *sambaram*. All the accompaniments are replenished throughout the meal.

Sambar

Tamil Spiced Lentil Broth

Much like *kheer*, or *aloo gobhi*, Sambar is a dish made all over the country and everyone has their own recipe for it. And the most contentious thing is that no two people can agree which recipe is better, let alone the best. This is Rakesh Nair's recipe, made by his family for Onam. It includes drumstick (also known as *moringa* or *moringakkai*), a vegetable available from south Indian shops.

Serves 6

150g toor dal
½ teaspoon ground turmeric
1 teaspoon salt
3 tablespoons vegetable oil
10 shallots, quartered
100g French beans, cut into 2.5cm pieces
2 carrots, diced into 2.5cm cubes
2 baby aubergines, quartered
1 drumstick, peeled and cut into 2.5cm pieces (optional)
50ml tamarind pulp
2 tomatoes, quartered

For the sambar masala
1 tablespoon coriander seeds
2 teaspoons cumin seeds
1 tablespoon chana dal
6 whole dried red chillies
1½ teaspoons peppercorns
2 tablespoons freshly grated coconut
½ teaspoon fenugreek seeds
a sprig of fresh curry leaves

For the tempering
1 tablespoon vegetable oil
½ teaspoon black mustard seeds
4 whole dried red chillies
¼ teaspoon asafoetida
a sprig of fresh curry leaves

Wash the toor dal lentils in cold running water, then place in a pan with the turmeric and salt. Add 750ml of water, bring to the boil, then simmer until completely mushy. Remove from the heat and set aside (there is no need to drain).

Prepare the sambar masala by dry roasting all the ingredients in a frying pan until they start to release their flavour. Grind them to a fine powder using a blender or food processor.

Heat the oil in a deep saucepan, add the shallots and sauté for a couple of minutes. Now add the remaining vegetables and sauté for another 5 minutes. Sprinkle in 1½ tablespoons of the spice mix and the tamarind pulp. Cover and cook for another 10 minutes until the vegetables are tender. Add this to the cooked lentils and stir well. Add the tomatoes and more water, if required, to adjust the consistency, which should be like a dal, i.e. a thick soup that can be poured, with chunks of vegetables. Simmer for 5 minutes and remove from the heat.

To prepare the tempering, heat the oil in a small frying pan, add the mustard seeds and when they crackle add the whole chillies, asafoetida and curry leaves. Stir for 30 seconds as the spices splutter, then immediately pour it over the sambar and mix well.

Clockwise from top left:
Sambaram (page 150); Pritvichakka Pachadi
(page 143); Sanku Khichadi (page 143);
Puliyinchi (page 147); Pulissery (page 146);
Narial Laddoo (page 151); Manga Chammanthi
(page 147); Puliyinchi (page 147)

Masala Dosa

South Indian Pancake with Spiced Potato Filling

Dosa pancakes are served as breakfast, as a snack or as a main meal at any time of the day and all over the country. Several good Asian stores now sell ready-made packs of batter, saving both time and the mess. The same applies to grating coconut from the shell, which is time consuming and can be messy – frozen grated coconut is also becoming increasingly easy to find these days.

Serves 6 (should make 10 pieces but allow for wastage as spreading a dosa can be tricky!)

For the rice pancake
50g split urad dal
150g basmati or dosa rice (parboiled rice is available in most speciality ingredient stores)
1 teaspoon salt
vegetable oil, for frying

For the spiced potato filling
2 tablespoons vegetable oil
1 teaspoon black mustard seeds
2 sprigs of fresh curry leaves (optional)
2 red onions, chopped
½ teaspoon ground turmeric
2 green chillies, finely chopped
2.5cm piece of ginger, finely chopped
1½ teaspoons salt
2 large potatoes, boiled in the skin, peeled and grated

To make the pancake batter, soak the rice and the dal together in water for at least for 3 hours. Drain and blend together in a food processor to a fine paste, adding enough water to make a smooth, spoonable mixture. Leave overnight to ferment in a warm place (about 35–40°C). The dosa batter is ready when bubbles begin to appear on the surface of the batter.

To make the filling, heat the oil in a pan, add the mustard seeds and let them crackle and pop for 30 seconds. Add the curry leaves and onions and sauté for 5 minutes or until translucent. Add the turmeric, chillies and ginger and sauté for 1 minute. Add the salt and the grated potatoes and mix well. Set aside at room temperature.

To make pancakes, add the salt to the batter and mix well.

Heat a non-stick frying pan over a medium heat, smear the base with a few drops of oil and pour in a small ladleful of batter (approximately 60ml). Using the ladle, spread it out into a thin circular pancake. The thinner the pancake, the crispier it gets, but this needs some practice. Drizzle a few drops of oil over the top while the pancake cooks. Normally dosas are cooked on one side only; however, if yours are thicker, it's okay to cook on both sides.

When crisp and golden, spoon approximately 50g of the filling into the centre of the pancake and fold the pancake over. Repeat with the remaining batter and filling. Enjoy with Onam chutneys (see page 147).

Pritvichakka Pachadi

Pineapple and Yoghurt Relish

This is a lovely, fresh and fruity addition to the *sadya* (a grand feast, usually vegetarian, served on special occasions), bringing the meal to life with its clean taste. Think of this as a cooked pineapple *raita* – it could make an interesting addition to your lunchtime wrap too.

Serves 4

35g grated fresh coconut
1 teaspoon cumin seeds
1 teaspoon black mustard seeds
1 pineapple, diced into 1cm cubes
1 teaspoon salt
½ teaspoon ground turmeric
15g jaggery or palm sugar
215ml plain yoghurt

For the tempering
1 tablespoon coconut oil
½ teaspoon black mustard seeds
2 whole dried red chillies
a sprig of fresh curry leaves

Grind the coconut, cumin seeds and mustard seeds to a fine paste using a little water and set aside.

Place the pineapple in a pan with the salt, turmeric and jaggery and 500ml of water and cook over a medium heat for about 30 minutes until soft. Reduce the heat to low, add the ground coconut paste and cook for about 5 minutes until the mixture becomes dry again. Add the yoghurt, mix well and remove from the heat (do not let the yoghurt boil).

To prepare the tempering, heat the oil in a pan, add the mustard seeds and when they splutter, add the red chillies and curry leaves. Pour the mixture over the pachadi.

Sanku Khichadi

Beetroot and Yoghurt Relish

Even though its name labels this recipe a *kichadi*, this accompaniment is more like a *pachadi* or tempered yoghurt. The brilliant beetroot colour adds drama to the feast, and it's unlike anything else you may have come across.

Serves 4

35g freshly grated coconut
2 shallots, sliced
½ teaspoon cumin seeds
1 raw beetroot, peeled and grated
4 green chillies, chopped
1 teaspoon salt
½ teaspoon black mustard seeds, crushed
215g plain yoghurt

For the tempering
1 tablespoon coconut oil
½ teaspoon black mustard seeds
2 dried whole red chillies
a sprig of fresh curry leaves

Grind together the coconut, shallots and cumin seeds to a smooth paste, adding 2 tablespoons of water.

Cook the beetroot in a pan with the green chillies, salt and 2 tablespoons of water, covered, over a low heat for about 5 minutes until soft. Add the coconut paste and the mustard seeds and mix well. Remove from the heat and stir in the yoghurt.

To prepare the tempering, heat the oil in a frying pan, Add the mustard seeds followed by red chillies and curry leaves. When they splutter, add to the kichadi and keep covered. Serve warm or at room temperature with rice, or chill it down and serve like a raita with kebabs.

Left: Cabbage Thoran (page 149)
Middle: Koottukari (page 148)
Right: Masala Dosa (page 142) and
    Manga Chammanthi (page 147)

Rasam

Spiced Tomato and Tamarind Soup

This hot, peppery soup from Kerala has travelled well to all parts of the world. In many hotels you will be served a refined version of the soup, i.e. strained to remove any whole spices, tomato skins and seeds, but at most events and in most homes the soup is served straight up with rice.

Serves 4

4 garlic cloves
1 tablespoon coriander seeds
1 teaspoon black peppercorns
1 teaspoon cumin seeds
2 tablespoons vegetable oil
a sprig of fresh curry leaves
12 tomatoes, cut into quarters
¼ teaspoon ground turmeric
½ teaspoon red chilli powder
1 teaspoon salt
1 tablespoon tamarind pulp
1 tablespoon freshly chopped coriander leaves

For the tempering
1 tablespoon vegetable oil
2 whole dried red chillies
½ teaspoon mustard seeds
a sprig of fresh curry leaves

Crush the garlic, coriander seeds, peppercorns and cumin seeds together using a mortar and pestle.

Heat the oil in a pan, add the crushed spices and curry leaves and sauté for 1 minute until they release their flavour. Now add the tomatoes, turmeric, chilli powder and salt and cook for a couple of minutes. Add the tamarind pulp and 600ml of water and simmer for about 20 minutes until the tomatoes are completely cooked. Sprinkle in the coriander leaves.

To prepare the tempering, heat the oil in a pan, add the red chillies and mustard seeds followed by the curry leaves and let them crackle. Plunge it into the hot soup and leave the soup covered with a lid until ready to serve.

Pulissery

Yoghurt and Coconut Gravy

Think of this as a warm yoghurt and coconut *kadhi*, except this isn't boiled for as long which results in a much lighter taste and cleaner flavours.

Serves 4

35g freshly grated coconut
2 green chillies
1 garlic clove
1 teaspoon cumin seeds
1 shallot, sliced
½ teaspoon ground turmeric
430ml natural yoghurt

For the tempering
1 tablespoon coconut oil
½ teaspoon brown mustard seeds
½ teaspoon fenugreek seeds
1 sprig of fresh curry leaves

Grind together the coconut, green chillies, garlic, cumin seeds, shallot and turmeric into a smooth paste, adding a little water if required. Mix it with the yoghurt and set aside. If the mixture is too thick, or isn't smooth, add a little water to thin it down.

To prepare the tempering, heat the oil in a pan, add the mustard seeds, fenugreek seeds and curry leaves. When they start spluttering, add the yoghurt and coconut mixture to the pan and cook over a low heat, stirring continuously, until the yoghurt is warm. Keep it warm for another couple of minutes, then remove it from the heat. Note: never allow the sauce to boil or it will curdle.

Serve warm, in a bowl, as part of the meal.

Puliyinchi

Sweet and Sour Ginger Chutney

This is a wonderfully spicy ginger chutney that lifts the entire meal in a tiny lick. Sweet, sour, warm and deep, it's a great one to have in your fridge for a rainy day in the UK.

Serves 4

3 tablespoons vegetable oil
7.5cm piece of ginger, sliced
½ teaspoon black or brown mustard seeds
½ teaspoon fenugreek seeds
2 green chillies, halved lengthwise
5 fresh curry leaves
½ teaspoon red chilli powder
1 tablespoon tamarind paste
40g jaggery or molasses sugar, dissolved in 3 tablespoons water
1 teaspoon salt

Heat the oil in a frying pan, add the sliced ginger and fry until golden brown and crisp. Drain the ginger and let it cool, then pound to a coarse powder.

Using the same oil, add the mustard seeds and fenugreek seeds to the pan and when they begin to crackle, add the green chillies and curry leaves. Add the ground ginger and red chilli powder and stir until the oil separates. Add the tamarind, the dissolved jaggery and salt and cook until the oil comes up on top. Remove from the heat and let the chutney cool before serving.

Manga Chammanthi

Green Mango and Coconut Chutney

I love the freshness, acidity and sourness from green mangoes that add another dimension to an otherwise rich coconut chutney. It is a brilliant accompaniment to most grilled fish.

Serves 8

3 green mangoes, peeled, deseeded and diced
70g freshly grated coconut
1 shallot, sliced
1 garlic clove
2 teaspoons red chilli powder
1 tablespoon vegetable oil
1 teaspoon salt
½ teaspoon sugar

Put all the ingredients in a food processor and blend to a smooth, thick paste, adding a little water (up to 3 tablespoons) if required. Refrigerate and serve with grilled seafood. This can be stored in the fridge for up to 2 days.

Parippu

Curried Moong Lentils with Coconut

This is the equivalent of dal in any other north Indian meal or feast, but here the lentils are first roasted and then cooked. This gives an extra depth of flavour and nuttiness to the lentils.

Serves 4 as an accompaniment

100g yellow moong lentils
35g freshly grated coconut
½ teaspoon cumin seeds
2 green chillies
¼ teaspoon ground turmeric
1 teaspoon salt
1 teaspoon ghee (optional)

For the tempering
2 tablespoons coconut oil
½ teaspoon black mustard seeds
2 dried red chillies
2 large shallots, chopped
a sprig of fresh curry leaves

Dry roast the moong lentils in a frying pan over a medium heat until they are lightly coloured.

Grind together the coconut, cumin seeds, green chillies and turmeric with 1 tablespoon water to a smooth paste.

Rinse the lentils in water, then place in a pan with 950ml of water. Bring to the boil, then reduce the heat to medium and cook for about 45 minutes until slightly mushy. Add the ground paste and salt to the pan and simmer for another 5 minutes. Add more hot water if required. Once cooked remove from the heat and set aside.

To prepare the tempering, heat the oil in a frying pan and add the mustard seeds. When they start to crackle, add the red chillies, shallots and curry leaves and fry until the shallots become golden brown. Pour over the cooked lentils and serve with rice.

If you wish, drizzle a teaspoon of ghee over the lentils just before serving to improve the taste even further.

Koottukari

Pumpkin, Gourd and Chickpea Curry

This is another one of the complex vegetarian combination dishes that form part of the Onam *sadya*.

Serves 4

100g black chickpeas, soaked overnight in water (available in Indian grocery stores)
1 teaspoon salt
70g freshly grated coconut
1 teaspoon cumin seeds
½ teaspoon black peppercorns
150g elephant yam, peeled and diced into 1cm cubes (alternatively, use potato)
150g ash gourd, peeled and diced into 1cm cubes (alternatively, use bottle gourd [doodhi] or cucumber)
150g red pumpkin, peeled and diced into 1cm cubes
½ teaspoon ground turmeric
1 teaspoon red chilli powder

For the tempering
3 tablespoons coconut oil
½ teaspoon black mustard seeds
a sprig of fresh curry leaves
35g freshly grated coconut

Drain the soaked chickpeas and place in a pan. Add 1.2 litres of water and a pinch of the salt, bring to the boil and boil for 45 minutes or until soft.

Grind together the coconut, cumin seeds and peppercorns. Set aside.

Place the yam, gourd and pumpkin with the turmeric, chilli powder and remaining salt in a pan with 235ml of water. Bring to the boil, then cover and cook over a low heat for about 15 minutes until tender. Add the chickpeas and their cooking liquid, followed by the ground coconut, and cook for another 5 minutes over a low heat. Remove from the heat.

To prepare the tempering, heat the oil in a frying pan, add the mustard seeds and when they crackle, add the curry leaves and coconut and stir until the coconut becomes golden brown. Add it to the koottukari, mix it in and serve.

Cabbage Thoran

Cabbage and Coconut Stir Fry

This is yet another of those easy, quick and simple dishes that is both great looking and great tasting. What's more, it is very good for you.

Serves 4

3 tablespoons coconut or vegetable oil
½ teaspoon black or brown mustard seeds
3 dried red chillies
10 fresh curry leaves
3 green chillies, finely chopped

1 onion, chopped
½ teaspoon ground turmeric
½ white cabbage, finely chopped
1 teaspoon salt
50g fresh or frozen grated coconut
1 teaspoon cumin seeds, roasted and crushed

Heat the oil in a frying pan. Add the mustard seeds and when they crackle, add the red chillies and curry leaves and fry over a medium heat until the chillies change colour and become darker. Add the green chillies and onion and sauté until the onion becomes translucent. Now add the turmeric, cabbage and salt and stir well. Cover, reduce the heat to low and cook for about 10 minutes, stirring occasionally, until the cabbage is cooked.

Stir in the grated coconut and cumin and cook for 1 minute. Serve hot as an accompaniment.

Avial

Mixed Vegetables in Coconut Curry

As you will probably see, this is a feast of vegetables, served as an accompaniment. If you can't find snake gourd or elephant yam, feel free to use more of the other vegetables.

Serves 4

100g carrots, cut into batons 5cm long and 1cm wide
100g cluster beans or French beans, trimmed
100g elephant yam (optional), peeled and cut batons 5cm long and 1cm wide
100g snake gourd, scraped and cut into batons 5cm long and 1cm wide
½ cucumber, peeled and cut into batons 5cm long

and 1cm wide, seeds removed
1 green plantain peeled and cut batons 5cm long and 1cm wide
½ teaspoon ground turmeric
1 teaspoon salt
70g grated coconut, fresh or frozen
4 green chillies
½ teaspoon cumin seeds
a sprig of fresh curry leaves
100ml plain yoghurt
1 tablespoon coconut oil, melted

Place all the vegetables in a pan with the turmeric, salt and 120ml of water, cover and cook for about 5 minutes until they are 50 per cent cooked. (Avial is traditionally a mishmash of vegetables and not all of them are expected to retain their shape after cooking.)

Grind the coconut, green chillies and cumin seeds into a coarse paste using a little water.

Add the ground paste to the pan and cook, covered, for about 5 minutes over a low heat. Add the curry leaves and yoghurt, mix gently and cook for another couple of minutes until the vegetables are well cooked but not mashed. Drizzle the coconut oil on top and keep covered until ready to serve.

Sambaram

Chilled Curry Leaf and Ginger Yoghurt Drink

Don't be fooled by the name – this isn't anything like *sambar*! This is rather like a very thin *lassi* or *chaas* – a thin yoghurt drink infused with curry leaves, chilli and ginger. In Rajasthan, they temper the drink with asafoetida, ginger and chilli, but this Keralan version is simply infused, chilled and served.

Serves 4

650ml low-fat plain yoghurt, stirred
475ml chilled water

1 green chilli
1 shallot, diced
1 sprig of fresh curry leaves
1cm piece of ginger
½ teaspoon sea salt

Whisk the yoghurt with the water. Crush together the green chilli, shallot, curry leaves, ginger and salt and add to the yoghurt. Mix well and refrigerate for at least 30 minutes. Strain and serve chilled.

Payasam

Kerala Rice Pudding

Much like the revered *kheer* in Bengal or the rest of northern India, this Keralan version uses raw red rice instead of basmati and a mixture of milk and water rather than just milk. In essence though, you can see how similar it is to the alternative version offered at other feasts and celebrations.

Serves 4

50g raw red rice, washed and soaked in water for around 20 minutes
710ml whole milk
½ teaspoon green cardamom powder

150g sugar
1 tablespoon ghee
1 tablespoon cashew nuts
1 tablespoon raisins
1 tablespoon dried coconut, diced into 5mm cubes

Drain the rice and place in a pan. Add half the milk and 175ml of water and cook over a low heat, stirring occasionally, until the rice is cooked. Now add the remaining milk and another 175ml of water and continue to simmer until you get the consistency of a rice pudding. Stir in the cardamom and sugar and allow it to dissolve completely. Remove from the heat and set aside.

Heat the ghee in a small frying pan, add the cashew nuts, raisins and coconut and fry until golden brown. Add it to payasam and mix well.

Payasam is traditionally served hot, but it also tastes just as good served chilled.

Narial Laddoo

Coconut Laddoo

In Kerala, any excuse to use up a bit of coconut is always welcome. Of all laddoos in the world, these are probably the easiest ones to make, so go for it!

Makes 36–40 small laddoos suitable for petits fours

200g coarse semolina
50g desiccated coconut
300g grated fresh coconut
400g sweetened condensed milk
50g caster sugar (optional)
½ teaspoon green cardamom seeds (pods removed and discarded, seeds crushed)

Roast the semolina in a dry pan over a medium heat, constantly stirring until it starts turning first golden and then light brown. Remove from the heat and set aside. In the same pan, toast the desiccated coconut and keep aside.

Add the grated fresh coconut to the semolina and allow the mixture to cool down.

Add the caster sugar, if using, to the cooled mixture, then add three-quarters of the condensed milk and mix well. If the mixture is not too wet to be shaped, add the remaining condensed milk. Add the ground green cardamom and mix well.

Make small balls of the mixture by taking a teaspoon of the mixture and rolling between your palms, then place on a plate.

Roll the balls in the toasted desiccated coconut. Place in the refrigerator for 30 minutes until chilled and set, then serve.

Kalan

Plantain Curry

Kalan takes its name from the Hindi word *kela*, or banana. Kerala loves its plantains as well as its coconut. Plantains are used extensively and pretty much every part of the tree is used – the leaves used as plates, the raw fruit in curries, as a snack in the form of plantain chips both sweet and savoury, and the ripe bananas used for dessert in *payasams*, or fritters.

Serves 4 as an accompaniment

2 green plantains, peeled and diced into 1cm cubes
3 green chillies, chopped
½ teaspoon coarsely ground black pepper
½ teaspoon ground turmeric
1 teaspoon salt
70g freshly grated coconut
½ teaspoon cumin seeds
650ml thick plain yoghurt

For the tempering

1 tablespoon coconut oil
½ teaspoon black mustard seeds
½ teaspoon fenugreek seeds
2 whole dried red chillies
a sprig of fresh curry leaves

Place the plantains in a pan with the green chillies, pepper, turmeric and salt with 235ml of water. Bring to the boil, then cover with a lid and let it simmer for about 30 minutes until the plantain is tender and cooked, and most of the water absorbed. Remove from the heat and set aside.

Grind the coconut with the cumin seeds with 3 tablespoons of water to a smooth paste, then mix with the yoghurt. Add to the pan containing the cooked plantain and mix together. Simmer, stirring continuously, for about 5 minutes until it thickens. Remove from the heat.

Heat the oil in a small pan and add the mustard seeds. When they crackle, add the fenugreek seeds, red chillies and curry leaves, let them splutter for 30 seconds or so then pour the mixture over the kalan and mix well.

Eid al-Adha

Eid al-Adha, also known as the Greater Eid or the Feast of Sacrifice, is the second most important festival in the Islamic calendar.

The day remembers the occasion when Allah appeared to the Prophet Ibrahim in a dream and asked him to sacrifice his son Isma'il as an act of obedience to Allah. The devil tempted Ibrahim by saying he should disobey God and spare his son. As Ibrahim was about to kill his son, Allah stopped him and gave him a lamb to sacrifice instead. It is not so much an act of disobeying the devil or obeying the wish of Allah, as it is about completely submitting oneself to the faith, as if to say 'If this is what you want of me, then who am I to question it? And whatever I have is actually yours, and whatever you want of me, I can only obey.' This complete submission and unconditional, unquestioned faith in Allah is what led to Allah to say 'I was merely testing your devotion'.

Eid al-Adha is observed after the Hajj – the annual pilgrimage to Makkah, or Mecca, in Saudi Arabia. The journey is seen as one of the Five Pillars of Islam, and it is a duty of each Muslim to go on the Hajj at least once during their lifetime, unless they are prevented by finances or ill health. Every year, millions of Muslims travel to Saudi Arabia from all around the world, a range of different colours, languages, races and ethnicities coming together in a spirit of universal brotherhood and sisterhood to worship Allah.

Muslims gather for prayers at Jama Masjid at Eid al-Adha. (Money Sharma/AFP/Getty)

The day of Eid al-Adha begins with Muslims dressed in their finest clothes going to the mosque for prayers and to thank God for all their blessings. These prayers often take place outside – sometimes due to the sheer number of Muslims in attendance! It is also a time for visiting friends and family and offering gifts. An animal is usually sacrificed as a symbol of Ibrahim's willingness to sacrifice his son. The meat from the animal sacrificed is shared among friends, family and the poor, with each receiving a third. Those principles of sharing and giving and helping others who are less fortunate ensures that everyone is given an opportunity to celebrate Eid.

Eid al-Adha is colloquially known as Bakri Eid in India, due to the common practice of sacrificing a goat, or a *bakri*. It is one of the most eagerly awaited festivals in India, even for non-Muslims like me, because each one of our Muslim friends or neighbours would invite us to their house to

partake in the celebrations and enjoy their feasts – which centred mainly around meat, and no Eid table would be complete without a biryani! In a city like Hyderabad, where such a large proportion of the population celebrates this festival, the abundance of meat and delicious food makes this one of the best times of the year to be living in the city!

Until I became a trainee at The Oberoi Hotel in Hyderabad in 1994, I had never encountered food like the dishes I saw there: I had never experienced aromas like I did in the city, nor had I ever come across people who had such passion for food, flavour, taste and, above all, a heart for hospitality as the Hyderabadis, all of which is bound up in the celebrations for Eid.

In my early days at the hotel, I would get hungry just smelling the fragrance of the biryani pot wafting through the service corridors. My friends said that during Bakri Eid the entire city smelled like one huge biryani pot and I didn't believe them. Well, I found myself in the city during the festival and saw first hand what they meant! No matter which direction you turned, you saw something being cooked, stirred, baked or served: kebabs, curries and biryani everywhere, being gifted, exchanged, sold and bought.

I vividly remember looking down at the city from Golconda Fort and seeing a film of haze – smoke from the numerous fires cooking in the city – suspended in mid-air over the townships. I quickly found that there was just so much meat going around, you couldn't even give it away. Often dishes would start off as a curry then, after being reheated a few times, would turn into a semi-dry bhuna kind of dish, then after further drying would become a kebab, finally being turned into a pickle. Some meat is also thinly sliced, seasoned and dried, then fried to turn it into a kind of jerky-type meat to prolong its life. And when all else fails, the Hyderabadis are also known to take their pots of curries and biryanis to the railway station and feed complete strangers who may be passing through their city on the train!

Chaney ki Dal Gosht

Deccan Lamb and Lentil Curry

This dish of lamb cooked with chana lentils is quite popular in the Deccan region and its origins are attributed to the kitchens of the Nizam of Hyderabad. Usually seen on menus during the celebration of Bakri Eid or Eid-al-Adha, this is one of the hundreds of types of dishes prepared using the meat widely available in the city of Hyderabad during those days.

Serves 4

750g mutton, boned and diced into
   2.5cm cubes
200g split yellow peas/chana dal
2 black cardamom pods
1 teaspoon ground turmeric
1½ teaspoons salt
4 tablespoons vegetable oil
1 bay leaf
4 cloves
4 green cardamom pods
5cm piece of cinnamon stick
4 black peppercorns
4 onions, finely chopped
1 tablespoon ginger-garlic paste (see
   page 260)
3 tomatoes, cut into quarters
10 curry leaves
½ teaspoon garam masala
1 tablespoon tamarind paste
1 tablespoon freshly chopped
   coriander
2 teaspoons desiccated grated
   coconut
juice of ½ lime
a pinch of sugar

For the fresh spice mix
50g coriander stems
3 garlic cloves
4 green chillies
½ teaspoon coriander seeds, roasted
½ teaspoon cumin seeds, roasted
½ tablespoon vegetable oil

Blend all the ingredients for the fresh spice mix to a coarse paste and set aside.

Wash the lamb in cold running water, drain, dry using kitchen paper and set aside.

Wash the lentils in cold running water. Place in a heavy-based pan along with the black cardamom and 1 litre of water, the turmeric and ½ teaspoon of the salt. Bring to the boil and simmer for 30–40 minutes until the lentils are almost cooked but still slightly crunchy. Remove from the heat, drain, reserving the liquid, and keep warm.

In the meantime, heat the oil in another heavy-based pan, add the whole spices and let them crackle for 1 minute or so. Add the onions and sauté for 8–10 minutes until they turn golden. Add the ginger-garlic paste and stir for 1 minute, then add the lamb, remaining salt and the fresh spice mix. Cook over a high heat, stirring continuously, for 6–8 minutes.

Add the tomato quarters to the lamb and cook over a high heat for 3 minutes until softened. Pour in 150ml of water, cover with a lid and allow the lamb to simmer for 45–50 minutes until it is almost cooked.

Pour in the lentils and two-thirds of the reserved cooking liquid and continue cooking over a medium heat for 6–8 minutes or until the lamb is tender. Stir in the fresh curry leaves, garam masala and tamarind paste, then finish the dish with the chopped coriander, coconut, lime juice and a pinch of sugar. If you wish, use the remaining lentil cooking liquid to let down the curry, otherwise serve as it is.

Serve hot with steamed rice or pilau rice.

Top left: Gosht ka Chudwa (page 161)
Bottom left: Kadhai ke Bheje (page 166)
Middle top: Thalasseri Kozhi Curry (page 167)
Middle bottom: Shami Kabab (page 165)
Top right: Hari's 'Hyderabadi' Kachhi Biryani (page 162)
Bottom right: Kaleji Kabab (page 164)

Hyderabadi Special Pathar ka Gosht

Tender Lamb Escalopes Grilled on Hot Stone

This is one of the most famed kebabs to originate from Hyderabad. Traditionally made with thinly sliced mutton leg which is marinated with black spices (black cardamom, cloves, peppper, allspice and rock moss) and tenderised using raw papaya paste, these would be cooked over hot stones, hence the term *pathar* – meaning stone in Hindi. In a domestic kitchen these cook just as well on a hot griddle pan. They literally take minutes to cook as they have been tenderised and they make for an excellent filling inside wraps. Alternatively, serve with a kachumbar salad (roughly chopped mixed vegetables, such as onion, carrot, cucumber and tomatoes, all mixed together).

Serves 4–6

750g deboned mutton leg, fat trimmed
    and sliced 5mm thick
3 tablespoons mustard or corn oil
juice of 1 lemon
bamboo skewers, soaked in water

For the marinade
2 teaspoons salt
1½ teaspoons red chilli powder
2 tablespoons ginger-garlic paste (see
    page 260)
1 tablespoon grated raw papaya or
    pineapple juice

For the spice mix
4 black cardamom pods
½ teaspoon peppercorns
1 teaspoon cloves
1 teaspoons allspice (optional)
1 tablespoon lichen or rock moss
    (optional)
3–4 tablespoons yoghurt
4 tablespoons crisp fried onions (see
    page 261)
1 teaspoon sugar
25g coriander stalks, stems and roots
    as available, finely chopped

Mix together the marinade ingredients in a large bowl. Add the mutton, mix well and set aside for 30 minutes.

Heat a small frying pan and dry roast the cardamom, peppercorns, cloves, allspice and lichen, if using, for 2–3 minutes, constantly stirring to roast evenly. Allow to cool, then grind coarsely.

Mix the ground spices with the yoghurt, onions and sugar and blend to a paste using a small blender or a mortar and pestle. Smear the spice mix on the mutton and sprinkle with the coriander. Set aside the marinated meat for at least 30 minutes (or it can even be prepared a day before and refrigerated overnight).

Thread the meat onto pre-soaked bamboo skewers. Heat the mustard or corn oil in the grill pan and cook the kebabs for 2–3 minutes each side in a very hot grill pan. Turn over and repeat on the other side, then let the kebabs rest for a minute or so. Sprinkle with lemon juice and serve with a bread of your choice.

Gosht ka Chudwa

Crisp Shredded Lamb

This snack has evolved mainly in an effort to preserve the very large quantities of meat available after the sacrifice or *qurbani*. Think of this as a lamb jerky, but fried rather than air dried.

Serves 6–8 as a snack

750g boneless lamb, from haunch or
   breast
1 teaspoon salt
1 tablespoon ginger–garlic paste (see
   page 260)
1 tablespoon red chilli powder
¼ teaspoon ground turmeric
vegetable oil, for frying
chaat masala (see page 261), to
   sprinkle

If cooking the meat in the oven rather than on the hob, preheat the oven to 160°C/140°C Fan/Gas Mark 3.

Cut the meat into 4–5 chunks and season with salt, ginger–garlic paste, chilli powder and turmeric. Place in a pan, add approximately 400ml of water (you need enough water to cover the meat) and cook, covered, either in the preheated oven or over a very low heat on the hob for about 3 hours or until the meat is tender and most of the water and spices have been absorbed in the cooking.

Let the meat cool, then shred with a fork or using your fingers.

Heat the oil in a deep fat fryer to 150–160°C. Fry the shredded meat for 3–4 minutes until crisp. Alternatively, heat a small amount of oil in a frying pan over a medium heat and fry the meat in batches for 6–8 minutes, stirring regularly to colour and crisp evenly. Take care as the lamb will spit while it crisps. Drain it well on kitchen paper to absorb any excess oil, then sprinkle with chaat masala and let it cool.

Store in an airtight container for 7–10 days. It can be enjoyed on its own as a snack with drinks or as a filling for a wrap with cooling raita or a chutney of your choice.

Hari's Hyderabadi Kachhi Biryani

Biryani of Mutton (or Goat)

Biryani is often called the king of dishes, but it's more than its lazy description of 'meat below, rice above'. There are many variations but in Hyderabad they follow the traditional recipe for *kachhi biryani*, as I have done here.

I have made and eaten many biryanis, but rarely have I had a better version than this, which comes courtesy of the Champ of Hyderabad, my long-time friend Hari Nagaraj!

Serves 6

1kg leg of mutton (or goat), diced into
   2.5cm cubes (meat on the bone is
   preferable)
a small pinch of saffron
50ml warm milk
1 tablespoon freshly chopped mint
50g ghee or butter, melted
250g plain flour (optional)

For the marinade
2 tablespoons vegetable oil
4 onions, sliced
1 tablespoon fresh green papaya
   paste (see method) or fresh
   pineapple juice (optional)
2 tablespoons ginger-garlic paste (see
   page 260)
1 tablespoon red chilli powder
1 teaspoon garam masala
1 teaspoon ground turmeric
a small bunch of mint leaves, chopped
6 green chillies, slit lengthways
¼ nutmeg, grated
juice of ½ lemon
a small pinch of saffron
1 tablespoon salt
100ml plain yoghurt

For the spiced rice
500g basmati rice
3 green cardamom pods
2 black cardamom pods
2 bay leaves
4 cloves
2 blades of mace
1 tablespoon cumin seeds
2 tablespoons salt

To make the marinade, heat the oil in a frying pan, add the sliced onions and fry until golden. Set aside a tablespoon of the onions to use as a garnish. If using green papaya rather than pineapple juice, blend a 5cm piece of papaya with some water in a blender to make a paste. Mix the onions (with the oil they were fried in) with all the other marinade ingredients in a large bowl. Add the cubed lamb and stir to coat in the marinade. Set aside to marinate for 4 hours (or overnight in the refrigerator).

Wash the rice in cold running water, then soak in a bowl of water for 30 minutes. Pour 2.5 litres water into a large pan and add the whole spices and salt. Bring to the boil, add the drained rice and boil for 10 minutes – the rice needs to be 50-60 per cent cooked or slightly less than al dente.

Transfer the marinated meat to the casserole. Soak the saffron in the warm milk for 5 minutes. Strain the boiled rice and layer it on top of the marinated meat in the casserole. Sprinkle over the mint, fried onions, ghee or butter and saffron (plus the soaking milk) over the rice. Cover the casserole with a lid and seal the sides with aluminium foil (or a stiff dough made with 250g plain flour mixed with 100ml of water, rolled into a long 'sausage' and used to seal the rim), leaving a small gap for steam to escape.

Place the casserole over a high heat for 8–10 minutes, making sure the heat is evenly spread across the base of the casserole. When you see the steam escape through the gap, turn the heat right down to low and cook the biryani for 20–25 minutes. Remove from the heat and set the casserole aside for 5 minutes Then open the lid and serve your aromatic biryani garnished with the reserved onions and with a thin yoghurt raita.

Gurdey ki Biryani

Kidney Biryani

This is another good recipe for using offal in a different and unusual way. It is said that during and just after the festival, a haze of perfumed smoke hangs just below the clouds over Hyderabad. The haze comes from the smoke fires lit all over town to cook the hundreds of versions of kebabs, curries and biryanis, and the aroma that starts off as roasty, barbecue and smokey on the first day turns into stronger sandalwood, saffron, rose, kewra and frankincense as the days go by and the meat gets older.

Serves 4 as a main, 6–8 as an accompaniment

400g basmati rice
100ml vegetable oil
2 white onions, finely sliced
2 tablespoons ginger-garlic paste (see page 260)
1½ teaspoons Kashmiri red chilli powder
½ teaspoon ground turmeric
2 teaspoons salt
500g lamb's or goat's kidneys, cut into halves, pith and connective tissue removed
120ml plain yoghurt, whisked
4 hot green chillies, broken into 2–3 pieces each
60g freshly chopped coriander
80g freshly chopped mint
4 green cardamom pods
5cm piece of cinnamon stick
4 cloves
2 bay leaves
4 tablespoons ghee
juice of 1 lemon
pinch of saffron, soaked in 100ml warm milk for 5 minutes
2 teaspoons ground garam masala

Rinse the rice well under cold running water, then soak in water for 20 minutes.

Heat the oil in a pan and fry the onions for 8–10 minutes until golden. Remove half of the fried onions and set aside.

Lower the heat, and into the remaining fried onions add the ginger-garlic paste, chilli powder, turmeric, 1 teaspoon of the salt and the kidneys. Fry for 2–3 minutes, adding a little water if the spices are sticking to the bottom of the pan, then add the whisked yoghurt. Cook for 8–10 minutes over a low heat, adding a little more water if needed. Sprinkle over the green chillies and half the coriander and mint, reserving the rest. Keep warm.

To cook the rice, add the remaining salt and the cardamom, cinnamon stick, cloves and bay leaves into 1.5 litres of water in a separate pan and bring to the boil. Simmer for 2–3 minutes, then add the soaked, drained rice and cook for 5–6 minutes or until the grains of rice are three-quarters cooked. Drain the rice and keep aside.

Assemble the biryani in a heavy-based, lidded pot or casserole dish. Melt 2 tablespoons of the ghee in the pan, then spread half the rice over the ghee. Next add the kidney mixture in an even layer and cover with a second layer of rice. Sprinkle over the reserved fried onions, the remaining mint and coriander, lemon juice, saffron milk, remaining ghee and ground garam masala. Cover and cook over a low heat for 7–8 minutes, then allow to rest for 2–3 minutes before serving.

Kaleji Kabab

Lamb Liver Kebab

Lamb or mutton liver (*kaleji*) is rather prized in the foodie community in Hyderabad. The Hyderabadi classic *bagara baingan* or aubergine cooked in a sesame tamarind curry is frequently enriched with the addition of livers and thick, fat, benign banana chillies. Lamb livers are good in a curry but great in a kebab, and here it is simply marinated, skewered and cooked in a hot grill pan. If you like livers, try this as it's really quick and easy.

Serves 4–6 as a starter or accompaniment

600g lamb livers, sliced into 1cm thick slices
6 fat chillies or Romano peppers (if unavailable, you can substitute 1 red onion)
2 tablespoons vegetable oil
juice of 1 lemon

For the marinade
1 tablespoon ginger-garlic paste (see page 260)
1 teaspoon dried red chilli flakes
½ teaspoon red chilli powder
½ teaspoon ground turmeric
1 teaspoon cumin seeds, lightly roasted
1 teaspoon salt
½ teaspoon sugar
2 tablespoons freshly chopped coriander, preferably stalks

Soak 6 bamboo skewers in water for 30 minutes.

Mix together all the ingredients for the marinade, add the sliced liver and set aside for 15–20 minutes.

Dice the chillies into 2.5cm pieces and discard the seeds (if using red onion, cut the onion into 6 wedges and separate the petals). Thread onto the soaked skewers, alternating the liver with chilli or onion. Refrigerate until ready to cook.

Heat up a grill pan and drizzle with a little oil. Arrange the skewers in the pan and cook for 2–3 minutes on each side. Serve drizzled with lemon juice.

If you don't have a barbecue or a grill pan to hand, you can simply cook the skewers direct on a hot frying pan. Usually at Eid al-Adha, when the animal is slaughtered, the liver is the first thing to get cooked, even before the rest of the animal has been jointed. The liver would be sent indoors to the family kitchen where the ladies would simply cook it in a pan or on skewers on open coal fire, immediately sending it back for the butchers to snack on.

Shami Kabab

Shallow-fried Ground Mutton or Beef Kebab

A good shami kebab is a thing of beauty and, although these are popular throughout the year and sold all over the country, during Eid al-Adha in Hyderabad shami kebabs turn into something of a genre. This version involves filling the kebabs with red onion and mint, referred to as *shikampur* – the one with a filled belly. By all means feel free to omit the filling if you find it daunting, in which case simply shape as flat, £2 coin-sized cakes and shallow fry.

Serves 4 (makes around 12 pieces)

1 tablespoon vegetable oil, plus extra for shallow frying
5 black peppercorns
1 bay leaf
2.5cm piece of cinnamon stick
500g mutton, beef or lamb leg, fat removed and diced into 1cm cubes
1 teaspoon salt
1 tablespoon ginger-garlic paste (see page 260)
1 teaspoon red chilli powder
½ teaspoon ground turmeric
3 green chillies, chopped
35g chana dal/chickpea lentils, soaked in water for 30 minutes, then drained
4 black cardamom pods, seeds removed and lightly crushed, pod discarded
2 tablespoons chopped coriander leaves
chaat masala (see page 261), to sprinkle

For the filling
½ red onion, finely chopped
½ green chilli, finely chopped
5g mint leaves, shredded
15g coriander, finely chopped
a pinch of salt
a pinch of sugar
1 tablespoon Greek yoghurt

Heat the oil in a deep pan, then add the whole spices and let them splutter for 30 seconds or so. Next, add the diced meat, and cook over a high heat for 5–6 minutes, then add the salt, ginger-garlic paste, red chilli powder and turmeric. Cook for another 5–7 minutes over a medium heat.

Add the green chillies, drained lentils and cardamom seeds. Add 475ml of water, reduce the heat to low and cook, partially covered, for 45–60 minutes or until the meat is tender and the liquid has almost dried up.

Add the chopped coriander, stir and remove the pan from the heat. Cool the mixture completely, then blend to a paste (do not add water) or pass through a mincer. Let the cooked mince rest in the fridge for 10–15 minutes. Check the seasoning and add salt if necessary.

Mix together all the ingredients for the filling except the yoghurt. Set aside for 10 minutes, then squeeze to remove the excess liquid from the vegetables. Stir in the yoghurt.

To fry, apply a little oil to your palms, and roll the mince into golf-ball sized portions. Press your thumb into each portion to create a cavity. Spoon in a small quantity of the filling, encase the mince around it and re-shape back into a ball. Press lightly, then shallow fry in a medium-hot pan for 2–3 minutes on each side until golden and crisp.

Sprinkle with chaat masala and serve with sliced red onion, lemon wedges and green coriander chutney (see page 51).

Kadhai ke Bheje

Lamb Brain Cooked in a Wok

During Eid al-Adha, when everyone has lots of meat in the house (probably more than any family can handle or consume!), it becomes important to follow a sequence of using the different parts, such as the offal, to avoid wasting anything. Livers, kidneys and brains are the first to be used as they cannot be stored for too long. This is a very simple and quick recipe using lambs' brains and goes very well with rotis or poories.

Serves 4–6

4 lambs' brains
80ml vegetable oil
4 red onions, finely sliced
1 teaspoon salt
½ teaspoon ground turmeric
1 tablespoon black pepper,
    freshly cracked
1 tablespoon white vinegar

To prepare the brains, carefully remove the surface brain, any visible veins on the surface and the white 'pearls' at the base of the brain. Cut each brain into 4–5 pieces.

Heat the oil in a wok, add the onions and cook, stirring constantly, for 8–10 minutes until they turn golden brown. Add the brains, salt, turmeric and cracked black pepper and cook for 3–4 minutes over a high heat. Add the vinegar and cook until the mixture dries up and the oil begins to float up the surface of the pan.

Remove from the heat and serve hot with poories or chapatis.

Rezala

Hyderabad-style Goat Casserole

This fascinating recipe comes from the kitchens of a very wealthy Begum in Hyderabad. It strangely resembles a pound cake recipe from the medieval era, where you put in equal quantities of everything, mix it and bang it in an oven to get a cake! In this case, just mix together all the ingredients and seal the pot. Cook it either in an oven or on the hob on a very low heat. Feel free to replace the goat with lamb or mutton as they work just as well.

Serves 4

1kg goat meat from the leg,
    diced into 2.5cm cubes

For the marinade
200g vegetable oil or ghee
200g fresh green chillies,
    slit lengthways and seeds
    removed
200g crisp fried onions,
    crushed coarsely (see
    page 261)
200g thick Greek yoghurt
25g piece of pineapple,
    blended
2 tablespoons ginger, finely
    chopped
1 tablespoon garlic paste
    (see page 260)
25g roasted gram flour
25g salt
1 teaspoon allspice
2 teaspoons each royal
    cumin, red chilli powder,
    ground cumin, ground
    garam masala (see page
    261)

For finishing
100ml single cream
2 tablespoons fried cashew
    nuts, made into a paste
    (see page 260)
120g freshly chopped
    coriander
1 tablespoon freshly
    chopped mint

Mix together all the marinade ingredients in a large bowl, add the meat and set aside for 10–15 minutes. Place the marinated meat in an ovenproof casserole or pot with a tightly fitting lid. Seal around the lid using dough (see page 162 for method). If need be, place a weight on the lid to prevent the steam from escaping.

Place the pot over a low heat and cook for 1½ hours. Open the lid after 1½ hours to check if the meat is cooked and tender or if it needs to cook for a little longer. This can also be cooked in an oven preheated to 140–150ºC/120–130ºC Fan/Gas Mark 1–2 for 2 hours.

Stir the sauce and finish by adding the cream and cashew nut paste. Bring to the boil and check the seasoning. Sprinkle with the chopped coriander and mint and serve immediately.

Thalasseri Kozhi Curry

Tellicherry Chicken Curry

Thalasseri in Kerala in recent times has become famous for its Tellicherry pepper which is one of the most prized varieties in the world today, but the town is also well known for its meat delicacies thanks to its resident Muslim community. This is a recipe they will cook at celebrations big and small.

Serves 4

4 tablespoons groundnut or vegetable oil
2 onions, finely sliced
15 curry leaves
2 green chillies, slit lengthways
10 black peppercorns, cracked
2 tablespoons ginger-garlic paste (see page 260)
1 tablespoon coriander seeds, coarsely crushed
1 teaspoon ground turmeric
1½ teaspoons salt
750g boneless chicken thighs
225ml water or stock
1 teaspoon garam masala
½ teaspoon freshly ground black pepper

Heat the oil in a large frying pan over a medium heat and add the onions, curry leaves, chillies and cracked peppercorns. Cook for 15 minutes, stirring often, until the onions are golden, then reduce the heat and add the ginger-garlic paste. Cook, stirring often, for 4–5 minutes, then add the coriander seeds, turmeric and salt and cook for another 2–3 minutes.

Add the chicken, stir to mix and cook for 2–3 minutes over a medium heat. Add the water or stock, cover and cook gently for 5–7 minutes until the chicken is cooked through.

Finish with the garam masala and finally with the freshly ground black pepper. Cover and set aside for 5 minutes. Serve hot with rice.

Sheermal

Rich Saffron Bread

This rich and flavoursome bread is a speciality in most Mughal courts all over India. Originally made in seldom-seen iron tandoors in India, this oven-cooked version produces an equally good result. This works well with a variety of kebabs, grilled meats, liver, etc. so abundantly seen and served after the sacrifice. The trick is to incorporate the ghee slowly into the dough by adding a little at a time, so that the fat is dispersed evenly through the entire dough.

Makes about 36

700ml milk
1 tablespoon melon seeds
75g sugar
2 pinches of saffron, dissolved in 1
   tablespoon milk
1 tablespoon salt
1kg plain flour
½ teaspoon ground green cardamom
300ml melted ghee, plus 2
   tablespoons for brushing

Place the milk and melon seeds in a pan and heat until simmering, then add the sugar and stir until it dissolves completely. Add the saffron milk (keep back a little for brushing) and allow the milk to cool, then add the salt.

Place the flour in a mixing bowl, add the green cardamom and cooled milk and mix well. Knead into a soft dough. Cover with a moist cloth and set aside at room temperature for at least 15 minutes.

Remove the cloth and knead the dough again. Add the ghee into the dough, little by little, and incorporate it into the dough using your fingers. Store it in cool place for 15 minutes.

Preheat the oven to 180°C/160°C Fan/Gas Mark 4.

Divide the dough into about 36 balls, each weighing about 50g. Cover and keep aside for another 10 minutes. Roll out the balls into discs approximately 3mm thick and prick all over with a fork. Arrange on a greased baking tray and bake in the preheated oven for 8 minutes. Remove from the oven, brush with the reserved saffron milk and bake again for 5 minutes. Serve immediately brushed with the melted ghee.

Top left: Sheermal (page 168)
Top right: Dhaniyey ki Hari Chutney (page 51)
Middle: Hyderabadi Special Pathar ka Gosht (page 160)

Navratri

Navratri is one of the largest Hindu festivals and is prevalent throughout India, but it is more prominent in the states of Gujarat and Maharashtra. It takes place at the beginning of October, around harvest time, and is dedicated to the worship of the Hindu deity Durga, who is said to have battled the demon Mahishasura in a battle lasting nine days and nights, a triumph of good over evil. Another legend is that Shiva gave Durga permission to visit her mother for nine days every year, and it is for this reason that the festival is celebrated over nine days, with Durga worshipped as the mother goddess.

The name Navratri comes from the Sanskrit – *nav* means 'nine' and *ratri* means 'night', thus, *navratri* means 'nine nights'. During the festival, the nine different forms of the goddess are worshipped, each of which is said to dignify a distinct power.

The number nine is seen in other ways throughout the festival. For example, to celebrate a good harvest women often plant nine different types of grains in small containers, one on each day of the festival, and then offer the young saplings to Durga.

Artists perform a traditional 'garba' dance in Gujarat. (India Pictures/UIG via Getty)

For women, Navratri is a time for shopping for new clothes and new pots. It is an auspicious time to buy gold or jewellery and the gold markets are open late each night. Women dress elaborately each day for the *puja* or rituals and nightly dances.

With a number of customs and traditions, each region of India has its own unique way of celebrating Navratri, honouring the various forms of Durga with its own rituals and ceremonies. In Gujarat, Navratri is a huge community event, and it is one of the only states in India that erupts into a full nine days of festivities, dance and devotion. In the villages and cities of Gujarat, people gather in large numbers to feast and perform traditional dances, such as the *garba*, while singing devotional songs. The *garba* is danced in a circle, with a small shrine to the goddess in the centre, and often begins slowly, speeding up gradually, with everyone moving around the central shrine. It is a time for even the most housebound of women to be out of the house and to join in with the dancing in order to worship Durga.

It is common for people to dress up in traditional costumes as part of the celebrations. In Gujarat painted earthen pots are filled with water with a lamp inside – the pot represents the human body, the flame symbolising the

divine power of the goddess and the water representing the body's transitory nature. Throughout the festival people worship young girls, who represent Durga, and feed them with sweets and different traditional foods.

As well as being seen as a lavish spectacle full of fun and dancing, it is also a time for introspection and purification. Beyond the outward celebrations, Hindus attend temple and prayers are offered for the protection of health and property. Navratri is traditionally an auspicious time for starting new ventures.

Although Navratri is indeed a significant Hindu festival, it also marks a wonderful opportunity for people of various cultures to socialise with each other. One can see the rich culture and tradition of India, especially in Gujarat where the festival is particularly celebrated, blossom in the nine-day long period of Navratri.

Many devotees of Durga observe a fast during the festival, or at least the first and last days. It is often used as an opportunity to detox, and to eat light, nutritious dishes. However, feasts of great variety and delicacy are offered to guests and family during the nine days, and there is a particular focus on vegetarianism.

Vrat Ke Aloo

Archana's Navratri Special Potato and Tomato Curry

During the nine days of Navratri twice a year, my wife, Archana, will religiously observe the rules of Navratri to the best of her ability, and she will insist that we do too. It's a particularly difficult time in our household as the kitchen will be cleared of all meat, fish, ham and bacon, and all kinds of animal protein, even eggs! For those nine days, we all turn vegetarian (albeit Eshaan, Maya and I do this under duress!). Although it's only Archana who observes Navratri, we are all expected to 'do the right thing'.

Serves 4

4 waxy potatoes, such as Cyprus, Desiree, Estima or Charlotte
4 large tomatoes
2 green chillies, 1 chopped and 1 left whole
2 tablespoons vegetable oil
1 teaspoon cumin seeds
1 teaspoon rock salt
2 tablespoons freshly chopped coriander

Boil the potatoes, peel and then set them aside.

Chop the tomatoes and place in a pan with the whole green chilli and 475ml of water. Bring to the boil and cook, covered, for 15–20 minutes, then blend to a purée if necessary.

Heat the oil in a pan over a medium heat, add the cumin seeds and cook for around 20 seconds or so until they start to crackle, then add the chopped green chilli.

Crush the boiled potatoes roughly and add to the pan. Cook over a high heat for 1–2 minutes, then add the rock salt and mix well. Add the tomato purée and mix while stirring for 1 minute. Reduce the heat and cook for 2–3 minutes or until the curry thickens slightly.

Garnish with coriander and serve the potato curry hot with buckwheat flour parathas (see page 180).

Palak Pakoda Chaat

Spinach Fritter with Tangy Mélange of Chutneys

Unlike most other *pakodas* where different vegetables are finely chopped and then mixed in a chickpea batter, these are much daintier and lighter. Individual spinach leaves are fried and then become the perfect vehicles to carry all the lovely dips, dressings and sauces that pack any chaat full of flavours. You may like to serve these as a base for canapés at a dinner party.

Serves 4

30–35 young spinach leaves, washed and dried using kitchen paper
vegetable oil, for deep frying
chaat masala (see page 261), to sprinkle

For the batter
100g chickpea flour (besan)
50g cornflour
1 teaspoon salt
½ teaspoon carom seeds
½ teaspoon nigella seeds
½ teaspoon fennel seeds
¼ teaspoon ground turmeric
½ teaspoon sugar
1 teaspoon red chilli powder

To serve
tamarind chutney (see page 51)
green coriander chutney (see page 51)
yoghurt dressing (see page 51)

Begin with the batter. Place all the batter ingredients in a large bowl and stir to combine well. Add 150ml of water and mix to make a thick batter.

Preheat the oil in a deep fryer to 170°C.

Dip each spinach leaf in batter to coat it evenly. Drop the leaf gently into the hot oil and fry it on a medium heat, turning once or twice until crisp. Remove from the fryer and drain on kitchen paper. Repeat with the remaining spinach leaves.

Sprinkle the fried leaves with chaat masala and serve drizzled with tamarind chutney, green coriander chutney and yoghurt dip to make a chaat.

Kaddu ki Subzi

Pumpkin and Coconut Curry

This is a very simple curry with coconut, curry leaves and chilli. You can make it as wet or dry as you like, depending upon your taste. During Navratri in India, which is usually in the autumn, this is one of the several vegetarian dishes that people reach out for to make it through the nine days of abstinence and fasting. In the UK, too, as autumn sets in and pumpkin is plentiful, the spices and coconut combine to make a delightful comfort meal.

Serves 4

1kg pumpkin or butternut squash, peeled and seeds discarded, diced into 4cm cubes
2.5cm piece of cinnamon stick
2 green chillies, slit lengthways
15 curry leaves
¼ teaspoon fenugreek seeds
½ teaspoon ground turmeric
2 teaspoons sugar
1 teaspoon salt
½ teaspoon red chilli powder
1 teaspoon mustard seeds
8–10 black peppercorns
3 tablespoons desiccated coconut
200ml coconut milk
2 tablespoons vegetable oil
1 small onion, finely chopped

Place the pumpkin in a pot with the cinnamon stick, green chillies, 10 curry leaves, fenugreek seeds, turmeric, sugar, salt, red chilli powder and 400ml of water. Bring to the boil, then cook, uncovered, for 12–15 minutes until the pumpkin becomes tender, but not mushy. You should be able to pierce the pumpkin with the tip of a knife or skewer, but it should not fall apart.

Meanwhile, using a blender or food processor, grind together the mustard seeds, peppercorns and 2 tablespoons of the desiccated coconut with the coconut milk. Pour this into the boiled pumpkin and allow it to simmer for a few minutes until the gravy thickens slightly. Taste for salt and turn off the heat.

In a separate small frying pan, heat the oil until smoking, then add the remaining curry leaves. As they turn crisp after about 30 seconds or so, add the chopped onion and fry for 3–4 minutes on a high heat until they turn pink. Add the remaining desiccated coconut and fry until crisp and golden in colour. Sprinkle on top of your curry as a garnish and serve with rice.

Left: Kaddu ki Subzi (page 178)
Right: Kuttu ke Aatey ka Paratha (page 180)

Kuttu ke Aatey ka Paratha

Buckwheat Parathas

These rustic buckwheat flour parathas are a firm favourite during Navratri
when most grains aren't allowed. It is during these nine days of abstinence when
all those that observe the fast turn strictly vegetarian, giving up even onion,
and garlic. Strict observers will substitute regular sea salt with rock salt.

Serves 4–6

500g buckwheat flour (kuttu ka atta),
  plus extra for dusting
1 large potato, boiled, peeled and
  mashed
1½ teaspoons rock salt
2 tablespoons chopped coriander
  leaves
1 red onion, finely chopped
1 green chilli, chopped (optional)
200ml warm water, to knead
ghee or oil, for brushing

In a bowl, mix the buckwheat flour with the mashed potatoes, rock salt, coriander, red onion and green chilli, if using. Add 2 tablespoons of the warm water and begin to knead. Keep on adding the rest of the water little by little, kneading until a dough forms and stays together, but don't overwork the dough or make it too soft. Divide the dough into 50g balls (about 18 in total).

Sprinkle some flour lightly over a clean damp cloth. Place a dough ball on the cloth, fold the cloth over the dough and roll the ball with a rolling pin to get a circle approximately 3mm thick. Repeat with the remaining dough balls.

Remove the cloth from the top of the rolled paratha and place the bread gently in a heated dry frying pan. Peel off the cloth and cook for 2–3 minutes over a medium heat. The bottom side will be partly cooked after 2–3 minutes, when brown spots begin to form on the bottom, so flip and let the other side cook for another 2 minutes or so. Brush ½ teaspoon of ghee or oil on top and then flip again. Cook for a few minutes and brush another ½ teaspoon of ghee or oil on the top. Flip once or twice until the bread has cooked through.

Repeat with the remaining dough balls and serve hot with a side vegetable dish or potato curry.

Sabudana Vada

Tapioca Cumin Fritters with Green Coconut Chutney

This is a recipe from Mumbai and Gujarat, and these fritters are often served as a snack during the Navratri *melas* (fairs). Given that there is no grain involved, this snack is deemed fit for the period of Navratri. Strict observers will use rock salt instead of regular sea/table salt. Peanuts add richness and texture and the green coconut chutney brings zing and freshness to the dish.

Serves 3–4 as snacks

200g tapioca, soaked in 400ml hot water for 2 minutes, then drained
150g boiled potato, mashed
1 teaspoon roasted cumin seeds
4cm piece of ginger, finely chopped
4 green chillies, finely chopped
1½ teaspoons salt
2 tablespoons finely chopped coriander
½ teaspoon garam masala (see page 261)
2 tablespoons peanuts, skin on, roasted lightly, cooled, then coarsely chopped
vegetable oil, for deep frying
green mango and coconut chutney (see page 147), to serve

Mix together all the ingredients except the peanuts and the oil, and leave the mixture to rest for 30 minutes. The tapioca will soak up some of the moisture from the potato and soften up a little.

Add the crushed peanuts to the mixture and mix well. Grease your palms with a little oil and divide the mixture into 8 portions. Flatten each ball with the palm of your hand to shape them like burgers. Deep fry in hot oil for 3–4 minutes or until crisp and golden on the outside.

Serve with the green mango and coconut chutney.

Smaller versions of these can be served as canapés or passed around as snacks at parties.

Tapioca Pearls Khichri

Tapioca, Potato and Peanut Kedgeree

This is another one of the go-to dishes during Navratri, as it is a quick and easy filling dish for when more people than expected turn up.

Serves 4–6, as an accompaniment

140g tapioca pearls
85g peanuts
1½ teaspoons rock salt
1 teaspoon sugar
4 tablespoons vegetable oil
1 teaspoon cumin seeds
1 green chilli, chopped
10 fresh curry leaves (optional)
1 teaspoon grated ginger (optional)
2 potatoes, boiled in the skin, peeled and diced into 1cm cubes
2 tablespoons freshly chopped coriander
juice of ¼ lemon

Soak the tapioca pearls in 950ml warm water for 10–12 minutes, then drain thoroughly and set aside in a bowl.

In a pan, dry roast the peanuts until browned, let them cool, then chop coarsely and set aside.

Mix the salt and sugar with the drained tapioca pearls

Heat the oil in a wok, add the cumin seeds and let them crackle for 10 seconds or so. Add the green chilli and curry leaves, if using. Fry for 30 seconds and then add the grated ginger, if using. Stir for 1 minute, then add the diced potato and sauté for 1–2 minutes.

Add the tapioca pearls. Continue cooking for 1–2 minutes, stirring gently, but don't overcook as they might become starchy and dense. Check the seasoning and adjust as necessary. Sprinkle over the roasted peanuts, coriander and a squeeze of lemon juice, then serve immediately.

Vrat ki Kadhi

Amaranth Flour and Yoghurt Soup

This is just like a *kadhi* or a yoghurt and chickpea soup, but there's no turmeric being used as this is not allowed during Navratri and the regulation chickpea flour is replaced by amaranth flour. If you can't find amaranth flour, it is easily substituted with arrowroot flour, water chestnut flour or buckwheat flour.

Serves 4

5 tablespoons amaranth flour
500ml full-fat fresh yoghurt at room temperature, whisked until smooth
4 tablespoons ghee or peanut oil
2 teaspoons cumin seeds
2 teaspoons ginger paste (see page 260)
4 green chillies, pounded to a paste in a mortar-pestle
1½ teaspoons rock salt
1½ teaspoons sugar
3 tablespoons freshly chopped coriander

Add the amaranth flour to the yoghurt, and whisk until smooth, then add 600ml of water. Mix well and check there are no lumps remaining, then set aside.

Heat the ghee or peanut oil in a pan. Add the cumin seeds and sauté for 30 seconds until they are fragrant and change colour. Then add the ginger and green chilli pastes and stir for a minute or so (the mixture spits a lot at this stage due to the water in the paste so I suggest using a high-sided pan to avoid getting burnt).

Reduce the heat to medium and add the yoghurt mixture, stirring continuously. Season with the rock salt and sugar, keep stirring until the mixture comes to the boil, then reduce the heat and let it simmer for 3–4 minutes until the kadhi thickens to a soup consistency.

Check the seasoning, finish with the chopped coriander and serve with sabudana vada (see page 181), kuttu paratha (see page 180) or one of the other Navratri dishes to accompany.

Singharey ke Aatey ka Halwa

Water Chestnut Flour Halwa

This is a simple yet very effective halwa commonly made during Navratri to serve either as a dessert or sometimes as a fudge for children and adults to snack on at any time of the day or night. I sometimes set this in trays and serve as petits fours at the end of the meal at The Cinnamon Club.

Serves 4

4 tablespoons ghee
40g cashew nuts, chopped
100g water chestnut flour
80g sugar
⅛ teaspoon ground cardamom

Heat the ghee in a deep, heavy-based pan to medium hot, add the cashew nuts and fry for 30–60 seconds until golden, then remove using a slotted spoon.

In the same pan, add the water chestnut flour and roast over a medium heat for 6–7 minutes, stirring continuously until the flour turns dark brown but not burnt. Add 250ml boiling water to the roasted flour and mix together well, avoiding any lumps. Cook for 2 minutes until mixed evenly, then add the sugar and keep stirring to mix well. The sugar will melt and the mixture will appear runny again, but keep cooking over a medium heat for 2–3 minutes or until the mixture thickens and the ghee begins to separate to the sides of the pan. Sprinkle over the ground cardamom and remove from the heat.

Take a shallow tray or plate deep enough to accommodate the mixture, sprinkle the nuts onto the plate and pour over the halwa. Spread to an even thickness and let it cool. It will set upon cooling; then cut into the desired shapes and serve.

The halwa can be enjoyed cold or warm, reheated for a few seconds in the microwave.

Thinai Kesari

Millet and Pineapple Kesari

This is a delicious, quick and easy, healthier halwa made using millet and pineapple. It is suitable for *phalahaar* or a meal made from fruits during Navratri.

Serves 6

2 tablespoons ghee
15 cashew nuts, cut in half
1 tablespoon raisins
170g millet, washed in a couple of changes of water, drained
75g sugar
a pinch of saffron
½ teaspoon ground cardamom
90g chopped pineapple

Heat the ghee in a pan, add the cashew nuts and stir fry until golden. As they are turning golden, add the raisins and stir until they puff up. Remove using a slotted spoon.

Add the millet to the same pan and stir fry for 4–5 minutes until it gives off a roasted aroma. Set aside.

Meanwhile, place the sugar, saffron and cardamom in a pan with 600ml of water and bring to the boil. Cook for 3–4 minutes until all the sugar has dissolved, stirring now and again. Add the pineapple and cook for 1 minute, then add the roasted millet over a medium-low heat, give it a stir and break up any lumps.

Reduce the heat to its lowest setting and cook for 12 minutes, stirring now and again to avoid it sticking to the base of the pan. Cook until all the water has evaporated and the millet is just cooked. Remove from the heat, cover and rest for 5 minutes. To serve, mix in the roasted cashew nuts and raisins and serve hot.

Durga Puja and Dussehra

The celebrations of Durga Puja and Dussehra are closely linked to Navratri. One of the largest festivals celebrated by Hindus in India, Navratri surrounds worship of the Hindu deity Durga and the last four days of Navratri are observed as Durga Puja. On the final day, worshippers take huge figures of the idol of Goddess Durga to the streets in a procession and there is plenty of dancing and a festive atmosphere. Although it is very much a religious festival, Durga Puja is celebrated with much revelry in comparison to other sacred events. Rather than a focus on fasting and prayers, feasting and socialising into the early hours are at the centre of this festival. Durga Puja is particularly spectacular in Bengal, but both in and outside Bengal, you can see representations of Durga Puja, with community congregations in huge decorated pandals (tents).

Bengalis from all over the world return home to celebrate Durga Puja and usually stay for several weeks until Kali Puja, which is three weeks after Durga Puja. The period in between is commonly referred to as *Bijoya*, or Victory – a time when everyone visits their friends and family to

Musicians celebrate the triumph of Lord Rama over the demon king, Ravana. (Eye Ubiquitous/UIG via Getty)

exchange gifts and sweets and generally entertain and be
entertained. Not going to visit a close friend or a relative
in this period is the same as dropping someone from your
Christmas card list in the UK!

Growing up, I had friends who would receive new clothes
and gifts during the festival, and even though my parents
didn't really celebrate Durga Puja, we'd all get new outfits
and toys then, so we didn't feel left out.

In many parts of the country, the tenth day of Navratri is
celebrated as Dussehra. There are varying interpretations
of Dussehra, with northern parts of India celebrating it as
the Day of Victory – Rama's victory over Ravana. Often
celebrations in most of north India and central Indian
states culminate with the burning of the effigy of Ravana.
North Indian towns and city squares turn into make-
shift street theatres where local residents participate in
performing *ramlila* – the enactment of the various scenes
from Ramayana.

Whatever the legend, the best part of Durga Puja for me
was going to different family friends' homes each night
and enjoying the feast that was laid out. Dishes would
include *bhapa* with lobster or king prawns, *kosha mangsho*
(see page 198) and *murgh makhan masala* (chicken
butter masala, see page 211), and I also remember the
khichuri served as a *bhog* or an offering to the Goddess,
then distributed among the devotees at the *pandal* when
the *puja* for the day finished. The fervour and passion
during this festival in Bengal is quite unmatched and the
atmosphere electric. I can't help but notice how many of
the dishes I remember for Dussehra or Durga Puja have
a Bengali influence and how, even after all these years, I
haven't been able to shake it off!

Bhuna Khichuri

Temple-style Kedgeree

Bhuna Khichuri is the bare basic rice dish which is offered as a *bhog* or *prasad* (offering) to the Goddess Durga; it's simple but the most important of all offerings. This dish is cooked in almost every home, and also in communal neighbourhood celebrations. Every family, irrespective of class, creed or colour, is given the option either to eat the food as a meal or to carry it back home as a token of the puja.

Serves 4–6 as an accompaniment

100g basmati rice
75g split yellow moong lentils
4 tablespoons ghee or melted butter, plus extra for drizzling
½ teaspoon asafoetida
1 bay leaf or cinnamon leaf
3cm stick of cinnamon
3 cloves
2 green cardamom pods
1 whole dried red chilli, broken, stalk and seeds discarded
1 tablespoon cumin seeds
2.5cm piece of ginger, grated
1–2 green chillies, chopped
2 teaspoons salt
1½ teaspoons ground turmeric
½ teaspoon red chilli powder
chopped vegetables, such as 60g carrots, 85g cauliflower and 2 tablespoons frozen peas (optional)
1 teaspoon sugar
1 teaspoon roasted cumin powder (optional)
juice of ½ lemon
1 tablespoon freshly chopped coriander

Wash the rice in 2–3 changes of water until the water runs clear. Drain, spread it out on a tray and let it dry for 15 minutes.

Meanwhile, dry roast the yellow moong lentils in a frying pan over a low-medium heat for 3–5 minutes until it turns deep golden and fragrant, stirring continuously. Take care and keep stirring as the lentils should not turn brown and black – some might have brown spots and that is okay. Once fragrant, remove the pan from the heat, tip the roasted lentils onto a plate, spread it out and let it cool.

Wash the cooled lentils in several changes of water until the water runs clear.

Heat the ghee in a heavy-based lidded pan over a medium-high heat. Add the asafoetida, bay leaf, cinnamon, cloves and cardamom. Let the spices sizzle and crackle, then add the dried red chilli and cumin seeds and stir to heat them evenly. After a few seconds, as the spices become fragrant, add the grated ginger and almost immediately add the rice, lentils and green chillies. Add the salt and turmeric, red chilli powder and vegetables, if using, and toss well until the ghee and the spices coat the lentils. Lower the heat, stir in the sugar and cook, stirring constantly so the contents do not stick to the bottom of the pan, for 5–8 minutes.

Add 1.6 litres of hot water; bring the water to the boil, then reduce the heat to low and cook for 15 minutes until most of the water from the surface has evaporated. Now cover the pot with a tightly fitting lid and cook until the lentils and rice have softened and are cooked (after adding water, they will take about 20 minutes to be cooked through). Although the usual khichdi is supposed to be almost mushed, this bhuna khichuri has less liquid and the grains of the rice and the lentils should remain distinguishable.

Serve warm with a drizzle of ghee or melted butter and a sprinkle of roasted cumin powder, if using. Finish with a squeeze of lemon juice and scatter over the chopped coriander.

Kankrar Chop

Bengali-style Crab Cakes

I have good memories of eating these as a child in West Bengal. These crab cakes are slightly uncommon due to their use of beetroot and raisins, but nevertheless they make a great little snack for Durga Puja.

Serves 4

300g cod fillet, skinned

For cooking the fish
½ teaspoon salt
1 teaspoon ground turmeric
½ teaspoon fennel seeds
½ teaspoon black onion seeds

For the fish cakes
3 tablespoons vegetable or corn oil
2 bay leaves
½ teaspoon cumin seeds
1 large onion, chopped
1 tablespoon ginger-garlic paste (see page 260)
½ teaspoon ground turmeric
1 teaspoon red chilli powder
½ teaspoon sugar
1 teaspoon salt
200g white crab meat
1cm piece of ginger, finely chopped
2 green chillies, finely chopped
1 large beetroot, boiled and diced into 5mm cubes
1 teaspoon Bengali garam masala (see page 261)
1 tablespoon raisins
2 tablespoons freshly chopped coriander

For crumbing
½ teaspoon fennel seeds
½ teaspoon black onion seeds
200g dried breadcrumbs, for coating
25g plain flour
2 eggs, beaten
vegetable oil, for deep frying

Cut the cod fillet into 4–5 even-sized pieces. Place them in a pan and add 100ml of water. Add the salt, turmeric, fennel seeds and onion seeds. Lightly poach over a medium heat, with the lid on, for about 5–6 minutes, until the fish is cooked. Remove and pat the fish dry on kitchen paper, then gently flake the fish using a fork and set aside. Reserve the liquid and reduce by half to make a concentrate.

To make the fish cakes, heat the oil in a large frying pan. Add the bay leaves and cumin seeds and when they release their flavour, add the onion and sauté until it turns golden brown. Add the ginger-garlic paste followed by the turmeric, chilli powder, sugar and salt and cook for 1 minute. Add the crab meat and sauté for 1 minute until mixed well, but take care not to break up the crab meat too much. Reduce the heat, add the flaked fish, ginger, green chillies and the diced beetroot and stir gently to mix them with the spices. Add the reserved cooking liquid. Sprinkle over the garam masala, add the raisins and coriander and mix well. Remove from the heat and leave to cool.

Divide the mixture into 8 portions and shape into balls. Mix the fennel and onion seeds into the breadcrumbs. Dust the balls with the flour, dip in the beaten eggs and roll them in the seasoned breadcrumbs until thoroughly coated. Flatten slightly and deep fry in a deep fryer or a deep saucepan for 2 minutes, until golden brown. Drain on kitchen paper and serve straight away with salad and lime pickle mayonnaise (see page 217).

Top: Achari Nimbu Mayo (page 217)
Bottom: Kankrar Chop (page 190)

Bhapa Lobster

Lobster with Coconut, Ginger and Chilli

The day after Dussehra (the tenth day of venerations for goddess Durga), the high society in Kolkata just kicks into action and with it begins a series of parties, invitations and celebrations. The period between Durga Puja and Kali Puja (otherwise known as Bijoya) is Bengal's equivalent of Christmas, the only difference being that the revelries go on for three weeks! If there is such a thing as making a statement or an impression with a dish, then this is the one! The use of coconut, mustard, chilli and ginger creates an interesting play of flavours, with the sweetness of lobster, cooked in its own steam, and coconut balanced by the heat from the chilli and ginger and the pungency of the mustard oil.

Serves 6

6 lobsters, about 450g each
75ml mustard oil
1 teaspoon black mustard seeds
50g coriander, finely chopped
1 teaspoon garam masala

For the sauce
60g yellow mustard seeds, soaked overnight in just enough water to cover, then drained and blended to a paste with 25ml white vinegar
250ml thick coconut milk
75ml Greek yoghurt
6 green chillies, slit lengthways
5cm piece of ginger, cut into matchstick-sized pieces
1½ teaspoons salt
1 teaspoon sugar
1 tablespoon ginger-garlic paste (see page 260)
¼ teaspoon turmeric

Slit each lobster in two lengthways, keeping the head and shell on. Clean and dry with kitchen paper, then remove the meat from the shell and claws and dice into 2cm cubes. Reserve the shells.

Preheat the oven to 180°C/160°C Fan/Gas Mark 4.

Whisk together all the sauce ingredients and set aside.

Heat the mustard oil in a pan to smoking point, then let it cool (this reduces the pungency from the mustard oil). Reheat the oil and add the black mustard seeds. Once the seeds crackle, add the sauce mixture and bring to the boil, whisking regularly over a low heat and taking care not to split the mixture. Once the sauce has boiled, reduce the heat and simmer for 6–8 minutes, then remove from the heat. The sauce should be thick and coat the back of a spoon.

In a separate pan, mix together the diced lobster meat and claws with three-quarters of the sauce, reserving the rest.

Place the lobster shells on a baking tray and fill the shells with the lobster meat coated with the sauce. Spoon the remaining sauce on top, cover with foil and bake in the preheated oven for 6–8 minutes, then place under a hot grill for 2–3 minutes.

Sprinkle with chopped coriander and garam masala and serve immediately with steamed rice.

Macher Dim Bora

Fried Fish Cutlets

This fish pakora is an unusual dish, often served as a snack or as a part of a meal at Durga Puja. Traditionally, thinly cut deboned *rohu*, or *rui* (a kind of Bengali carp) would be used, but feel free to replace it with cod or perch.

Serves 4

- 600g cod or perch fillets, shredded into thin strips
- 1 large onion, finely chopped
- 4 green chillies, finely chopped
- 2.5cm piece of ginger, peeled and finely chopped
- 1 teaspoon salt
- 2 teaspoons red chilli powder
- 2 tablespoons freshly chopped coriander
- 2 tablespoons rice flour
- 120g besan or chickpea flour
- juice of 1 lime
- mustard oil, for frying
- chaat masala (see page 261), to sprinkle (optional)

Mix the strips of fish in a bowl with the onion, green chillies, ginger, salt, chilli powder and coriander.

Mix together the rice flour and chickpea flour, add the lime juice and the fish mixture and let the mixture sit for 10–15 minutes. Shape the mixture into 8 equal flat, round patties.

Heat the mustard oil in a shallow frying pan to smoking point, then reduce the heat to medium. Shallow fry the patties for 3 minutes on each side until golden brown on both sides and cooked.

Serve hot sprinkled with chaat masala, if using, and with a simple salad of chopped red onions and cucumber.

Paka Macher Pulao

Mature Fish Pulao

This dish in Bengal would be made with large *bekti* or *hilsa*, but any large fish would do. In Europe you could use salmon, halibut or a large monkfish.

Serves 4

- 600g fish, cut into 4cm dice
- 2 onions, ½ onion blended to a purée and the rest thinly sliced
- 2 teaspoons garlic paste (see page 260)
- 1½ teaspoons salt
- ½ teaspoon ground turmeric
- 100ml vegetable oil
- 2 tablespoons ghee
- 4 bay leaves
- 4 green cardamom pods
- 400g basmati rice, washed in 2 changes of water
- 2.5cm piece of ginger, cut into strips
- 800ml hot water or chicken stock
- 1 teaspoon sugar
- a pinch of saffron (optional), soaked in a few teaspoons hot water
- 1 teaspoon ground garam masala

Marinate the fish with the blended onion, 1 teaspoon of the garlic paste, ½ teaspoon of the salt and the turmeric and set aside for 5 minutes.

Heat the vegetable oil in a shallow frying pan and slowly fry the fish in 2 batches until light brown, turning over after about 2–3 minutes to cook evenly and on all sides. Remove from the pan and set aside.

Heat the ghee in a heavy-based lidded pan. Add the bay leaves, cardamom and sliced onions. Sauté over a high heat for 3–4 minutes until the onions are translucent and just turning soft. Add the remaining garlic paste, fry for 1 minute, then add the rice and ginger and cook for 3–4 minutes until the rice is roasted and evenly coated in the spices and ghee.

Add the hot water or stock, the sugar and the remaining salt and cover the pan. Bring to the boil, then reduce the heat to a simmer. After 6–8 minutes, when the water has reduced to the level of the rice and holes appear on the surface, place the fried fish over the surface of the rice and pour over any leftover oil from frying the fish. Add the saffron water, if using, and the garam masala, then cover the pan and place over a very low heat for 15–20 minutes until the rice is cooked, all the water is absorbed and the grains are fluffy. (The last stage may be carried out in an oven at 180°C/160C Fan/Gas Mark 4.)

Top left: Macher Dim Bora (page 193)
Bottom left: Bhapa Lobster (page 192)
Top right: Panthar Ghuguni (page 199)
Bottom right: Kosha Mangsho (page 198)

Kashmiri Keema Kofta

Dried Fruit and Meatball Curry

These *koftas* could be from anywhere, and in fact no one in Kashmir
recognises the dish as particularly Kashmiri, but we in the rest of the country
call them Kashmiri due to the use of dried fruits and nuts along with the mince.
The use of crisp fried onions to add texture and sweetness to the *kofta* is
a nuanced technique originally employed in the cooking of palaces.

Serves 4

For the koftas
600g lean minced lamb
1 onion, finely chopped
4 garlic cloves, finely chopped
1½ teaspoons salt
4 dried apricots, finely chopped
4 dried figs, finely chopped
2 tablespoons roasted cashew nuts,
   coarsely chopped
2 tablespoons salted roasted
   pistachios, coarsely chopped
1 teaspoon garam masala
1½ teaspoons red chilli powder
2 tablespoons crisp fried onions (see
   page 261)
4 dry-roasted cloves, finely ground
1 tablespoon each of freshly chopped
   mint and green coriander
2 tablespoons ghee or clarified butter
3 tablespoons roasted chana dal (daria
   dal), ground

For the sauce
4 tablespoons vegetable oil, plus extra
   for frying
2 bay leaves
4 cloves
1 teaspoon royal black cumin seeds (or
   regular cumin if royal not available)
3 onions, finely chopped
5cm piece of ginger, peeled and finely
   grated using a microplane
4 garlic cloves, finely grated using a
   microplane
2 tablespoons freshly grated coconut

4 large ripe tomatoes, puréed
1½ teaspoons red chilli powder
2 teaspoons ground cumin
1 teaspoon garam masala
3 green chillies, finely chopped
1 teaspoon salt
325g plain yoghurt
1 teaspoon rose water or screw pine
   essence
pinch of saffron (optional)
2 tablespoons freshly chopped
   coriander

Prepare the koftas by mixing together the mince with the remaining
ingredients. Chill for 15–20 minutes, then knead to form a smooth mix.
Divide the mince into 40–50g size balls (slightly smaller than golf balls).

Heat the oil for frying in a heavy-based pan and sear the koftas over
a medium heat for a minute or so, turning to colour them evenly on all sides.
When browned on all sides, drain on kitchen paper. (You can either finish
cooking the koftas in an oven preheated to 180°C/160°C Fan/Gas Mark 4 for
4–6 minutes or simply simmer them in the sauce – see below.)

Heat the oil for the sauce in a heavy-based pan and add the bay leaves
and cloves. Let them sizzle in hot oil for 30 seconds, then add the royal cumin
seeds. As they crackle and pop, add the chopped onions and sauté for 8–10
minutes until golden in colour, then add the ginger and garlic and sauté for 2–3
minutes. Add the coconut and stir for 2 minutes, then add the tomato purée,
all the ground spices, the green chillies and the salt. Cook well over a moderate
heat for 10–15 minutes until the oil begins to separate from the masala.

Add the yoghurt and 120ml of water to the cooking spices. Mix well and cook
for a further 2 minutes. Now add the prepared koftas to the gravy and fold in
very gently to coat on all sides. Finish the dish with either rose water or screw
pine essence and saffron and infuse for 2 more minutes, then remove from the
heat. Garnish the dish with chopped fresh coriander. Serve hot with rice
or chapatis.

Kosha Mangsho

Lamb Cooked in Rich Onion Sauce

This is a lamb curry from West Bengal, also popular in the state of Bihar and neighbouring areas. The term *kosha* literally translated means 'tightened', which refers to the drying up of spices to give a rich, finished product. It is often served with a soft *khichri* (the original kedgeree) on a cold day, and the combination is both comforting and invigorating.

Serves 4 if the only main meat dish, or 6 as part of a selection of curries

1kg leg of lamb, diced into 2.5cm cubes
2 teaspoons salt
3 tablespoons ginger-garlic paste (see page 260)
1 heaped tablespoon red chilli powder
1½ teaspoons ground cumin
1½ teaspoons ground coriander
50ml mustard oil
50g ghee or vegetable oil
3 bay leaves
5 black peppercorns
3 black cardamom pods
4 dried red chillies, each broken into 2–3 pieces
3 blades of mace
6 large red onions, finely chopped
5 large tomatoes, puréed
250ml of water or lamb stock
1 teaspoon sugar
2 teaspoons Bengali garam masala (see page 261)
1 tablespoon finely chopped coriander
juice of ½ lemon (optional)

Mix the meat with 1 teaspoon of the salt, the ginger-garlic paste, red chilli powder, cumin and coriander and set aside.

Heat the mustard oil in a deep pan and bring to smoking point, then add the ghee or vegetable oil (this will lower the temperature so when the spices are added, they don't instantly burn). Next, add the whole spices and let them crackle for 30 seconds or so. Add the chopped onions and cook over a low heat, stirring constantly, for 10–12 minutes until they turn light brown. Take care to stir the onions continually to prevent them colouring or cooking unevenly.

Next, add the marinated lamb and cook over a high heat for about 20 minutes, stirring frequently.

Add the puréed tomatoes and remaining salt and cook, still over a high heat, for a further 15 minutes. Next add the water or stock, reduce the heat and simmer with a lid on for 20 minutes or until the lamb is tender.

When the meat is tender, if the sauce still looks quite wet, increase the heat and reduce the sauce further until it becomes thick and coats the lamb.

Correct the seasoning with salt if required and stir in the sugar to balance the spiciness of the dish. Finally, stir in the Bengali garam masala. Sprinkle generously with freshly chopped coriander and a squeeze of lemon if you like, and serve with poories or a bread of your choice.

Panthar Ghuguni

Lamb Mince and Chickpea Curry

This dish is a firm favourite on Bijoya Dashami – the tenth and final day of celebrations during Durga Puja.

Serves 4

4 tablespoons mustard oil
2 onions, finely sliced
1 potato, peeled and diced into 1.5cm cubes
2 teaspoons salt
1 teaspoon ground turmeric
3 tomatoes, finely chopped
1 tablespoon ginger paste (see page 260)
2 teaspoons chilli powder
1½ teaspoons ground cumin
1 teaspoon ground coriander
500g lamb mince
4 tablespoons yoghurt
240g can of chickpeas, rinsed and drained
1 teaspoon Bengali garam masala (see page 261)
2 green chillies, finely chopped
1 tablespoon freshly chopped coriander

Heat the mustard oil in a wok, add the onions and cook over a high heat for 5 minutes until golden, then add the diced potato, half the salt, the turmeric and the tomatoes. Continue cooking over a medium heat for 5–6 minutes while stirring to get the onions to an even brown colour.

Add the ginger paste, chilli powder, cumin and coriander, the remaining salt and the lamb mince, and cook over a high heat for 10 minutes or so until the fat begins to separate and the mince starts to brown at the edges. If needed, add just a little water if you feel the potatoes aren't completely cooked.

Reduce the heat to low, add the yoghurt and cook, covered, for 5 minutes. Add the chickpeas and cook over a high heat until very little gravy remains. Correct the seasoning. Finish with ground garam masala, sprinkle over the chopped green chillies and coriander and serve.

Vadai

Rice Flour and Urad Lentil Bread

This wheat-free, gluten-free bread is a must-try. Maharashtrians make a spicy chicken or goat dish at Dussehra and have this bread with it. I find it works just as well with Kosha Mangsho (see page 198) or even a dal.

Makes 12–15

100g white urad dal
1 tablespoon coriander seeds
1 tablespoon fenugreek seeds
2 tablespoons fennel seeds
10g black peppercorns
500g rice flour
1 tablespoon cumin seeds
1 tablespoon freshly chopped coriander
2.5cm piece of ginger, peeled and finely chopped
1½ teaspoons ground turmeric
1 teaspoon red chilli powder
15g salt
oil, for frying

Mix together the urad dal, coriander seeds, fenugreek seeds, fennel seeds and peppercorns, and grind to make powder. Mix the powder with the rest of the ingredients, except the oil.

Add 480ml warm water to the mixture and mix to form a soft dough, then set aside for 20–30 minutes.

Place a length of clingfilm on your work surface, place the dough on top and divide into 12–15 small balls. Cover with another piece of clingfilm and press down on the dough, until the discs are now about 5mm thick.

Heat the oil to 160–170°C.

Remove the clingfilm, lift the flattened dough discs carefully, and place in the hot oil. Deep fry until the balls have puffed up and turned golden on the underside, then turn over and fry the other side until golden; this should take 30 seconds on each side.

Diwali and Kali Puja

Every year the sound of firecrackers announces the celebration of India's favourite festival, Diwali. Homes are decorated, sweets are distributed and thousands of lamps are lit to create a world of fantasy. Of all the festivals celebrated in India, Diwali is the most vivid. Throughout India, Diwali is enjoyed by people of every religion, and the celebrations are similar to those associated with Christmas in other countries.

The Diwali story differs from state to state and from region to region, but essentially Diwali commemorates the victory of good over evil. It's a time to look forward to with optimism and hope, whilst praying for success and prosperity of your loved ones.

In the north, it is a celebration to mark the return of Lord Rama after his victory over Ravana, the demon king of Lanka. The tale is of Prince Rama and his wife Sita who were banished from their home in Ayodhya by their father, the king. It's believed that the people of Ayodhya lit oil lamps in rows to guide Rama and Sita back from exile in the forest to Ayodhya, and on their return Rama

Children light candles as part of traditional Diwali celebrations. (Suvankar Sen/ Pacific Press/LightRocket via Getty)

was crowned king. In the business communities of India, such as Gujarat, Lakshmi – the Goddess of Wealth – is worshipped to give thanks and to pray for prosperity, while in Bengal and the east, Diwali is linked to the worship of the demon-goddess Kali, a festival in its own right that coincides with Diwali.

Regardless of the differences across India, Diwali signifies the renewal of life, so it is common to wear new clothes on the day of the festival. Similarly, it signifies the approach of winter and the beginning of the sowing season.

Known as the Festival of Lights, Diwali is nothing short of a colourful and happy occasion. Families prepare their homes and themselves for special festivities that symbolise the victory of spiritual goodness and the lifting of spiritual darkness. Flower garlands are made, candles float in bowls of water outside homes and sweets are shared. Light is an important physical and spiritual symbol of the holiday: people commonly light small oil lamps

called *diyas*, as it is believed that deceased relatives come back to visit their families on earth during Diwali, with the lights guiding the spirits home.

The sound of firecrackers exploding is common as the noise is said to ward off evil spirits. However, in reality it is the fumes produced by the firecrackers that kill a lot of insects and mosquitoes, found in plenty after the rains, so it has proven quite useful, no matter how raucous the noise can be! In recent times there has been more awareness around reducing the use of firecrackers in order to reduce the pollution and the damage they cause to the environment, especially in big cities. There is a definite move towards finding other symbolic forms to celebrate the spirit of the festival.

Diwali is celebrated between mid-October and mid-November, and is commonly celebrated over a number of days: in some cases five! Day one is commonly known as Dhanteras, where it is considered auspicious to buy something metallic, whether it's a new pot for the kitchen

or a small amount of gold or silver. Day two is celebrated as a little Diwali, followed by the main festival night of Diwali on the third day, which takes place on the darkest night: the first night of the new moon. Day four is a day of worship, and recovering from the previous night's partying, and on Day five in most parts of the country it is a day to acknowledge the bond between brothers and sisters. In the old days, brothers would visit their sisters, reinforce their family ties and give gifts to one another.

Kali Puja is a festival prevalent in West Bengal, and is celebrated on the first night of the new moon, coinciding with Diwali. In fact, Kolkata's most popular temple is actually called Kali temple, located in Kalighat – some say that the city is named after Goddess Kali. In Hindu mythology, Goddess Kali is the first of the ten incarnations of the goddess Durga. Regarded as the more aggressive form, as she is depicted with a fierce face and terrifying look, she is known to destroy all evil and is a fierce fighter for the cause of justice. For this reason people offer prayers to her during the festival in the belief that she will protect them from evil.

Celebrations and excitement around Kali Puja are the same as seen for Diwali across the rest of India, and people often light lamps in honour of Kali.

The dishes surrounding Diwali and Kali Puja truly embrace the essence of sharing and celebration. It is often a social occasion for the women of the household, getting together in each other's kitchens in the weeks leading up to Diwali to prepare some of the snacks. Whilst there are plenty of sweets to indulge in such as *rasmalai* (see page 219) and *gajar ka halwa* (carrot halwa, see page 218), speciality dishes eaten on each day of Diwali vary from region to region. As it is a custom to make dishes at home for the celebrations, I've included a homely chicken curry (see page 214) and some Bengali celebratory favourites.

Phuljhari Murgh

Firecracker Chicken Wings

These chicken wings are an easy recipe to prepare in advance, and then simply fry before serving. You can use the entire wing if you like, but these are best with just the wing drumsticks (the piece of wing from the shoulder joint to the next). It gets a little messy to eat the whole wings with fingers, but the drumsticks work just fine to eat standing up and with fingers. Feel free to leave the skin on as it becomes crisp when fried.

Serves 4–6

900g chicken wings, skin on
vegetable oil, for deep frying

For the marinade
2 teaspoons garlic paste (see page 260)
1½ teaspoons salt
1½ teaspoons red chilli powder
1 teaspoon sugar
4 tablespoons malt vinegar
½ teaspoon black peppercorns, coarsely crushed
1 teaspoon Sichuan pepper (optional)
1 green chilli, finely chopped
1 tablespoon freshly chopped coriander, plus extra for garnishing
50g rice flour
100g cornflour

For the dipping sauce
1 tablespoon vegetable or corn oil
½ star anise
1 banana shallot, finely chopped
50g pineapple, diced into 5mm cubes
5-mm piece of fresh ginger, finely chopped
5 tablespoons tomato ketchup
1 teaspoon soy sauce
1 teaspoon sugar
juice of ½ lime

For the green chilli mayo
4 green chillies, chopped
20g coriander, finely chopped
120ml vegetable oil

1 egg yolk
1 teaspoon mustard
a pinch of salt
juice of 1 lemon

Mix together all the ingredients for the marinade except the rice flour and cornflour and rub the mixture over the chicken wings. Place in the fridge to marinate for 4 hours (or if possible overnight).

In the meantime, make the dipping sauce. Heat the oil in a pan, add the star anise and stir for 30 seconds, then add the shallot and sweat over a high heat for 2–3 minutes, stirring continuously. Add the pineapple and continue cooking over a high heat for another 2 minutes until the pineapple is caramelised at the edges and is beginning to soften. Reduce the heat, add the ginger, tomato ketchup, soy sauce, sugar and 120ml of water and bring to the boil. Cook for 1 minute or two until the sauce turns glossy, check the seasoning and remove from the heat. Add the lime juice, cool and set aside.

To make the green chilli mayo, blend the chillies and coriander with the oil in a blender until fine. Whisk together the egg yolk and mustard, then make an emulsion by adding the blended chilli-coriander oil a little at a time, until all the oil is used. Season with salt and lemon juice and set aside.

When the chicken has been marinated, drain the excess liquid that has come out of the chicken. Mix together the rice flour and cornflour, then dredge the chicken wings in the flour a few at a time, so the chicken wings are dry.

Heat the oil to 180°C and fry the chicken for 6–7 minutes in small batches until cooked through and crisp. Take care not to crowd the oil with too many wings at the same time as the coating comes off and the wings won't be as crisp.

Drain on kitchen paper for 5 minutes, then sprinkle over a little chopped coriander. Serve accompanied with the dipping sauce and the green chilli mayo.

Left: Shorshe Bata Maach (page 208)
Top right: Lao Chingri (page 209)
Bottom right: Peper Plastic Chatni (page 217)

Shorshe Bata Maach

Bengali Fish in Mustard Sauce

The simplest of fish dishes, this recipe is traditionally cooked using *rohu* (or rui) – a river fish similar to pike or perch. Thick darnes of the fish are cut on the bone and fried in mustard oil before being simmered in a sauce made out of mustard paste, green chillies and yoghurt. In the UK, as well as bass, you may use either grey mullet or large red mullet, if you can find any.

Serves 4

35g black mustard seeds
4 sea bass steaks on the bone
2 tablespoons vegetable oil, plus extra for shallow frying the fish
2 tablespoons mustard oil
1 teaspoon panch phoran (equal quantities of the following seeds: nigella, fenugreek, mustard, fennel, cumin, available from good Bengali stores; alternatively use only nigella seeds)
300ml plain yoghurt
½ teaspoon ground turmeric
2 green chillies, slit lengthways
1½ teaspoons salt
1½ teaspoons sugar
300ml of water or fish stock
juice of ½ lemon
1 tablespoon freshly chopped coriander leaves

For the marinade
1 teaspoon salt
½ teaspoon sugar
½ teaspoon ground turmeric
½ teaspoon nigella seeds
1 teaspoon red chilli powder

Soak the mustard seeds in enough water to cover, then set aside for 2 hours or overnight if possible. Drain, and then blend the mustard seeds with 50ml of water to a fine paste.

Meanwhile, mix together the marinade ingredients in a bowl, add the fish steaks, mix well and set aside for 15 minutes.

Heat some vegetable oil in a pan large enough to fit the fish, and pan fry the fish over a medium heat for 3–4 minutes on each side until they are crisp on the outside and cooked inside.

Meanwhile in a separate wok or pan, heat the mustard oil and vegetable oil. Add the panch phoran and let it crackle and pop for 10 seconds or so. Add the mustard paste and cook for a couple of minutes over a medium heat, stirring continuously, then stir in the yoghurt and mix well to prevent splitting.

Add the turmeric, green chillies, salt and sugar, then cook for 2–3 minutes. Check the seasoning, add enough stock or water to thin the sauce and simmer for 2–3 minutes until you get a good coating consistency (add the stock or water gradually as you may not need to add all of it). Add the fried fish and simmer for 2–3 minutes, coating the fish with the sauce, until heated through.

Finish with a squeeze of lemon and sprinkle the coriander over. Serve hot with plain boiled rice.

Lao Chingri

Prawns with Bottle Gourd

Lao or *lauki* or *doodhi* – this vegetable goes by many names. A member of the marrow family, it has a high water content and doesn't have a very prominent taste of its own, but it does take on the flavours of other ingredients and spices it is cooked with. This version, cooked with tiny prawns or shrimp, is a particular favourite at Kali Puja and Bijoya parties.

Serves 4

1 large doodhi, 500–600g, peeled, pith and seeds discarded and diced into 1cm cubes
1 teaspoon ground turmeric
1½ teaspoons salt
1 teaspoon sugar
60ml mustard oil
2 dried whole red chillies, broken, seeds and stalk removed
1 teaspoon cumin seeds
400g prawns, heads and shells removed, cut into 2 or 3 pieces
1½ teaspoons ground cumin
1 teaspoon red chilli powder
1 teaspoon radhuni (fine ajowan or wild celery seeds, or replace with regular ajowan/carom seeds)
70g garden peas or petits pois (frozen is fine)
½ teaspoon garam masala
squeeze of lemon juice

Place the diced marrow in a pan with ½ teaspoon of the turmeric, ½ teaspoon of the salt, the sugar and 250ml of water. Bring to the boil and simmer, covered, until the marrow is cooked and most of the water is absorbed (this takes 15–20 minutes). Set aside.

In a large separate pan, heat the mustard oil to smoking point, then let it cool for 2–3 minutes (this is to reduce the extra pungency in the mustard oil). After 2–3 minutes, add the dried red chillies and cumin seeds and fry until they crackle and pop. Add the prawns, the remaining turmeric and salt, ground cumin, chilli powder and ajowan seeds and cook for a couple of minutes over a high heat. If the spices appear to stick or burn, sprinkle in some water and continue cooking for a couple of minutes until the prawns are pink, cooked and coated in spices.

Add the cooked gourd into the prawns, reduce the heat and cook for 2–3 minutes. Add the peas and cook until most of the liquid has evaporated and the oil begins to separate on the sides of the pan. Finish with the garam masala and a squeeze of lemon juice and serve with rice or poories.

Murgh Makhan Masala

Chicken Butter Masala

Similar to chicken tikka masala in Britain, chicken butter masala is a very famous and widely interpreted dish all over the country, but especially in Orissa, Bengal and the eastern part of the country when I was growing up. Much as Punjab restaurants would be judged by the quality of their black dal, in the east restaurants would often be judged on the quality of their chicken butter masala. It was always such a treat to eat, so I learnt this recipe from the banquet cooks from Orissa who catered for my sister's wedding, preparing this dish for 1200 people.

Serves 4

750g chicken breast, cut into 1cm
    thick strips or dice

For the sauce
4 tablespoons ghee or vegetable oil
½ teaspoon cumin seeds
4 green cardamom pods
2 black cardamom pods
1 bay leaf
1 large onion, finely chopped
1½ teaspoons salt
1 teaspoon ground white pepper
1½ tablespoons ginger-garlic paste
    (see page 260)
1½ teaspoons red chilli powder
4 ripe tomatoes, puréed
2 tablespoons whole milk powder
1 tablespoon full-fat Greek yoghurt
1 tablespoon boiled cashew nut paste
    (see page 260)
1 tablespoon dried fenugreek leaves
½ teaspoon garam masala
½ teaspoon sugar
3 tablespoons single cream
25g cold butter
1 tablespoon freshly chopped
    coriander
juice of ½ lemon

For the sauce, heat the ghee or oil in a heavy-based casserole dish. Add the cumin seeds, green and black cardamom pods and the bay leaf and let them crackle. Add the onion and sauté over a medium heat for 4–5 minutes, stirring constantly. Then add the salt and reduce the heat to low, cover with a lid and cook for 8–10 minutes, until the onion has softened and reduced to bring out its natural sweetness.

When the onion is reduced and soft, add the white pepper, ginger–garlic paste and red chilli powder and cook for a further 3–5 minutes over a low heat, stirring constantly. Now add the puréed tomatoes and cook for a further 10–12 minutes over a low heat until the tomatoes are reduced by half and the entire mixture comes together or the ghee begins to separate from the sides of the pan.

Add the milk powder and incorporate well, then add the yoghurt and mix well with constant stirring, add the cashew nut paste and cook for another 3–5 minutes. Add the chicken and stir for a couple of minutes, taking care to stir continuously. Add the dried fenugreek leaves, garam masala and sugar, stir in the cream and simmer for 1–2 minutes, covered. The chicken should be thoroughly cooked but don't let it overcook.

Finally, add the cold butter and stir to emulsify the butter in the sauce but do not allow it to boil. Sprinkle with coriander, squeeze over the lemon juice and serve with pilau rice or paratha of your choice.

Tip
The cooking of onions over a slow heat with the lid on is the secret to getting a really lovely, silky, velvety sauce that is so unique about chicken butter masala, so take your time to get the onions right and you will enjoy the dish that much more.

Top left: Cholar Dal Narkel Diye (page 215)
Bottom left, top middle and top right: Gajar ka Halwa (page 218)
Middle: Murgir Jhol (page 215)
Bottom right: Methi Begun (page 216)

Murgir Jhol

Home-style Chicken Curry

The basic chicken curry differs from household to household. Every cook has his or her own recipe and each swears by theirs. *Jhol* refers to the thin curry – or 'gravy' as it's called in India – that makes it so special. This is quite a simple and rustic method of cooking – true home-style. You could use boneless chicken if you prefer, but it tastes better with a whole bird cut up into small pieces, as you would for a coq au vin.

Serves 4–6

75ml corn or vegetable oil
1 teaspoon cumin seeds
2 cinnamon leaves or bay leaves
6 green cardamom pods, 3 left whole and 3 roasted and then ground
4 black peppercorns
5 large red onions, finely chopped
2 large potatoes, peeled and each diced into 6 equal pieces (optional)
2 teaspoons salt
1.2kg chicken on the bone, skinned and cut into 8–10 pieces (you can ask your butcher to do this for you)
2 tablespoons ginger-garlic paste (see page 260)
1 tablespoon ground coriander
1 tablespoon ground cumin
1 tablespoon mild chilli powder
1½ teaspoons ground turmeric
4 tomatoes, chopped or blended to a purée
400ml of water or chicken stock
5cm piece of cinnamon stick, roasted and ground
1 tablespoon finely chopped coriander leaves
juice of ½ lemon

Heat the oil in a large pan and add the whole spices. When they crackle, add the onions and fry over a medium heat until golden brown. Stir in the potatoes, if using, and cook for 5 minutes. Add half the salt, then add the chicken and cook for 5–8 minutes until lightly browned.

Add the ginger-garlic paste, ground coriander and cumin, the remaining salt, chilli powder and turmeric. Cook for a further 10 minutes, stirring constantly, until the spices begin to release their aromas. Stir in the tomatoes and cook for 5 minutes, then pour in the water or stock. Bring to the boil, then reduce the heat to low and simmer for 20–25 minutes until the chicken is cooked and the potatoes are tender but not disintegrated.

Taste and correct the seasoning, if required. Sprinkle over the roasted ground cardamom and ground cinnamon and finish with the chopped coriander and lemon juice. Serve with steamed rice.

Cholar Dal Narkel Diye

Chana Lentils Cooked with Coconut

This is perhaps the signature celebration dal in Bengal. Chana lentils are cooked mostly on special occasions rather than every day, when either toor lentils or masoor (red lentils) would be used. Also, rather than a simple thin dal, chana lentils are thick, have a rich taste due to the use of coconut, and are heady with cinnamon and fennel seeds. This version is great as part of a meal, but equally good with bread, chapatis, parathas or poories on its own!

Serves 6

200g chana dal, washed in 2 changes of water
1 teaspoon ground turmeric
1 tablespoon ghee or vegetable oil
5cm piece of cinnamon stick, broken
2 bay leaves
2 dried whole red chillies, broken, seeds and stalk removed
1 teaspoon cumin seeds
2 tablespoons fresh coconut pieces (optional)
100ml coconut milk
1½ teaspoons salt
1 teaspoon sugar
1 tablespoon fennel seeds, dry roasted in a pan for 1 minute and coarsely ground using a mortar and pestle
½ teaspoon Bengali garam masala (see page 261)

Rinse the lentils under cold running water, then place in a pan with the turmeric and 1.2 litres of water. Bring to the boil, cover with a lid and cook for 25–30 minutes until the lentils are cooked thoroughly. Stir the lentils so that half break up but the rest remain whole for some texture.

In a separate pan, heat the ghee or oil, then add the cinnamon, bay leaves and dried red chilli. Let the spices infuse in hot oil for 30–60 seconds, then as the chillies change colour and darken, add the cumin seeds and coconut, if using, and fry for 30 seconds or until fragrant, taking care not to burn the cumin and coconut. Immediately add the boiled lentils, salt and sugar and cook for 5 minutes. Add the coconut milk and cook for another 5 minutes. Finally, add the ground roasted fennel and garam masala. Check the seasoning and serve.

Methi Begun

Aubergine with Fenugreek Leaves

The Bengalis have a weakness for a bitter taste, often opening the meal with something bitter and ending with sweet. This dish makes for an excellent accompaniment.

Serves 4 as an accompaniment

75ml mustard oil
1 large aubergine or 2 medium aubergines, diced into 2.5cm cubes
100g bunch of fenugreek leaves, chopped
1cm piece of ginger, finely chopped
1 tablespoon mustard (English mustard or Dijon grain is fine)
1 teaspoon salt

Heat 60ml of the mustard oil in a wok and add the aubergine. Fry for a couple of minutes until starting to brown, then cover and cook for 2 minutes or so until starting to soften. Remove the lid and stir fry until the aubergine is cooked but not broken. Remove from the wok and set aside.

Add the remaining oil to the same pan and fry the fenugreek leaves for 4–5 minutes, until the moisture dries up. Add the ginger, and cook for 1 minute, then add the mustard, salt and fried aubergine and cook, stirring, for another 2 minutes to mix well. Serve as an accompaniment.

Peper Plastic Chatni

Green Papaya Chutney

Green papaya chutney is the chutney that changed my life! I remember this was one of the first things I cooked when I moved from Kolkata to Rajvilas in Jaipur in 1998 – it's something people had never eaten in Jaipur and was an instant hit. This rather queer name is derived from its plastic-like appearance, which is obtained by very finely slicing the peeled raw papaya and then cooking it in syrup with enough acid in it to render the papaya almost transparent, like plastic.

Serves 12–15

1kg raw green papaya, peeled, seed removed, sliced as thinly as possible using a mandolin (alternatively you could simply grate the peeled seeded papaya)
½ teaspoon pickling lime or calcium hydroxide (optional)
1 tablespoon vegetable oil
2 dried whole red chillies, broken
½ teaspoon nigella or black onion seeds
1 teaspoon fennel seeds
2.5cm piece of ginger, grated
250g sugar
½ teaspoon salt
juice of 3 limes or 100ml white wine or cider vinegar

If using the pickling lime, soak the sliced papaya in 200ml of cold water into which you have dissolved the pickling lime. Soak for 20–30 minutes, then drain. The pickling lime makes the papaya turn clear in appearance but firm in texture. If not using pickling lime, simply wash and drain the papaya in chilled water.

Heat the oil in a pan, add the dried red chillies, nigella and fennel seeds and let them crackle and pop for 30 seconds or so, then add the papaya. Stir to mix for 1 minute, then add the ginger, sugar, salt and an additional 200ml of cold water. Cook for 8–10 minutes over a medium heat until the sugar is dissolved, the syrup appears glossy and thick and there is very little moisture left. Finally, add the lime juice or vinegar. Cook for a couple of minutes, then remove from the heat and allow to cool.

Store in an airtight container in a refrigerator for up to 2 weeks.

Achari Nimbu Mayo

Lime Pickle Mayo

An easy, cheat's way to add some interest into a condiment, and a great convenience for dinner parties. It goes well with chicken wings (see page 204), but would also work as a spread inside sandwiches.

Makes enough to fill a 150g jar

2 tablespoons ready-made lime pickle
100ml good-quality mayonnaise (shop-bought is fine)
juice from ½ lime
1 tablespoon finely chopped coriander

Coarsely chop the lime pickle, or use a blender. Mix in the mayonnaise, then, if necessary, slacken the mixture with hot water, adding a little at a time (no more than 2–3 tablespoons). Add the lime juice and coriander, and mix well. Chill until ready to serve.

Gajar ka Halwa

Carrot Halwa

For many people carrot halwa marks the onset of autumn and winter, which is also synonymous with festival time in India. I remember this as a treat my mother used to make when we were little. Back then it was only made in the winter months when carrots were plentiful. These days, however, carrots are available pretty much throughout the year, and this dish is now cooked all year round. There's still something special about carrot halwa at Diwali – but much as I love it, the idea of having bowl after bowl of rich, sweet halwa seems less and less appealing, hence my 'cheffy' twist of turning them into spring rolls. Properly cut up and presented, they make for an interesting dessert canapé too.

Serves 6

60g ghee or clarified butter
500g carrots, peeled and grated
100g sugar
2 tablespoons raisins
250ml evaporated milk
3 green cardamom pods, ground

For the spring roll option
6 sheets of spring roll pastry
melted butter
vegetable oil, for frying

Heat the ghee in a frying pan, add the grated carrots and sauté for 10–12 minutes over a low heat until the carrot juices evaporate.

Add the sugar and raisins and continue to cook until the sugar melts, then add the evaporated milk and cook for about 20 minutes until the mixture takes on the look of orange-coloured fudge. Mix in the ground cardamom.

To serve, divide among 6 dessert bowls and serve with an ice cream of your choice.

If you wish to jazz up the halwa a little and make it suitable to serve at parties, then try this fantastic way of serving them.

Cool the mixture, then take a spring roll pastry sheet and brush with melted butter. Place one heap of carrot 'fudge' towards one corner. Take the same corner of the pastry and fold it over the carrot and continue rolling it until you almost reach the end of the sheet. Tuck in from both sides, roll again and seal the edges with a few drops of water. Repeat the same process with the remaining sheets. Deep fry the spring rolls at 160–170°C until they are golden brown. Drain on kitchen paper. Serve hot with ice cream.

You could also make these smaller, and pass them around as a dessert canapé at the end of a meal too.

Rasmalai

Milk Dumplings Served with Saffron and Cardamom Milk

After *rossogolla* (see page 257), *rasmalai* is possibly the second most loved pan-Indian sweet. Right enough, you start with 20 *rossogollas*!

Makes 20

2 litres whole milk
150g sugar
4 green cardamom pods
3 drops of rose water
a pinch of saffron
20 rossogollas (see page 257),
   squeeze out as much of the syrup
   as possible without breaking them
2 tablespoons chopped pistachio nuts

Place the milk in a pan with the sugar and the cardamom and rose water, bring to the boil and reduce to about 1.2 litres. Remove from the heat, then add the saffron and let it infuse for 5 minutes.

Add all the squeezed rossogollas to the reduced milk and saffron mixture, return to the heat and simmer for 3–4 minutes. Divvy up in small bowls (serve about 3 per person) and chill. To serve, garnish with chopped pistachios.

Christmas

Christianity had been in existence in India much before the arrival of the Portuguese in the fifteenth century. It is believed that Saint Thomas – one of the twelve apostles of Jesus Christ – introduced Christianity to India around the first century. Today, Christianity is the third largest religion in India and is mainly concentrated in south and north-east India, and particularly in Kerala which is home to the Saint Thomas Christian community.

In comparison with other festivals, Christmas is quite a small occasion in India. This is due to the percentage of Indians who are Christians (about 2.3 per cent) compared to those who belong to other religions (Hinduism makes up nearly 80 per cent and Islam around 14 per cent). Nevertheless, the population of India is over 1 billion, so there are over 25 million Christians in India, and Christmas is a national holiday. One of the largest Indian urban Christian communities is in Mumbai, most of whom are Roman Catholic, and today what we see is an Indian adaptation of the western Christmas celebration.

Decorations, such as this nativity scene at Sacred Hearts Cathedral in New Delhi, are a common sight in the run up to Christmas. (Sunil Ghosh/Hindustan Times via Getty)

Midnight Mass on Christmas Eve (24th December) plays a significant part in the Christmas traditions in India, especially for Catholics. Families often walk to Mass together and a feast with family and friends follows, as well as the giving and receiving of gifts. After the service, the church bells ring to announce that Christmas Day has arrived.

Most Christian families display a nativity scene featuring clay figures – everyone wants to have the best nativity scene, and Mumbai is famous for its lavish scenes. Churches are decorated with poinsettia flowers and candles illuminate the Midnight Mass services. Lights are central to the festival, and streets in southern India are lit up, as Christians place small oil-burning clay lamps on the flat roofs of their homes.

Some of the most vibrant Christmas celebrations can be seen in Goa, where over a quarter of the state's population are Christian, and of those most are Catholic. Goa flaunts its culture to its best during Christmas time; it's a party and a spectacle for both locals and international tourists, with the beaches playing host to an array of music, dance and celebrations taking place throughout the festivities.

Goans have incorporated many western customs into their Christmas celebrations, most likely as a result of Goa's historical connections with Portugal. Carol singing in your neighbourhood in the run-up to Christmas is not uncommon, as well as decorated Christmas trees – some families even use banana or mango trees! On Christmas Eve Christians in Goa hang giant star-shaped paper lanterns between the houses so that the stars float above you as you walk down the road.

Beyond the Christmas merrymaking, as with all Indian festivals, food plays a central role. On Christmas morning a lavish brunch is often enjoyed, often featuring an array of dishes from mutton curry and chicken stew to a traditional roast, fish curries and steamed rice cakes, and of course several sweet treats. Lots of sweet treats are eaten at Christmas time in India, and one of my favourites is a rich Christmas fruit cake (see page 237). Families often make sweets together to share with their friends and neighbours, and it doesn't matter if neighbours are Hindu, Christian or Muslim – all are given some goodies and are wished a happy Christmas!

Growing up in Asansol in West Bengal, Christmas was a big festival that we looked forward to with much anticipation. With a long holiday from school and plenty of time for revelling with friends, my childhood memories are based around Christmas Day, and all the indulgence in cakes and sweets.

For this book, I have mainly focused on Christmas dishes from Kerala where an ancient Christian community resides, as they have some of the most fascinating cross-cultural cooking. One might say that Christmas in India has been particularly influenced by western traditions, but nevertheless it is an occasion for reunions with family and friends, and the spirit and joy around the festival link back to the culture and traditions of the place where it is being celebrated.

Top left: Ishtew (page 227)
Bottom left: Meen Kudampuli
Curry (page 228)
Top right: Appams (page 232)
Bottom right and far right:
Hans Mappas (page 230)

Puff

Chicken and Pastry Patties

These puff pastry parcels are relatively quick to make and very versatile as far as fillings go. You can fill these with halved boiled eggs, a spicy shrimp filling or just a regular *dosa* filling of vegetables. These are a great snack to offer to kids at festivals and are frequently seen on Christmas menus when feeding large families.

Makes 20−24

450g boneless chicken thighs (or leftover roast chicken, shredded)
1½ teaspoons salt
2 teaspoons red chilli powder
4 tablespoons vegetable oil
5cm piece of cinnamon stick
12−15 curry leaves
3 red onions, thinly sliced
1 tablespoon ginger-garlic paste (see page 260)
½ teaspoon ground turmeric
1 teaspoon garam masala
1 teaspoon peppercorns, coarsely cracked
2 green chillies, finely chopped
2.5cm piece of ginger, peeled and finely chopped
juice of 1 lime
2 x 320g rolls of puff pastry sheets
1 egg, beaten, for brushing
fennel seeds, to sprinkle

Preheat the oven to 180°C/160°C Fan/Gas Mark 4.

Place the chicken thighs in a roasting dish, sprinkle with ½ teaspoon of the salt, 1 teaspoon of the red chilli powder and 1 tablespoon of the oil, and roast in the preheated oven for 15−20 minutes until cooked through and the juices run clear. Alternatively, place in a pan with 150ml of water and bring to the boil, then simmer, covered, for 15−20 minutes until the chicken is cooked and the water is almost absorbed. Cool and shred the chicken, reserving any leftover juices.

Heat the remaining oil in a separate pan. Add the cinnamon stick and let it infuse for 30 seconds, then add the curry leaves and sliced onions and cook for 5−6 minutes until the onion is translucent. Next add the ginger−garlic paste and sauté for 2 minutes. Add the remaining salt and chilli powder, plus the turmeric and garam masala, and sauté for another minute or two. Add the shredded chicken and mix until well combined. Add the coarsely crushed peppercorns, chopped green chillies, chopped ginger and any reserved cooking juices and mix well. Finish with a squeeze of lime juice. Remove from the heat and allow the mixture to cool.

Turn the oven down to 170°C/150°C Fan/Gas Mark 3½. Line a baking tray with baking parchment or grease with oil or butter.

Unroll the puff pastry sheets (if using a block of puff pastry, roll out to approximately 3−4mm thick). Cut into 7.5cm squares. Brush the edges of the pastry with water or egg wash and place a tablespoon of the filling in the centre. Fold in the pastry edges to make a triangular or rectangular shape and gently press down on the pastry edges to seal the parcel.

Once all the puffs are made, brush the tops with the remaining egg and sprinkle fennel seeds on top. Arrange the puffs on the prepared baking tray and bake in the preheated oven for 12−14 minutes or until they are golden brown and crisp.

Ishtew

Suriani Home-style Chicken Stew

This stew is served in Syrian-Christian households in Kerala for breakfast
and is a firm favourite at the Christmas table. Traditionally served with *appams*
(fermented rice batter pancakes cooked in a heavy iron wok), it can also be
accompanied by rice vermicelli or plain rice. Fiddly as they may be, *appams* have
thin, crisp sides, soft fluffy centres and look beautiful as they take the shape
of the wok they are cooked in.

You could use boned chicken in this recipe if you wish, but chicken on the
bone provides much more flavour. If using boned chicken, use just the thighs
and cook them slowly and long for a great result and depth of flavour.

Serves 4–6

3 tablespoons coconut or sunflower oil
5cm piece of cinnamon stick
6 cloves
4 green cardamom pods
4 garlic cloves, thinly sliced
5cm piece of ginger, cut into small
    matchsticks
2 red onions, thinly sliced
8 green chillies, slit lengthways
15 fresh curry leaves
1 free-range chicken, cut on the bone
    into 8 pieces
2 teaspoons salt
1 tablespoon black peppercorns,
    coarsely crushed
590ml coconut milk
5 tablespoons toddy (palm) vinegar
    (substitute with sherry vinegar or
    sweet white wine vinegar if you can't
    find toddy)
1 teaspoon ground garam masala

For the sweet and sour rice
240g basmati rice, washed under
    running water and soaked for 20
    minutes
4 tablespoons vegetable oil
2 star anise
4 green cardamom pods
2 bay leaves
1 onion, thinly sliced

10 fresh curry leaves
1½ teaspoons salt
1½ teaspoons sugar
4 tablespoons white vinegar
160ml coconut milk

To cook the chicken, heat the oil in a pan, add the cinnamon, cloves
and cardamom, followed by the garlic, ginger, onions, chillies and curry leaves
and cook over a medium heat until the onions are soft. Add the chicken, salt
and pepper and stir for 1 minute. Stir in the coconut milk and 125ml of water,
reduce the heat to low and simmer, covered, for about 45 minutes or until
the chicken is cooked.

While the chicken stew is cooking, prepare the sweet and sour rice. Heat
the oil in a pan, add the star anise, cardamom and bay leaves and stir for 30
seconds or so until they release the flavours into the oil. Add the onion, curry
leaves, salt and sugar and cook until the onions are translucent. Add the
vinegar, coconut milk and 300ml of water and then the drained rice. Mix well
and stir for 5 minutes or so over a medium heat, then lower the heat, cover the
pan with a tightly fitting lid and cook the rice for another 7–8 minutes. All the
liquid should be absorbed by this stage. Remove the lid, stir the rice to open
the grains, cover with the lid again and set aside for another 10 minutes
to finish cooking in its own steam.

When the chicken is cooked through, add the vinegar to the stew, sprinkle
over the garam masala and mix well. Remove from the heat and serve with
sweet and sour rice.

Meen Kudampuli Curry

Pan-seared Bream in a Kerala Curry Sauce

It's the use of kokum berries (black mangosteen) that gives this dish a distinct sourness that is noticeably different than if you used tamarind or lemon juice, and makes this dish so unique. If you can't find kokum, which is available online, fear not, just substitute with tamarind or lemon juice if necessary. If you wish you could also use boneless filleted fish, but I find using darnes on the bone keeps the fish moist and creates beautiful form on the plate.

Serves 4

4 small whole black bream, cut into
    darnes 2.5cm thick
½ teaspoon salt
1 tablespoon vegetable oil, plus extra
    for frying
½ teaspoon cracked black
    peppercorns
1 green chilli, finely chopped
1 teaspoon fennel seeds

For the sauce
2 tablespoons vegetable oil
½ teaspoon fenugreek seeds
1 teaspoon black mustard seeds
2 sprigs of fresh curry leaves
2 white onions, chopped
1½ teaspoons red chilli powder
2 tomatoes, chopped
1 tablespoon kokum berries
150ml coconut milk
125ml fish stock
1½ teaspoons salt
juice of 1 lime

Place the fish in a bowl. Mix the salt into the oil, sprinkle in the peppercorns, green chilli and fennel seeds and pour over the fish. Set aside to marinate for 10–15 minutes.

Meanwhile, make the sauce. Heat the oil in a deep pan, add the fenugreek seeds and mustard seeds and let them crackle and pop for 20–30 seconds, then add the curry leaves and onions, and sauté for 6–7 minutes or until the onions turn pink. Add the red chilli powder and cook further for 30 seconds. Add the tomatoes with the kokum berries and cook until the tomatoes cook off and are almost dry. Add the coconut milk and simmer for 3–4 minutes, until it begins to thicken. When the sauce thickens, add the fish stock to thin it, bring to the boil and reduce to a flowing consistency. Add the salt, check the consistency and finish with a squeeze of lime.

To cook the fish, heat some oil in a flat-based pan, sear the fish darnes for 2–3 minutes on each side, cooking them until they are crisp. Pour the sauce on to 4 serving plates, place the fish on top and serve.

Mackerel Moilee

Masala Fried Mackerel Moilee

This crisp fried masala fish can easily be the centrepiece at pretty much any celebration, but it is often seen at the Christmas table. Mackerel is good for this dish as it handles the spices well, but in Kerala they can use pomfret or pearl spot. Here in the UK, feel free to try this dish with sea bass or sea bream if you aren't too fond of mackerel.

Serves 4

4 x 350g whole mackerel, cleaned
vegetable oil, for deep frying
juice of 1 lime

For the marinade
2 tablespoons ginger-garlic paste (see page 260)
1 tablespoon red chilli powder
2 teaspoons ground coriander
1 teaspoon black peppercorns, crushed
¼ teaspoon ground turmeric
1½ teaspoons salt
1 tablespoon rice flour
2 tablespoons cornflour

For the sauce
3 tablespoons corn or vegetable oil
½ teaspoon mustard seeds
a sprig of fresh curry leaves
1 white onion, sliced
2.5cm piece of ginger, peeled and cut into fine strips
4 green chillies, slit lengthways
1 teaspoon salt
½ teaspoon ground turmeric
500ml coconut milk

Mix all the ingredients for the marinade together. Slash the fish 2 or 3 times on each side with a sharp knife and rub in the marinade. Set aside for 20 minutes.

For the sauce, heat the oil in a pan, add the mustard seeds and curry leaves and when they start to crackle, add the onion, ginger, green chillies and salt and cook until the onions are soft. Add the turmeric and stir for 1 minute. Pour in the coconut milk and simmer over a low heat until the sauce thickens to the consistency of double cream. Remove from the heat.

To fry the fish, heat the oil in a wok or deep pan large enough for the fish to fit in. Deep fry the fish in medium-hot oil for about 10–15 minutes, turning them over occasionally to cook all sides, until cooked through and crisp on the outside. Remove gently and place on kitchen paper to remove the excess oil.

Squeeze the lime juice over the fish and serve it with the moilee sauce and steamed rice or green salad as accompaniments.

Hans Mappas

Roast Goose Breast Mappas

At Christmas many Christian families roast goose breast and serve it with its own juices deglazed with a little vinegar. Feel free to substitute duck breasts or even large chicken breasts with the skin on.

Serves 4

2 large goose breasts, skin on, slashed on the skin side to make incisions
1 tablespoon vegetable oil

For the marinade
5cm piece of cinnamon stick
2 bay leaves
4 cloves
1 teaspoon peppercorns
1 teaspoon fennel seeds
¼ teaspoon ground turmeric
½ teaspoon red chilli powder
1 teaspoon salt

For the sauce
3 tablespoons vegetable oil
2.5cm piece of ginger, peeled and cut into matchsticks
12 curry leaves, preferably fresh
1 red onion, sliced
4 green chillies, slit
¼ teaspoon ground turmeric
1 tablespoon ground coriander
235ml duck stock
2 tablespoons red wine vinegar
1 teaspoon salt
1 teaspoon garam masala
235ml coconut milk

Finely grind all the marinade ingredients together and rub the goose breasts with the mixture. Take care to rub the spices into the incisions made on the skin side of the breasts too. Set aside for 30 minutes.

Preheat the oven to 160°C/140°C Fan/Gas Mark 3.

To make the sauce, heat the oil in a pan, add the ginger, curry leaves and onion and sauté over a medium heat for 4–5 minutes until soft. Add the green chillies, turmeric and coriander and sauté for 2 minutes. Add the stock, vinegar and salt and simmer for 5–6 minutes. Add the garam masala and coconut milk and simmer until the sauce thickens enough to coat the back of the spoon.

Heat a tablespoon of oil in an ovenproof, heavy-based frying pan and sear the goose breasts on the skin side over a medium heat for 6–8 minutes until the skin is crisp and much of the fat is rendered down in the pan. Turn over and sear the second side for a couple of minutes, then place in the preheated oven for 3–4 minutes, then remove and rest for 5 minutes.

Slice and serve the goose breast with the sauce and Podimas-style roasted new potatoes (see page 233).

Chukka Steak

Spice-crusted Seared Sirloin in Onion, Chilli and Coconut Masala

This is inspired by a traditional Kerala toddy shop favourite, beef chukka – a double-cooked beef dish where strips from chuck of beef, or topside or skirt, are first braised, then stir fried with onions, curry leaves and more spices to make an excellent accompaniment to drinks. This version uses a better cut as it's a family celebration, and the meat tastes much better being simply grilled and folded in with the masala, rather than braised.

Serves 4–6

800g sirloin steak, 2.5cm thick
4 tablespoons vegetable oil
5cm piece of ginger, peeled and cut into thin matchsticks
5 garlic cloves, chopped
4 green chillies, halved lengthwise
20 curry leaves
3 red onions, cut into slices 5mm thick
1½ teaspoons salt
1 teaspoon sugar
120ml coconut milk
1 tablespoon freshly chopped coriander
juice of ½ lime

For the spice mix
2 whole dried red chillies
1 tablespoon coriander seeds
½ teaspoon ground turmeric
1 tablespoon fennel seeds
1 teaspoon cumin seeds
1 teaspoon black peppercorns
5cm piece of cinnamon stick
3 cloves
2 green cardamom pods

To make the spice mix, dry roast all the spices in a pan for 1 minute or so until they smell fragrant, then crush them coarsely using a mortar and pestle. Sprinkle 2 pinches of the coarse spice mix on each side of the steak and set aside for 5 minutes.

Heat 1 tablespoon oil in a frying pan or griddle pan over a medium-high heat, then sear the steak over a high heat on one side for 2–3 minutes without moving it in the pan. Turn over and cook the other side for 3 minutes. Remove from the heat and set aside to rest for 5 minutes.

While the meat is resting, into another frying pan add the remaining 3 tablespoons of oil and heat to medium, then add the ginger, garlic, green chillies, curry leaves and onions. After 30 seconds or so, increase the heat to high and sauté for a couple of minutes until the onions have softened. Sprinkle in the remaining ground spice mix, salt and sugar and stir fry for another 2 minutes.

Reduce the heat to medium, stir in the coconut milk and continue cooking until the liquid has reduced by half. Slice the seared steak into strips 1cm wide and add back in the pan. Scatter over the chopped coriander and squeeze in the lime juice. Mix the onion masala well to coat the sliced steak and serve immediately.

Appams

Fermented Rice Pancakes

This recipe uses yeast to make the pancakes spongy and delicious. In Kerala they are known as *appams*, whereas in Sri Lanka they are called *hoppers*. The vessel they are cooked in is typical to the area – a small, wok-shaped *kadhai* that has a round bottom. When the batter is spooned into the hot wok, it is swirled around in circular motion and forms a thin coating. When the pan is returned to the heat, the batter settles down in the centre of the pan, forming a thick, pillowy centre with crisp, thin edges. This duality of texture is the beauty of *appams*.

Serves 4

350g rice
950ml thin coconut milk
½ teaspoon fresh yeast (or 1 teaspoon active dry yeast)
2 tablespoons sugar
1 teaspoon salt
vegetable oil, for frying

Wash the rice in a couple of changes of water, then soak it in a bowl of water for 1½ hours, then drain.

Reserve 235ml of the coconut milk and set aside. Add the remaining coconut milk to the drained rice and grind to a smooth paste (you can use a wet grinder or a blender/food processor).

Once the rice mixture is smooth, place 2 tablespoons of it in a pan with the reserved coconut milk and add 235ml of water. Bring this mixture to the boil, then reduce to a simmer and let it thicken into a paste, stirring continuously. Let it cool down completely.

Once that mixture is completely cooled, add it to the ground rice flour mixture in the food processor along with the yeast and grind for another couple minutes. Transfer the resulting batter to a bowl, cover with clingfilm and let it ferment at room temperature (26–32°C) for about 4 hours, then refrigerate until you need it.

When ready to cook the appam, take the bowl out of the fridge and add the sugar and salt straight away. Mix the batter using a whisk or a paddle spoon – this helps to mix the salt and sugar evenly as well as aerating the batter and quickly bringing it to room temperature. If the batter is too thick to spread, add a little water to bring it to the right consistency (aim for the consistency of single cream) and let it come to room temperature before use.

Appam batter should be quite flowing so that when you use the swirling technique during cooking, the edges are light and crisp. If your batter is thicker, you get appams of more uniform thickness and sponginess. There's no need to flip them. Keep the heat medium-low at all times. If you don't have an appam kadhai to hand, you can simply pour a ladleful of the batter into a frying pan or omelette pan oiled with a teaspoon of vegetable oil and cook like a flat pancake – they taste just as good.

Serve warm, with Suriani chicken stew (see page 227) or a similar dish. This quantity will make a stack of appams, to be shared among 4 people.

Aloo Podimas

New Potatoes Tempered with Mustard Seeds and Curry Leaves

These are like the filling you find inside *dosa* pancakes, but instead of being crushed or mashed the new potatoes are left whole or cut into marble-sized pieces. Think of these as curried roast potatoes, but the potatoes are first boiled in the skin then peeled, as this gives a richer texture to the *podimas* rather than boiling them after peeling.

Serves 6–8

600g new small potatoes, unpeeled, but thoroughly washed
1 red onion, finely chopped
a pinch of asafoetida
2 green chillies, slit lengthways
2.5cm piece of fresh ginger, peeled and finely chopped
1 teaspoon ground turmeric
1½ teaspoons salt
2 tablespoons freshly chopped coriander
juice of 1 lemon

For tempering
1 tablespoon vegetable oil
10 fresh curry leaves
1 dried red chilli
2 teaspoons black mustard seeds

Bring a pan of salted water to the boil. Add the potatoes and simmer for about 12–15 minutes or until tender. Drain well and set aside.

When the potatoes are cool enough to handle, peel them and set aside. They need to be marble sized so cut them into two if they are very large.

For the tempering, heat the oil in a large, heavy-based frying pan to smoking point and add all the tempering ingredients. When the seeds crackle and the curry leaves crisp up, add the red onion and cook over a medium heat for 3–4 minutes stirring continuously. Next add the asafoetida, green chillies, ginger, turmeric and salt and stir over a high heat for 30 seconds. Add the potatoes and stir to mix the tempering evenly through the potatoes. Cook for another 2–3 minutes, then sprinkle over the coriander and finish with lemon juice.

Sabudana aur Ananas Payasam

Pineapple and Tapioca Kheer

This *kheer* is unusual owing to the jewel-like appearance of tapioca pearls and the refreshing use of pineapple. It tastes just as good in its vegan version which omits the sweetened condensed milk, replacing it with coconut milk and sugar.

Serves 6–8

75g sago pearls (large grain size), soaked in warm water for 20 minutes
½ ripe pineapple, peeled, core removed and diced into 1cm cubes
2 tablespoons sugar
475ml coconut milk
200g sweetened condensed milk
½ teaspoon ground cardamom
½ teaspoon ground ginger
1 tablespoon ghee
1 tablespoon whole cashew nuts
1 tablespoon raisins

Drain the sago pearls, transfer to a pan, add 475ml of water and simmer for about 15 minutes until they start to become translucent. Add a little more hot water if the mixture is too thick. Now add the pineapple and sugar and simmer for another 15–20 minutes until the pineapple is tender. Add the coconut milk and condensed milk and simmer for about 5 minutes until the mixture thickens again. Stir in the cardamom and ginger and remove from the heat.

Heat the ghee in a small frying pan, add the cashew nuts followed by the raisins and fry until the cashew nuts are golden brown in colour. Add to the payasam and mix well.

It can be served either hot or cold.

Left: Mackerel Moilee (page 229)
Middle: Puff (page 226)
Right: Sabudana aur Ananas Payasam (page 233)

Thalasseri Bakery Special

Malabar Christmas Cake

Unlike the traditional western Christmas pudding, this is a much lighter, cake version that is delicious served on its own or with custard. I find the spices are much better expressed in this cake than in a traditional Christmas pudding where they get too cloyingly intense as the texture is much denser and the fruit closely packed. Give this a go!

Serves 10

200g dried fruits (such as raisins, prunes, figs, dates, cherries), chopped

200g mixed candied orange and lemon peel, chopped

40ml dark rum or inexpensive brandy, to soak the fruits (optional)

3 tablespoons sugar, for the caramel syrup

300g plain flour

1 tablespoon baking powder

5 cloves

5 green cardamom pods

5cm piece of cinnamon stick

½ teaspoon ground ginger

¼ teaspoon grated nutmeg

200g caster sugar

250g butter, softened, plus extra for greasing

4 eggs

1 teaspoon vanilla extract

60g cashew nut halves

If you wish to soak the dried fruits in the rum or brandy, place them in a bowl and set aside for 2 hours (or overnight).

Preheat the oven to 180°C/160°C Fan/Gas Mark 4. Grease a round 25cm diameter cake tin.

To prepare the caramel syrup, heat the sugar in a pan until the sugar melts and turns a dark brown colour. Mix with a wooden spoon to even out the colouring, then carefully pour 75ml of water into it and mix in well. The liquid is very dark and close to burnt (it's referred to by some pastry chefs as Black Jack and used to impart a very dark colour to cakes/sponges). Remove the liquid from the heat and set aside to cool.

Sift the plain flour with the baking powder and set aside. Grind the whole spices to a fine powder.

Cream the caster sugar and butter together for 5–7 minutes to incorporate all the sugar into the butter and get the mixture light and fluffy. Add the eggs into it one by one and mix well between adding each egg. Add the vanilla extract and cooled caramel syrup, followed by the powdered spices and flour. Finally, add the dried fruit and candied peel and fold in slowly (adding the fruit last ensures that no pockets with lumps of flour are formed).

Pour the mixture into the prepared cake tin and decorate the top with cashew nuts. Bake in the preheated oven for 20 minutes, then reduce the heat to 165°C/145°C Fan/Gas Mark 3 and bake for a further 45 minutes or until a knife inserted in the centre of the cake comes out clean. Let it cool well before cutting.

Bengali Wedding

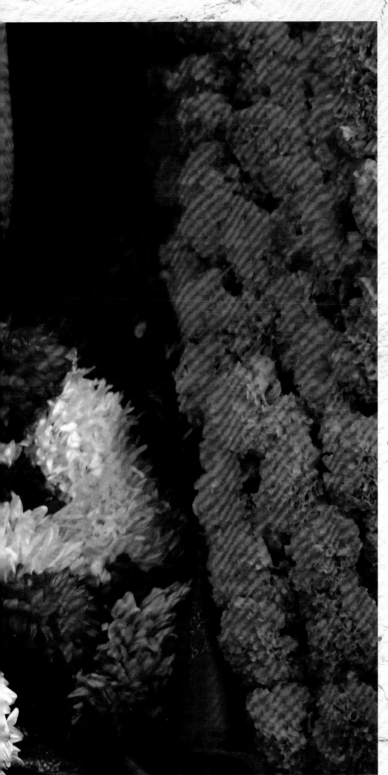

I have always had a personal weakness for weddings. Whether the bride and groom were people close to me or not, it didn't matter. In fact, during my time in college, where the food in the hostel was terrible, every time the wedding season came about I took it as a great opportunity to gatecrash weddings and help myself to some wonderful food, along with a few of my friends, of course. At the time my view was that they're already feeding 800 people so what damage could I do?

Weddings are beautiful, vibrant, colourful landscapes on a culture's canvas. Most weddings in India are an ensemble of rituals and traditions, from pre-wedding ceremonies to the wedding-day events, and even more ceremonies post-wedding. The style of a Bengali wedding is no different, and involves a spread of these elaborate and colourful ceremonies. Whilst being of great significance to the start of marital life, weddings are the ultimate occasion to bring together friends, families and communities to celebrate.

A traditional Indian bride on her wedding day: the henna, the garlands and the bangles are all important elements. (Antara Sarkar/Getty)

Different cultures across India have their own unique traditions and rituals for weddings, but wherever you celebrate a marriage in India, it will always be full of energy and vibrant colours, involving lots and lots of people. There is a sense of community, an all-encompassing celebration, where everyone and anyone is invited – even if you don't know them all that well. For a parent, marrying off one of their sons or daughters is seen as a huge achievement in their lives, after having raised their child and seen them grow, and families want to share this achievement and joy with the community which is why we often have such big weddings.

The sense of celebration is evoked in the emphasis on hospitality, and the efforts to look after the elders and all the wedding guests. No matter how expensive it is to have a wedding, no matter how many dishes are being cooked and how many people they have invited, the warmth and hospitality of the event are always at the forefront.

The rituals of a Bengali wedding are generally quite elaborate and involve the family members on both sides. There are elements of music and dance, with a particularly peculiar – but attractive – feature of Bengali weddings being the blowing of conch shells and ululation by the women during most of the ceremonies. Some of the other rituals are based around the principles of mischief and fun; this sense of informality, fun and frivolity is all part of the occasion, and can even involve food, such as a *rossogolla* eating competition!

A Bengali wedding can often be separated into many elements. The first is the *paka-dekha* – the ceremony to formalise the alliance between families which is marked with sweet treats such as *rossogollas* and *mishti doi* (see pages 257 and 256). This is done some time ahead of the actual wedding, and marks the start of all the planning. The actual wedding day begins with the *nandi much* ceremony, where a priest or elder pays tribute to the deceased ancestors of the bride and groom, requesting their spirits to bless the couple. Following this is the *gaye holud*, or 'yellowing of the body', where turmeric is applied to the skin of the bride and groom. The groom's family also travel to the bride's home, bringing with them the bride's wedding dress and other decorations and gifts.

The main ceremony begins later in the day, when the groom arrives at the venue or bride's home, where his arrival is heralded with the women blowing conch shells and ululation. He is then given his wedding clothes from the bride's family. The actual wedding ceremony is begun without the bride present, and she joins later, accompanied by her brothers and her female friends. Her face is often covered with betel leaves, which she removes during the *shubhodrishti*. The groom places the *sindoor* (a red powdered pigment) in the parting of the bride's hair, and the ceremony is complete – they are married. They exchange flower garlands, and the loose ends of their clothes are knotted together for the evening.

The celebrations and rituals seen during the Bengali wedding period are often for the enjoyment and entertainment of family and guests, rather than for the bride and groom, who are usually the least of everyone's concerns, and who may be the ones having the least fun! Often the couple are fasting for the whole day, or being subjected to numerous rituals and traditions – a lot of which they may not even understand. In a society like India, where many of the marriages are arranged, it's not uncommon for the bride and groom not to have met many times, and if they have, they may not know each other all that well. All of these complex traditions and rituals serve as a mechanism to help break the ice and help the families to get to know each other. But the reason why I think we have so many convoluted traditions and rituals is so that the couple are suitably distracted, and might not fully grasp the seriousness of what they're getting into. And that is the paradox of The Big Fat Indian Wedding.

Generally speaking, food at weddings is great, but at Bengali weddings it is even more so. Very often the success of the wedding is judged by the quality of food on offer and the other hospitality arrangements. In the old days, weddings would be a two- or three-day affair with different meals being served throughout the day, but the main meal is usually in the evening when the groom's procession arrives at the bride's house. The welcome, the arrangements and this meal are what everything hinges on!

Traditionally the wedding party is accommodated in a large marquee where they will be offered sweets and cool drinks. In an adjoining tent, long tables are set up where people are seated with plates and bowls placed in front of them – almost like an assembly line. Served first would be a little salt, a wedge of lime and a chutney of some description. Next up would be the *bhaja* – a fried snack (see page 245), such as fried aubergine or fried fish. Next would be a rich, semi-dry curry with prawns, meat or vegetables. This would be distributed with care, making sure everyone got some, and there is enough to offer to the more important guests who may eat later. Next are poories, more vegetables, lentils, wet curries, followed by rice. After rice, seconds of everything are served again! Finally, desserts like *rossogolla* (see page 257) and *mishti doi* (see page 256) are brought out and guests are affectionately force-fed until they feel they're about to die!

One of my most enduring memories of weddings is that warmth and hospitality, the love of feeding and making sure everyone had a great time. Of course, at any big event, all guests should be treated as equal, but as it is with life, some are more equal than others. One of my first lessons on the varying importance of guests was at a Bengali wedding. When I was young I would help with dispensing the food; perhaps you would be on lime duty, or rice duty, or if you were really good you would be put on *rossogolla* duty! It was important to ensure everyone was being served. When serving in the *pandal* (the huge decorated marquee where hundreds of guests were being fed) sometimes you would be scouted out to look after certain people who were more important than others and who needed special attention, for example the groom's father or his brother-in-law. This was my first lesson in the hierarchy of guests. These days, of course, some of the format has changed, and people prefer to set up buffets where guests can help themselves, which saves a lot of effort for the host's family.

Matarshutir Dhoka

Green Pea Gnocchi

Dhoka is a term used for describing something which doesn't turn out as it was expected to! In this case, what appears to be diced meat in a curry turns out to be cubes made from green peas. This sort of trick-playing often happens at weddings when chickpea masquerades as paneer and jack fruit is passed off as mutton. It's a light-hearted joke that the bride's family would often play on the groom's guests. If you wish, you can use chickpea flour instead of green peas.

Serves 4

For the dhoka

500g garden peas or petits pois (frozen will do)

4 green chillies, stalks removed

3 tablespoons mustard oil

1 tablespoon ginger paste (see page 260)

2 teaspoons fennel seeds, lightly roasted and ground

1 teaspoon ajowan seeds, lightly roasted and ground with the fennel seeds

½ teaspoon red chilli powder

3 tablespoons chickpea flour or besan

½ teaspoon sugar

1 teaspoon salt

For the sauce

3 tablespoons ghee

1 teaspoon cumin seeds

100g potatoes, peeled and diced into 5-mm cubes

½ teaspoon ground turmeric

1 teaspoon red chilli powder

100ml plain yoghurt

1cm piece of ginger, finely chopped

1 teaspoon salt

½ teaspoon sugar

½ teaspoon garam masala (see page 261)

a pinch of asafoetida (optional)

For the dhoka, grind the peas with the green chillies, adding as little water as possible until the mix is a smooth purée and is not too wet. (If using frozen peas, defrost them first.)

Heat the mustard oil in a wok and add the green pea and chilli purée and the remaining dhoka ingredients. Cook over a very low heat for 15–20 minutes, stirring constantly, or until the mix begins to leave the sides of the wok and is holding its shape.

Meanwhile, grease a shallow tray large enough to contain the mixture. When the pea mixture is cooked enough to leave the sides of the pan, transfer it to the tray and spread evenly to a thickness of 1.5cm. Let the mixture cool. Once cooled, cut into squares and set aside.

Heat 1 tablespoon of the ghee in a frying pan and shallow fry the cooled pea squares. Cook them in 2 or 3 batches. Set aside while you make the sauce.

For the sauce, heat the remaining ghee in the same frying pan and add the cumin seeds. Let them crackle and pop for 30 seconds or so, then add the diced potatoes and fry for 3–4 minutes. Next, add all the remaining ingredients except the garam masala and asafoetida, stir well to combine and cook over a medium heat for about 5 minutes.

Add 350ml of water to the pan, cover and cook until the potatoes are cooked through but don't break up. Don't worry about having too much liquid in the sauce as the pea cubes will soak it up quite quickly. Add the dhoka and simmer for a minute or so, then sprinkle over the garam masala and asafoetida, if using. Serve immediately with rice or bread of your choice.

Radha Bollobhi

Urad Dal Poories

There are several theories about how the name Radha Bollobhi came about, but the most plausible one is that it combines Radha and Krishna together, their love for each other being well established in Indian mythology.

The pairing of these poories with a spicy Bengali *dum aloo* is the foodies equivalent of Radha-Krishna's love story. This combination is often served at weddings and at most family gatherings, and is a favourite Sunday morning breakfast in most Bengali households.

Makes around 20

For the filling
200g white urad lentils
2 teaspoons cumin seeds
2 teaspoons fennel seeds
2 dried red chillies
4 peppercorns
1 teaspoon salt
2 tablespoons vegetable oil
½ teaspoon sugar

For the dough
500g plain flour
1 teaspoon salt
1 teaspoon sugar
3 tablespoons vegetable oil
400ml warm milk

vegetable oil, for deep frying

First prepare the filling. Start by soaking the urad lentils in warm water for an hour or so, then drain and grind to a fine paste.

In a separate pan, dry roast the cumin and fennel seeds, chillies and peppercorns in a frying pan over a medium heat for a minute or so until the spices smell roasted and aromatic. Grind the spices to a medium-fine consistency or pound in a mortar and pestle. Add the salt and pounded spices to the lentils and stir to combine.

Heat the oil in a wok, add the lentil paste and fry for 8–10 minutes over a medium heat, stirring constantly, until the paste is thick and begins to resemble to consistency of the dough. Add the sugar to the pan, check the seasoning and allow the mixture to cool. When cool, divide the mix into 20 equal balls and set aside.

To make the dough, mix the flour, salt, sugar and oil together to obtain a sandy, crumbly mixture (this will make the poories crisp). Stir the warm milk into the mixture and knead well to obtain a soft, smooth and elastic dough. Divide the dough into 20 equal parts and cover with a damp cloth or clingfilm to prevent it drying out.

Take a ball of dough, make an indent in the centre with your thumb and keep pressing and rotating the dough in the palm of your hand to make the cavity slightly larger than the size of the ball of filling. The edges of the cavity of dough should be slightly thinner than the rest of it. Sit the ball of filling in the cavity and bring together the edges to cover the stuffing on all sides. Do not leave any cracks or the filling will come out while rolling the parathas.

On a very lightly oiled work surface, roll out the filled dough ball carefully to obtain discs 10–12cm in diameter, taking care that the dough doesn't tear or the filling come out.

Deep fry in oil preheated to 150–160°C for about a minute or so, turning over when it puffs up and until both sides are golden. Cook one or two at a time and drain on kitchen paper. Serve hot with Aloor Dum (see page 244).

Notun Aloor Dum

New Potato Dum Curry

This dish's pairing with Radha Bollobhi (see page 243) is the representation in food form of the eternal love story of Radha and Krishna. As two people exchange vows and prepare to be joined in a union, the serving of this food pairing is considered auspicious. The fact that neither onion nor garlic is used in this recipe makes it suitable to make and serve at most religious and social events. The quantities given here are for a side dish or to serve as part of a feast; to serve as a main course, simply double up.

Serves 4 as an accompaniment

7 green chillies (5 for the paste, 2 to be slit and used for garnish)
2.5cm piece of ginger, peeled
1½ teaspoons cumin seeds
20–24 marble-sized new potatoes
50ml mustard oil
1 teaspoon nigella seeds
2 tablespoons ghee
2 green cardamom pods, lightly crushed
2.5cm piece of cinnamon stick
2 cloves
a pinch of asafoetida
4 tomatoes, puréed
1½ teaspoons salt
¾ teaspoon sugar
pinch of ground turmeric
1½ teaspoons red chilli powder
½ teaspoon Bengali garam masala (see page 261)
2 tablespoons finely chopped coriander

Start by making the paste – place 5 chillies, the ginger and ½ teaspoon of the cumin seeds in a blender, add a splash of water and blitz to a paste consistency.

Parboil the potatoes in their skins for 10–12 minutes or until they are about three-quarters cooked. Once cool enough to handle, peel them. Heat the mustard oil in a frying pan, then add the nigella seeds and potatoes. Fry over a medium heat until they turn a golden colour, but do not brown them. Drain them in kitchen paper and keep aside.

Heat the ghee in a pan, add the cardamom, cinnamon and cloves and let them splutter for 30 seconds. Next add the asafoetida, then the remaining cumin seeds and as they crackle and pop, immediately add the chilli–ginger paste and sauté for 2 minutes.

Add the puréed tomatoes, salt, sugar, turmeric and red chilli powder and cook for 2–3 minutes over a high heat, then add 200ml of water and bring to the boil, stirring constantly. Reduce the heat and simmer for 5 minutes, then add the potatoes. Bring back to the boil, then reduce the heat and simmer for another 10 minutes or so until the potatoes are cooked through and the gravy thickens. (Many people like this dish completely dry but since it is usually paired with Radha Bollobhi, it helps to have a bit of sauce to dip the bread in.)

Cut into a potato and check the seasoning, adjusting the salt as needed. Sprinkle over the garam masala and stir in to mix. Garnish with freshly chopped coriander and the remaining slit green chillies.

Begun Bhaja

Aubergine Fritters with Poppy Seeds

A complete Bengali meal comprises all the flavours – sweet, salty, sour, bitter – and also includes different cooking techniques, such as steaming, frying, braising, broth and so on. Traditionally a big feast would start off with something sour like a fragrant lime sweet chutney and then gradually progress towards a fried snack of some description, which could be a *bora*, *pora* or *bhaja*. This aubergine fritter is one of the most popular *bhajas*.

Serves 4 as a starter

2 long Japanese aubergines (or courgettes), sliced lengthways 3–4mm thick, using a mandolin slicer or sharp knife
1½ teaspoons red chilli powder
1 teaspoon ground turmeric
1 teaspoon salt
½ teaspoon nigella seeds
½ teaspoon sugar
2 garlic cloves, finely chopped
1 green chilli, finely chopped
1 tablespoon freshly chopped coriander
juice of ½ lemon
3 tablespoons cornflour
2 tablespoons coarse semolina
1 tablespoon white poppy seeds
vegetable oil, for deep frying (anything with a high smoking point works, nothing fancy or expensive)
chaat masala (see page 261), to sprinkle

Arrange the aubergine slices on a tray. Mix together the chilli powder, turmeric, salt, nigella seeds and sugar in a small bowl. Mix together the garlic, green chilli and coriander in a separate bowl. Sprinkle the 2 mixtures evenly over the aubergines and squeeze the lemon juice over. Turn the aubergines and sprinkle over the other side too. Set aside for 10–15 minutes.

Mix together the cornflour, semolina and poppy seeds.

Taking one aubergine slice at a time, dip in the cornflour mixture and pat with your fingers to make the coating stick.

Deep fry the aubergine slices in hot oil at 180°C for 3–4 minutes, a few pieces at a time, until crisp. Turn over halfway through the cooking time to cook through and get both sides crisp. Remove from the hot oil with a slotted spoon and drain on a plate lined with kitchen paper. Sprinkle with chaat masala and serve hot, either with your main meal or as a starter with tomato or green coriander chutney (see pages 254 and 51).

Ilish Macher Paturi

Steamed Hilsa in Banana-leaf Parcel

Ilish – or hilsa – is known as *macher raja*, the king of all fish in Bengal.
A member of the herring family, it swims upstream from the sea to the river,
similar to salmon, for the purpose of spawning. In the course of its migration,
it is believed to travel 1,200–1,500km up and down the river. This particular dish
is a little similar to the Parsi delicacies on page 125.

Serves 4

250g grated coconut (frozen will do)
2 tablespoons brown mustard seeds,
    soaked in 75ml hot water for 30
    minutes
2 tablespoons ready-made English
    mustard
4 green chillies, chopped
1 teaspoon ground turmeric
2 tablespoons mustard oil
1½ teaspoons salt
2 large seabass (approx. 600g each),
    filleted and each fillet cut into 3
    pieces (you should have 12 pieces
    in all, with 2 pieces per portion)
12 banana leaves, cut into 25cm
    squares (or use foil and greaseproof
    paper)

Grind the coconut with the soaked mustard seeds, English mustard and green chillies. Mix the ground paste with the turmeric, mustard oil and salt, then add 4 tablespoons of water to loosen the paste. Spread this over the fish pieces and marinate for 30 minutes.

Wrap each piece of fish in a clean banana leaf, folding it to secure the fish like a parcel. If you can't find banana leaves, simply use foil lined with greaseproof paper and fold it to make an envelope to enclose the fish.

Steam the fish parcels for 12–15 minutes or until cooked. If you do not have a steamer, these are just as good roasted in a hot frying pan for about 6–8 minutes on each side or cooked simply on a barbecue. In Bengal, the traditional way to cook these parcels is to place them in large containers of freshly boiled rice and the heat from the rice itself cooks the fish perfectly whilst still keeping it moist.

Serve the fish in the banana-leaf parcels, so that guests open the parcels at the table and can enjoy the full aroma.

Top left: Radha Bollobhi (page 243)
Bottom left: Meetha Tamatar Chutney (page 254)
Right: Notun Aloor Dum (page 244)

Chingri Malai Curry

Prawns in Coconut Curry Sauce

If I ever had to pick a dish to attribute the start of my love for food, it would have to be this dish that I first had at a Bengali wedding in Asansol in the late 1970s. It was quite simply the best thing I had ever eaten in my life! It's my first luxury food memory and kickstarted my passion for food, but also demonstrates my love for attending weddings. Well, I was mostly invited, but when I was in college in Orissa, I would sometimes sneak into strangers' weddings uninvited too! No doubt this is one of the all-time favourite Bengali dishes, reserved for very special guests, big celebratory dinners, weddings and so on.

Serves 4

750g freshwater prawns, peeled and deveined (the largest size you can find)
1 teaspoon ground turmeric
1½ teaspoons salt
4 tablespoons vegetable oil
4 bay leaves
2 black cardamom pods, bruised
4 red onions, blended to a fine paste
1 tablespoon ground cumin
3 tablespoons ginger-garlic paste (see page 260)
4 green chillies, slit lengthways
100ml coconut milk
250ml shellfish stock
1 teaspoon sugar (optional)
½ teaspoon ground green cardamom
1 tablespoon freshly chopped coriander
juice of ½ lime

Marinate the prawns with half the turmeric and half the salt for 10 minutes.

Heat the oil in a pan and add the bay leaves and black cardamom and let them sizzle for 30 seconds or so. Next add the onion paste and sauté over a medium heat for 10–12 minutes until light brown.

Mix the remaining turmeric in a pan with the ground cumin and ginger-garlic paste in 100ml of water, add to the sautéed onions, reduce the heat and cook for 2–3 minutes, stirring regularly. Add the remaining salt and the green chillies and stir for 1 minute. Mix in the coconut milk and shellfish stock and simmer for 3–4 minutes or just until the sauce begins to get slightly thick and glossy.

Add the prawns and lower the heat: let it simmer for 3–5 minutes until the prawns just curl up and are cooked. Remove from the heat, correct the seasoning with salt and sugar and sprinkle on the ground cardamom and chopped coriander. Cover the pan with a lid and let it sit for 1 minute or two, then squeeze over the lime juice and serve immediately. A good chingri malai curry waits for no one, not even the son-in-law.

Macher Jhol

Mixed Seafood in a Bengali Vegetable Broth

This is my take on the classic Bengali dish *macher jhol*. A proper celebration dish for the entire family, this versatile sauce goes well with many different types of seafood. Traditionally the choice of seafood would often depend upon the importance and status of the guest, so for a wedding we'd use the very best.

Serves 4–6

300g piece of halibut fillet or small fish such as red mullet, scaled, pin-boned and diced into 5cm cubes
4 large prawns, shells and veins removed
4 large scallops, cleaned and cut from the half shells
meat and claw from 1 lobster, diced into 2.5cm cubes
1 squid, cleaned and sliced into 1cm thick rings
2 small potatoes, boiled, peeled and sliced 1cm thick
2 baby aubergines, cut into 1cm thick slices
8 cherry tomatoes on the vine
1½ teaspoons salt
½ teaspoon sugar
3 tablespoons vegetable oil
1 teaspoon ground turmeric
½ teaspoon each of red chilli powder, nigella seeds and fennel seeds
coriander cress, to garnish

For the broth
2 tablespoons mustard oil
4 green cardamom pods, crushed
10 black peppercorns, crushed
2 bay leaves
1 large onion, finely chopped
¼ teaspoon ground turmeric
1 teaspoon red chilli powder
1½ teaspoons ground cumin
2 tomatoes, chopped finely
2 green chillies, finely chopped
750ml shellfish stock, made from the shell/bones
1¼ teaspoons salt
½ teaspoon sugar
2 tablespoons freshly chopped coriander
juice of 1 lemon
a pinch of ground cardamom

To make the broth, heat the mustard oil in a pan over a high heat. When the oil is hot, add the cardamom, peppercorns and bay leaves and let them crackle. Add the onion and cook over a high heat for about 10 minutes until it is golden brown. Add the turmeric, chilli powder and the ground cumin and sauté for 1 minute. Add the chopped tomatoes and green chillies and sauté for 3 minutes. Now add the fish stock, salt and sugar, reduce the heat and simmer for 10 minutes.

Meanwhile, wash the seafood and pat dry with kitchen paper. Place on a large plate with the potatoes, aubergine and tomatoes and sprinkle with the salt, sugar and oil, and sprinkle the turmeric, chilli powder, nigella and fennel seeds over the seafood. Set aside for 5 minutes.

Finish the broth with chopped coriander and a squeeze of lemon. Allow the flavours to come together for 2 minutes, then strain the broth through a sieve lined with muslin to obtain a smooth shiny soup. Finish with ground cardamom and keep warm.

Heat a separate large non-stick pan (you may need to use two pans, or cook the vegetables first and set aside, then cook the fish and seafood). Add the tomatoes, potatoes and aubergines and cook over a medium heat for 2 minutes, then add the fish, prawns and scallops and cook for a further 2 minutes. Next add the lobster and cook for another minute or so. Add the squid rings and as they colour, carry on turning the fish, prawns and vegetables, then the lobster. Cook the second side for another 2 minutes until the seafood and vegetables are just cooked. Remove from the pan and arrange the fish, seafood and vegetables in a serving dish, sprinkle with coriander cress, then pour over the strained soup. Serve immediately with hot boiled basmati rice.

On the platter: top: Begun Bhaja (page 245); bottom: Chingri Malai Curry
(page 250); right: Matarshutir Dhoka (page 242)
Top right: Mishti Doi (page 256) and Rossogolla (page 257)
Bottom right: Aloo Posto (page 254)

Meetha Tamatar Chutney

Sweet Tomato and Raisin Chutney

This is my mother's recipe for the tomato chutney I've loved ever since I was a child. Hot, sweet and complex, this is just the best chutney there is. It works well as a spread in breads too; I've devoured many poories with nothing else but just this chutney!

Makes approx. 450g (1 jar)

3 tablespoons vegetable oil
1 bay leaf
2 whole dried red chillies
½ teaspoon black onion seeds
500g tomatoes, chopped
1¼ teaspoons red chilli powder
1 teaspoon salt
2 tablespoons raisins
200g sugar

Heat the oil in a pan to smoking point; add the bay leaf, whole red chillies and the onion seeds. When they crackle, add the chopped tomatoes and cook over a medium heat for 10–12 minutes until they are soft and disintegrated.

Add the chilli powder, salt and raisins and cook for 15 minutes over a medium heat until most of the moisture has evaporated and the chutney turns glossy. Stir in the sugar.

Cool and store in an airtight jar in the fridge for up to 2 weeks.

Aloo Posto

Potato and Poppy Seeds

By nature, Bengali home cooking is quite humble. Poppy seeds are a relatively inexpensive ingredient. Rarely a meal on its own, this dish is a great accompaniment to other main dishes as part of a feast. The use of roasted poppy seeds adds both richness and interest to potatoes.

Serves 4–6

100g white poppy seeds
8 green chillies, slit lengthways
80ml mustard oil
1 teaspoon panch phoran
600g potatoes, peeled and diced into 1cm cubes
1½ teaspoons salt
1 teaspoon ground turmeric

Dry roast the poppy seeds in a wok for 2–3 minutes until they smell toasted and turn a couple of shades darker. Keep 2 teaspoons aside and grind the rest to a paste with 2 of the green chillies and 100ml of water.

Heat 60ml of the oil in a wok and season with panch phoran. This will crackle and pop! Stir and, as it settles down, add the potatoes and fry for 3–5 minutes until golden.

Add 200ml of water, the remaining green chillies, salt and turmeric and cover with a lid. Cook over a moderate heat for 8–10 minutes until the potatoes are cooked but still retain their shape. Add the poppy seed paste and remaining oil and cook until it is thoroughly mixed and the moisture has dried up.

Remove from the heat, sprinkle with the reserved roasted poppy seeds and serve.

Chhena Payesh

Cottage Cheese Crumbled Milk Dumplings

Chhena payesh is yet another of the hundreds of variants originating from *rossogolla* and *rasmalai* (see page 219). What I like about *chhena payesh* is you don't need to worry about shaping the *chhena* and cooking it. It's particularly effective when you have small quantities to use up, and although it's not authentic, you can even cheat by using a small quantity of grated paneer, to make a quick *chhena payesh*.

Serves 4

For the chhena
1½ litres whole milk
3 tablespoons white vinegar

For the rabri sauce
1½ litres whole milk
6 green cardamom pods
100g sugar
a pinch of saffron

To finish
½ teaspoon rose water
2 tablespoons pistachios, roasted and chopped roughly
2 tablespoons flaked almonds, roasted

Heat the milk for the chhena in another pan over a medium heat. Once it comes to the boil, turn off the heat and leave for a few minutes so a skin forms. Scrape the skin off and return to the heat. When the milk comes back to the boil, turn the heat down to low and pour in the vinegar. Shake the pan a little to disperse the vinegar. Once the milk has curdled, pour into a strainer lined with a damp muslin cloth or a clean tea towel and set over a large bowl.

When the milk has drained, place the muslin containing the fresh curds into a bowl of cold water to cool quickly, being careful not to allow any to fall out of the cloth. When the curds are at room temperature, hang the cloth for around an hour to fully drain.

While the curds are draining, make the rabri sauce. Place the milk and cardamom pods in a pan over a medium heat and bring to a simmer. Turn the heat down slightly and simmer for 10 minutes, stirring occasionally. Add the sugar, stir and continue to simmer until the milk is reduced to half its original volume, then take the pan off the heat and add the saffron to infuse for a few minutes.

Place the drained curds in a bowl and mix well with your fingers to make the chhena smooth. Add to the hot rabri and gently break the chhena up into large pieces. Simmer for 2 minutes, stirring gently. Remove the cardamom pods and add the rose water and half the nuts. Gently mix in and remove from the heat to allow to cool.

Serve in small dishes garnished with the remaining nuts sprinkled on top.

Mishti Doi

Caramelised Yoghurt

Mishti doi is possibly one of the Bengalis' two favourite dishes in the wedding feast (*rossogolla* is the other favoured dish – see page 257). People go to great lengths to customise the earthenware pots in which the yoghurt will be set. And often the brightest and the most switched-on people will be put on *rossogolla* and *mishti doi* duties in order to ensure the most important guests are served and their importance is duly acknowledged.

Serves 6

1.4 litres whole milk
120g sugar
8 green cardamom pods
4 heaped tablespoons plain live
   yoghurt, whisked

Pour the milk into a heavy-based pan, bring to the boil, then reduce the heat and simmer for 5 minutes. Add 40g of the sugar and the cardamom pods to the hot milk. Continue simmering for about 30 minutes until the milk has reduced by half.

Preheat the oven to 80°C/60°C Fan/the lowest gas setting, then switch off the oven.

Meanwhile, heat the remaining sugar in a pan over a low heat until the sugar has caramelised. Turn off the heat. Add 2 tablespoons of water to the sugar and stir with a spoon.

Add the caramelised sugar mixture to the milk and stir well. Let the milk cool down until it is just above body temperature, but not hot (approximately 37–40°C), then add the yoghurt and stir to mix well. Remove the cardamom pods and discard.

Pour the mixture into 6 earthenware ramekins, cover with foil and set for 2–3 hours or overnight in the warm oven. Once the yoghurt is firm, place it in the refrigerator for a few hours before serving.

Rossogolla

Poached Milk Dumplings

The most discerning foodies and purists will declare *rossogolla*, pillowy dumplings of clotted milk, as India's national sweet. For 3,000 years milk, rice and sugar has always been considered the food of the gods, and used in many different ways. The simplest dessert using all three ingredients is *kheer*, the Indian equivalent of rice pudding. Since refrigeration wasn't possible, the only way to prolong the life of milk was through boiling it every few hours. Gradually the milk would thicken and would then be referred to as *rabri*, or as *kheer* in Bengali. When reduced even further, milk would turn into *khoya* (where the solids set almost as fudge). If the milk split or curdled, it was considered inauspicious and almost always thrown away or given to animals. Purposely curdling milk through the addition of acid was a turning point in Indian cuisine, but here we are, 500 years later, and *rossogolla* is the pride and joy of Bengal.

Makes 20

1.5 litres whole milk
2 tablespoons white vinegar
1 teaspoon plain flour

For the syrup
400g sugar
6 green cardamom pods
juice of ½ lemon
2 teaspoons rose water

Bring the milk to the boil in a pan, then let it cool. As it cools, a skin will form on the surface. Carefully remove and discard the layer of skin using a sieve or a slotted spoon, then bring the milk back to the boil again. As soon as it comes to the boil, remove from the heat and add the vinegar, a little at a time, until the milk curdles. Drain through a fine muslin cloth to remove the whey (the whey is discarded), then dip the muslin into cold water to cool the curds or otherwise they will overcook. When the curds are at room temperature, remove them from the cold water and hang them for an hour to drain (I tie the cloth around a wooden spoon and suspend it over a large jug). This is the chhena.

Remove the curds from the muslin and mash using the heel of your palm, adding the flour until the mix is smooth. Divide the mix into 20 balls and roll them in your palm to obtain smooth balls without any cracks on the surface. Set aside on an oiled flat tray or the back of a metal plate (this makes it easier to drop the balls into the syrup later).

For the syrup, pour 4 litres of water into a wok, add the sugar and cardamom and bring to the boil. Once the syrup has boiled for 2–3 minutes and the cardamom has infused, reduce the heat and add the lemon juice to the syrup. If any scum forms on the top, remove it using a slotted spoon or a sieve. Carefully drop the chhena balls into the syrup and boil for 4–5 minutes. The balls will float and grow in size as they cook. Cover with a lid, reduce the heat and simmer for an additional 10 minutes for the balls to cook through. If the syrup appears to thicken, sprinkle over a splash of water and continue cooking. Remove from the heat, let the balls cool down in the syrup and then add the rose water.

Serve a couple of rossogollas per person, with a few spoons of the syrup. (The leftover syrup can be reused to make 1–2 more batches if you wish.)

Basics and Measures

A cow statue in the midst of Holi. (Atid Kiattisaksiri/LightRocket via Getty)

Ginger Paste

Makes about 6 tablespoons

175g fresh ginger, peeled
5 tablespoons water

Chop up the ginger and process it to a paste with the water in a food processor or blender. The paste will keep for 1 week in the fridge.

Garlic Paste

Makes about 6–8 tablespoons

175g garlic, peeled
5 tablespoons water

Chop up the garlic and process it to a paste with the water in a food processor or blender. The paste will keep for 1 week in the fridge, but if you substitute oil for the water it should keep for 2 weeks.

Ginger-Garlic Paste

Makes about 10 tablespoons

100g fresh ginger, peeled
100g garlic, peeled
175ml of water

Chop up the ginger and garlic and process them to a paste with the water in a food processor or blender. The paste will keep for 1 week in the fridge.

Boiled Cashew Nut Paste

Makes about 400g

200g cashew nuts
a blade of mace
1 green cardamom pod
300ml of water

Soak the cashew nuts in enough water to cover for 10 minutes, then drain. Put them in a pan with the mace, cardamom and water, bring to the boil and simmer for 25 minutes. Remove from the heat and leave to cool. Blend to a smooth paste in a food processor or blender with 100ml of water. The paste will keep for 4 days in the fridge.

Garam Masala

50g coriander seeds
50g cumin seeds
20 green cardamom pods
10 cinnamon sticks, about
    2.5cm long
2 tablespoons cloves
10 blades of mace
10 black cardamom pods
½ nutmeg
1 tablespoon black
    peppercorns
4 bay leaves

Put all the ingredients on a baking tray and place in a low oven (about 110°C/90°C Fan/Gas Mark ¼) for 3–5 minutes; this intensifies the flavours. You could even dry the spices in a microwave for 20 seconds or so. Allow to cool, then grind everything to a fine powder in a spice grinder. Sift the mixture to remove any husks or large particles. Store in an airtight container and use within 2 weeks.

Bengali Garam Masala

1 teaspoon cumin seeds
1 tablespoon coriander
    seeds
1 cinnamon stick
seeds from 4 green
    cardamom pods

Heat a small heavy-based frying pan over a medium heat and dry-roast the cumin, coriander and cinnamon for a couple of minutes, then add the green cardamom and stir for 30 seconds or so until aromatic. Remove from the heat and allow to cool to room temperature then grind to a fine powder in a spice grinder. Store in an airtight container for up to 2 weeks.

Chaat Masala

Makes about 7 tablespoons

1 tablespoon cumin seeds
1 teaspoon black
    peppercorns
¼ teaspoon ajowan seeds
1 teaspoon white pepper
¼ teaspoon ground
    asafoetida
1 tablespoon rock salt
2 tablespoons dried mango
    powder
1 teaspoon ground ginger
½ teaspoon garam masala
¼ teaspoon tartaric acid
    (optional)
½ teaspoon dried mint
    leaves, crushed
1½ teaspoons dried
    fenugreek leaves, crushed
    between your fingertips
1 teaspoon salt
1 tablespoon icing sugar

Heat a small heavy-based saucepan and dry roast the cumin seeds lightly over a medium heat for 2–3 minutes until the flavours just begin to release. The cumin should not be allowed to change colour or become too roasted. Allow it to cool down, then add all the other ingredients. Grind them in a spice mill and pass them through a sieve. Stored in an airtight jar, this will keep for months.

Crisp Fried Onions

Makes about 100g

600g onions, sliced
at least 600ml vegetable or
    corn oil for deep-frying

Deep-fry the onions in medium-hot oil until golden brown, then remove and drain on kitchen paper. Store in an airtight container for up to 1 week.

Dhansak Masala

Makes 220g

1–2 teaspoons vegetable oil
5g cinnamon stick
5g green cardamom pods
20g black peppercorns
100g coriander seeds
25g cumin seeds
6g royal cumin seeds
5g black mustard seeds
5g poppy seeds
5g fenugreek seeds
5g cloves
5g curry leaves, ideally fresh
5g dried bay leaves
5g dried orange peel
5g dried lime peel
2g ground turmeric

Heat 1 teaspoon of the oil in a frying pan and roast each of the ingredients separately for just a couple of minutes until the aromas are released. Add the remaining teaspoon of oil as necessary. Let the mixture cool, then grind it and store in an airtight container for up to 6 months.

Botal Masala

Makes 180g

30g dried Kashmiri red chillies
1cm piece of cinnamon
2 green cardamom pods
4 cloves
½ star anise
4 whole allspice
a blade of mace
½ teaspoon black peppercorns
1½ tablespoons coriander seeds
1 teaspoon sesame seeds
1 teaspoon poppy seeds
1 teaspoon mustard seeds
1 teaspoon chana dal
½ teaspoon cumin seeds
1 tablespoon wheat grain (or bulgur wheat)
¼ teaspoon royal cumin
⅛ nutmeg, grated
a sprig of black stone flower
½ teaspoon ground turmeric

Slowly dry roast all the ingredients except the turmeric separately, until they start to give off an aroma.

Starting with the dried red chillies, begin pounding the largest spices first, then adding the small ones as you go along. Finally add the turmeric and pound everything into a fine powder. It is believed that pounding by hand is best as blending in a machine causes the volatile oils to be lost due to the generation of heat.

Store in clean, dry beer bottles. Pack the spice in as tightly as you can, to ensure as little air as possible remains in the bottle. This will help to prolong the flavour. To use, simply use either a barbecue skewer or knitting needle to release as much spice as you need. After use, place the lid back, and store in a cool, dark cupboard until next required.

Conversion Tables

Weights

Metric	Imperial
15g	½oz
20g	¾oz
30g	1oz
55g	2oz
85g	3oz
110g	4oz / ¼lb
140g	5oz
170g	6oz
200g	7oz
225g	8oz / ½lb
255g	9oz
285g	10oz
310g	11oz
340g	12oz / ¾lb
370g	13oz
400g	14oz
425g	15oz
450g	6oz / 1lb
1kg	2lb 4oz
1.5kg	3lb 5oz

Liquids

Metric	Imperial
5ml	1 teaspoon
15ml	1 tablespoon / ½fl oz
30ml	2 tablespoons / 1fl oz
150ml	¼ pint / 5fl oz
290ml	½ pint / 10fl oz
425ml	¾ pint / 16fl oz
570ml	1 pint / 20fl oz
1 litre	1¾ pints
1.2 litres	2 pints

Length

Metric	Imperial
5mm	¼ in
1cm	½in
2cm	¾in
2.5cm	1in
5cm	2in
10cm	4in
15cm	6in
20cm	8in
30cm	12in

Useful conversions

1 tablespoon = 3 teaspoons
1 level tablespoon = approx. 15g / ½oz
1 heaped tablespoon = approx. 30g / 1oz
1 egg = 55ml / 55g / 1fl oz

Index

Prayers are offered at the start of Eid al-Fitr at the Taj Mahal. (STRDEL/AFP/Getty)

Acknowledgements

Jon Croft for getting me to agree to yet another recipe book. After *Spice at Home* I wasn't sure I had another cookbook left in me!

A million thanks to Meg Avent for supporting with the research and kicking off the book when I was getting cold feet.

To Emily North and Kim Musgrove who made this book their own with their enthusiasm and support in researching.

To Gillian Haslam and Amy Stephenson for painstakingly scouring through the recipes, challenging, suggesting amendments by editing and testing... The book is much better for it.

Jodi Hinds, you are possibly the easiest photographer I have worked with so far, on what was a challenging book to photograph! Thank you.

James Mossman – every recipe needs to be cooked at least once by someone who hasn't cooked it before, so thank you for cooking every dish once and for all your suggestions.

Rakesh Ravindran Nair for his incredible support with photography and sharing his childhood stories and recipes of Onam, thank you.

Ramachandran Raju of The Cinnamon Kitchen for his contribution to the Pongal chapter.

Sankar Chandrasekaran, Surendra Nathawat, Narendra Yadav and Santosh Shah at The Cinnamon Club for all their assistance with the photography and for our lunches, thank you all.

To a long-time friend Parizad Mody Katyal for her enthusiasm, support and terrific insight into Navroze. I can't thank you enough for the several telephone calls and Skype chats we had and your enthusiasm whilst sharing the story of the festival. I hope you love the book as much as I do.

To my sister Vineeta, who I requested to research Eid al-Adha for me, only because she said she had taken up learning Urdu, and of course as she lives a five minute walk away from the Nizamuddin mosque where devotees from all religions throng to celebrate the life and lessons from the Sufi mystic Hazrat Nizamuddin.

Firdaus Takolia, who has been a terrific assistant from the very beginning and at every stage of writing this book. Firdaus has also been kind enough to contribute her family's recipe for Khajoor Biscuit (page 117) and share her childhood stories of Eid. I'm not wrong in feeling that *Indian Festival Feasts* is as much her book as it's mine.

To Maya, Eshaan and Archana who to me make every day a celebration and every meal a feast.

Publisher Jon Croft
Commissioning Editor Meg Avent
Design Matt Inwood, Marie O'Mara and Kim Musgrove
Cover Design Matt Inwood
Art Direction Kim Musgrove
Photographer Jodi Hinds (jodihinds.com)
Photographer's Assistant Tristan Fennell
Food Styling Vivek Singh and Firdaus Takolia
Project Editor Emily North
Recipe Editor Gillian Haslam
Proofreader Margaret Haynes
Indexer Zoe Ross